THE HANGING OF

Mary Ann

Published by Brolga Publishing Pty Ltd
ABN 46 063 962 443
PO Box 12544
A'Beckett St
Melbourne,VIC, 8006
Australia

email: markzocchi@brolgapublishing.com.au

National Library of Australia Cataloguing-in-Publication entry
        Badger, Angela, author.
        The hanging of Mary Ann
        9781922175526 (paperback)
        Women murderers--Australia--Fiction.
        Hanging--Australia--Fiction.
        Women's rights--Australia--Fiction.
        A823.3

Printed in Australia
Cover design & Typesetting by Wanissa Somsuphangsri
Photography by Daphne Salt
Cover image: A portrait of Clara Rice as Mary Ann
        Rural scene: the South Australian Alps by George Edwards Peacock,
        Courtesy of the Mitchell Library, State Library of NSW.

BE PUBLISHED

Publish through a successful publisher. National distribution, Macmillan
& International distribution to the United Kingdom, North America.
Sales Representation to South East Asia
Email: markzocchi@brolgapublishing.com.au

THE HANGING OF

Mary Ann

Based on a true story,
this colonial woman was a victim of the times

ANGELA BADGER

CHAPTER I

They came for her mid-afternoon.

They should have come early in the morning but the gaoler's wife had whispered, "We're still waiting luvvy, still time," and put the bowl of porridge down, then hurried away. What can you say to someone waiting to die?

Every day a reprieve had been expected. Each afternoon the Sydney coach rumbled into Goulburn and half the townsfolk turned out.... hoping.

Surely there would be word from the Governor? Tomorrow, the next day, maybe the day after. Time was running out.

Her hair had been cut off. Nothing must tangle with the hangman's rope.

As the scissors snicked through her thick dark locks she thought of another whose hair had also been shorn. Another barely ten years older than she, whose hair had turned white with the terror and who listened for the grinding wheels of the tumbril with no possible hope of rescue.

There was still time for Mary Ann. Even if the coach had nothing in the mail, a horseman could yet come galloping down the highway with the papers in his saddlebag. Everyone in the town waited... waited and hoped.

But nothing came.

"We will kneel together." The Rev Sowerby touched her on the shoulder. "We will pray together and give Him thanks." even Samuel Sowerby felt a twinge of unease as he spoke those words.

Thanks… for what?

He had christened, married and buried Mary Ann's family and all those other families around Lake George for three generations but had never had to watch anyone, let alone a young woman in her prime, take those last fatal steps.

For several days her ears had been filled with the sound of hammering; now, as they led her from the building, she saw the gallows waiting for her.

Spite, fury, screaming impotence filled the air as shrieking women prisoners crowded round the windows yelling down abuse at the prison guards.

She heard none of it as she halted for a moment at the first step. Instead she took a deep breath and then paused at the next one, and the next after that, savouring the memory of all that she would never know again. The cry of the plovers down by the dam, a baby's warm breath on her cheek, the touch of a loving hand, the taste of fresh baked bread and honey, the sound of a fiddler tuning up for the dance, the bleat of a new born lamb, the early morning challenge of the rooster and the cawing of the crows as they circled high above the lake… the crows. She even managed a smile as she looked up at the sky and the wheeling birds; they were old friends. They had always been part of her life, everything about them was familiar. Not like the rough stuff of the hood they pulled over her head, nor the hard bite of the noose they put about her neck.

Panic snatched at her.

Fear gripped her throat, then her chest, her bowels, her

bladder as she strained to hold back her water. That other woman must have struggled as her body betrayed her fear, certainly she had bled. For many days before she faced the guillotine her womb had shed itself. White-haired and bleeding, head held high, that woman had faced her end, had never faltered.

Now Mary Ann must follow in those footsteps. She shut her eyes, she squeezed them tightly shut till all that was left of her world were pinpoints of light in the darkness.

Try as she might, the fear surged inside her. Then soft hands took hold of her bound ones and a wise, sad voice whispered, "Fear not, I have trodden this path before you."

CHAPTER 2

"Sit here, Grand-père. You're just a bit out of breath." Why was it that old people never could keep up? Always huffing and puffing and lagging behind when old cats still climbed trees, old dogs ran faster than she could and old crows still flew across the sky.

Three of those birds were mourning their way across the heavens at that moment. Black flakes from the bonfire of a disappearing life, they swooped to earth and settled on a ring-barked tree.

The great crows had for centuries ranged over forest, plain and bush. Nowadays paddocks patchworked the land and, where bush had once cloaked the terrain, shrivelled lagoons and dusty ridges stretched as far as the eye could see. Those beady eyes missed nothing – water, faltering prey, safe places for nesting, all that made up the life of a predator.

From Collegdar to Gundaroo and beyond the countryside stretched, a vast canvas on which the new race of human beings had begun to paint its own picture. Those who had settled near the stretch of water known as Weereewaa had changed its name in honour of a distant king, and now strived to bring some semblance of civilisation to their isolated lives. Seventeen miles long, six miles wide, Lake George stretched into the distance whilst over the Cullarin Range scattered dwellings marked the beginnings of settlements.

Mary Ann perched herself on one of the flat rocks that crowned the hill and patted the surface beside her.

"You promised! You said you'd tell me more. You said you'd tell me about that ball, remember?"

"The Ball of the Yew Trees! Patience! Patience, for heaven's sake. Let me get my breath back."

Whenever Richard Guise rode out his granddaughter clamoured to be taken with him. Even when very small he'd tucked her in front of him. Now she had her own pony.

"Why can't you be content to stay with your sisters?"

He'd half grumble and half smile to himself as he experienced the glow of flattery when she replied, as she always did, "You know, I'd rather be with you, Grand-père." For Mary Ann had no time for the chit-chat of family life. Where others chose to sew and embroider, read and gossip, she preferred the broad open paddocks and the lake, always the lake.

Lake George displayed its bounty for all to see. A vast stretch of water with distant hills hinting at mountains beyond. Seagulls flocked overhead while brolgas, herons and spoonbills waded in the shallows and bobbing ducks busied themselves amongst the reeds. Flotillas of black swans glided across the surface while pelicans scythed their way down from the sky to land upon the water and search for fish.

In the palm of its hand the great lake held the fate of all who settled near the shores. The ancient owners had now begun to move away as the white men took over the land for themselves and their lumbering beasts. If any of the newcomers had thought to ask those who'd dwelt upon its shores for all those generations they might have learnt the real secret of Lake

George and been more wary of its blandishments.

From their vantage point the two of them could see the lake glimmering in the distance. The Guise property stretched as far as the eye could see, and besides this farm there were acreages at Liverpool, Parramatta, Macquarie Fields and much else besides. But this was where the Guise family chose to make its home.

"Sit down, child, you're making me quite giddy. Don't stand up on that rock. If you fall you'll do yourself real damage."

"I can see for miles. Miles and miles… I can see as far as the river…and there's a hut there. Oh Grand-père, there's a girl there, she's throwing sticks for a dog, and he's barking and barking."

"Sit down at once."

"If we went past the dam and took the other path, down to the river, I could say hello."

"No, you could not, young miss."

"Why not? She's bigger than me but she'd play with me, I know she would."

At a loss for words, for a moment the old man did not answer. He stared at the distant ramshackle dwelling with a frown on his face.

"Why not?"

"Peasants! No better than tinkers! Enough! Don't try to argue… most definitely not! Now, what were you asking? Ah…The Ball of the Yew Trees. Give me a moment while I put on my thinking cap."

Narrowing his eyes he blinked in the sunlight. For a minute or so he sat in silence, then a faint smile touched his lips. "Yes, I remember, everyone wore green masks and the ladies had their hair dressed so cleverly it was as much as three feet high above their heads."

"How could it?" Mary Ann scorned, "They'd never get into their carriages."

"Oh yes, they could, Miss Cleversticks," her grandfather laughed. "They knelt on the floor... think of that!"

"But three feet! How could it stand up that high?"

"Their coiffeuse would put a horsehair cushion on the top of their scalp and comb the lady's hair, and possibly false hair, over it. To secure it they'd drive steel pins into the cushions. Then they'd be decorated with flowers or jewels or whatever the lady wanted. For the Ball of the Yew Trees they used sprigs of green yew."

"What if they needed to scratch?"

"Ladies don't scratch. Nevertheless, you're quite right. Sometimes it must have been unbearable.

"They had long sticks with small ivory claws at the end. These reached right in so they could at least get some relief. Anyhow, stop interrupting, you wanted to know about the Ball of the Yew Trees."

"Was it in the Hall of Mirrors?"

"Yes, the *Galerie de Glace*. Being such a long room the Queen commanded that an orchestra played at each end. Hundreds of candles reflected the dancers all along those looking glass walls. The paintings on the ceilings and golden scrolling round the windows turned that ballroom into a fairyland."

"What was her dress like?"

"Let me think," the old man paused and pursed his lips in concentration. "She wore emerald brocade with Brussels lace, the neckline was low and the sleeves slashed with velvet. Of course, everyone wore green masks. The most noble ladies and gentlemen of France had been invited. Always a de Guise would be there, close by. The Queen liked to have one of her kinsmen at her side.

"A great family indeed. De Guise is a name to be proud of, connected to every royal house in Europe, married into many a

8

noble family in France. Such brave men, such great soldiers. Why, François de Guise became one of the most famous soldiers in Europe, François the Scarred was often called Le Balafré – twice so badly wounded he nearly died. Oh, a great family amongst all those other great families… Orléans, Bourbons, Longuevilles… the names are endless…" The old man's eyes closed as he mused to himself. "Oh, a great family."

"But the ball Grand-père, did you dance with the Queen?"

"The Queen had her favourites, remember I was very young, I had to assist with the guests, make sure every lady danced and any lady on her own had an escort for supper." He paused. "Such suppers! There were boars' heads with apples in their mouths, pheasants and quails and platters of meats arranged in all their colours so they looked more like tapestries than food. We were all so hungry by the time we went in that our mouths were watering. Because of course we had to wait for Her Majesty, and the Queen never wanted to stop dancing. Night after night she liked nothing better than the company of her friends, if it wasn't dancing it was the opera, or playing cards, always the same friends."

"Wish I had a friend," grumbled Mary Ann, "I wish I had someone to play with."

"Well, you're not a queen, are you, or even a princess!" he smiled at her downcast face. "Her greatest friend was the Princess de Lamballes, a lovely woman with the face of an angel, kindest woman I've ever met. Seems like yesterday, my first day at court and me being so gauche and tongue-tied, remember I was no more than a lad. This charming lady came up to me and smiled, such eyes and hair as golden as the wheat. She held out her hand, and ladies would not usually do such a thing to a young unknown, of course, and she said, 'Don't concern yourself unduly, young sir, come and ask me anything you need to know.' Ah! I think it's nearly time for us to make for home, look at the shadows, they're lengthening by the minute and...."

"You've not finished yet."

"Oh yes, I have."

"A de Guise never goes back on his word! You told me that. You've not finished yet."

"I've told you about the Ball of the Yew Trees."

Mary Ann pouted. "But it's too soon to go back. Tell me about the Queen. Did she wear her crown when she got up in the morning? Did she wear it at breakfast? Did she say, 'Off with his head' if someone made her cross?"

Grand-père laughed and straightened up. "Never. She always acted according to etiquette. Remember she'd been trained to be a queen from the cradle. But like all little girls, she would have played around the palace just as you have your games out in the yard back at Bywong and now that's enough! Time to go home. Your father will be wondering where on earth we've got to... and didn't I feel the first drops of rain?"

"We could go down to that shepherd's hut down there."

"We could not, young miss. Even if he's away with his flock it's still his home. You can't go pushing in like that."

Flicking at the grasses with her crop Mary Ann followed him down from the hill to where their horses were tethered.

A contented smile touched her lips. She'd had her own way once again. Nothing was as exciting as her grandfather's stories. The world that Grand-père conjured up became more real than the vast scorched plains and the distant shimmer of the lake. When life is lived in remote places there are none of the distractions of the crowd that buzzes and hums around a city dweller. When books are few and letters from the old country are months arriving, journals are pored over till the pages fall apart. There is a great emptiness that can only be filled with stories.

So much wisdom and knowledge to be handed down from generation to generation. Just as the Canberri and Ngunawal passed on the tales of Dreamtime sitting around their fires, so the white folk mulled over their memories whenever time hung heavily on their hands.

Grand-père rarely spoke of the past when the rest of the family were around, though. Perhaps the day-to-day problems took precedence over reminiscences, perhaps the bored looks that passed around the table whenever the conversation drifted back towards that distant time put him off. Alone amongst the grandchildren Mary Ann pounced upon every snippet the old man dropped.

"Filling the child's head with all those fancies," his son grumbled that evening when Mary Ann was telling her sister about the Ball of the Yew Trees. "Any daughter of mine needs to know her alphabet. If she's not at her lessons she should be out helping in the dairy, not having her head filled with all those fancies. Don't you agree, Charles?" More and more frequently William asked the opinion of his eldest son. He had become his father's right-hand man.

"I'm sure you're right, Father."

"We should remember. No one should forget." Richard Guise persisted.

"Now, son." William wasn't going to be distracted by the old man. "We've got to decide about whether we need that new harrow this year or can scrape by till next. Can you call by…"

"Father, I'm off tomorrow, off to Gundagai. I'll think about it. Remember, you wanted me to look over that stock down the river." Charles spent most of his time away, overseeing the scattered properties of the Guise family.

"Well, I still say we should not forget. It's wrong to let

everyday matters cloud our memories." Richard was like a dog with a bone.

William gave an exasperated sigh. "Of course we ought to forget. What does our family need to know about those Frenchified ways. Think, Papa! You may have been Richard de Guise all that time ago, and you've told us often enough about the Duke de Guise and the family and so on, but soon it was plain Richard Guise and sometimes they even called you Richard Guys, remember? Times change."

"Possibly. But the past is always with us. Remembering the past is what separates us from the animals, isn't it? That is what makes us human beings." He shrugged and looked down at his plate.

Mary Ann's eyes sparkled as she stared at the old man. Grand-père was the only person she knew who said things like that. When everyone else talked about crops and cattle and the weather, and the latest gossip from Gundaroo fizzed around the table, he could be relied on to say something that made a person think.

Mary Ann liked to think. The great world outside their property enthralled her with its mystery. Why, where and when were the most used words in her vocabulary and she yearned to know more about that enthralling place. Much as she loved her family, her quicksilver mind wove circles around their placid contentment.

Each night the Guise family gathered round the large table in the kitchen for their evening meal. Ever since she could remember there had been sisters, brothers, cousins, and many a guest rubbed shoulders down its length. With the passing of the years, the marriages and some sad absences, there were no longer so many under the roof of Bywong. Her father, William, sat at the head of the table with her brother Charles on his right hand, Grand-père presided over the far end and in between she sat with her sister.

Every evening Mary Ann basked in the contented glow which marked this precious moment in their hard-working days when the family came together. As knives and forks scraped upon plates and the tea cups chattered to the saucers she looked around the table and knew she loved every one of them.

"And I just hope Mr Sowerby doesn't take the opportunity to give us all one of his sermons," her sister Elizabeth grumbled, her approaching wedding being the topic on everyone's lips. "He never knows when to stop!"

"Well, my dear, it'll be the last for a long while. There won't be another wedding till our Mary Ann's turn. You won't have to sit and listen to him when you've moved to Woodbury." Grand-père firmly sliced the last of his mutton into neat pieces and regarded his granddaughter with a hint of disapproval.

"He never stopped rabbiting on at our Hannah's wedding, didn't he? Went on and on he did, telling us how wicked we were not to be there regular every Sunday."

"He's a good man. Many a wise word I've heard him speak."

"Well, as you say, it'll be the last time... till our Mary Ann."

"And coming back to that, have you decided if you'll use Hannah's veil or…"

As Mary Ann's thoughts drifted and conversation flowed all around the table her fancy took flight and their faces gleamed with the transient glow of fish rising to the surface of the river, leaping for insects, snapping at any particle floating upon the water, as they snatched at every topic of conversation and bandied words around the table. All the while her grandfather sat nodding and listening, just like the wise old cod who lurked in the deep pool under the shade of the willow tree down by the river. Years and years of survival, eluding the hooks of the fishermen had honed that ancient fish to perfection. He had escaped the lures, he'd survived the droughts in the depths of the river and never allowed himself to be swept out when the deluges came and the waters spilled over every bank and spread across the countryside.

Grand-père had survived so much, he'd escaped from the guillotine and come to this place and prospered. What was his secret? How had he turned the disaster of his life into such success?

Mary Ann caught his gaze and they exchanged glances, the bond she shared with him was enduring and deep. Alone amongst the family she had inherited his spare features, the aristocratic bones and the dark, searching eyes. When she looked around at her siblings she knew she'd also inherited that fierce pride which they did not even begin to understand.

"Well, it's different for us," her father muttered. "We don't want to hear all about that… that King Louis, Queen Marie Antoinette and all that, it's past. It's gone for ever. Some things are best laid aside and forgotten."

"Forgotten! I tell you this my lad, no one is forgotten until the last person on earth no longer speaks his name." Grand-père laid down his knife and fork and glared disapprovingly at his son.

CHAPTER 3

"He can't go all that way on his own," William muttered. "He'll have Job with him."

"Keep your voice down, Elizabeth, his ears are that sharp."

"I know, I know, Papa, but Dr Morton says he must have some help. He says, if he falls, then how will he be able to get up. Job's not always there. And even after the surgeon's done his work, of course he can rest at Hannah's, but still, on the return he'll need someone beside him."

A pall of silence enshrouded the house. Year in and year out, each day had commenced with Grand-père making his way over to the stables, and just as surely the day ended when he nodded off over *The Herald*. Now he lay tight-lipped and sweating in his bed while the family muttered together, closeted in the parlour.

"He needs help with everything he does. Five days on the road. You'll have to go with him Papa."

"Impossible! If only this had happened last week, he could have had Charles for company. Place'll go to rack and ruin if I'm away more than a couple of days. We are talking about weeks. And I can't spare any of the lads for that length of time.   Job'll drive him, he'll have to manage. You know it's difficult enough to find anyone reliable these days. We need every hand to finish off those last two paddocks and then in two weeks' time there's that sale on. I have to be there, After that it's…"

"And I certainly can't leave Woodbury for all that time. It's just the same for all of us these days, but the fact remains, someone has to accompany Grand-père. What about Mary Ann, then?"

William shook his head and frowned at his daughter. "Too young. She's far too young."

"Times are changing, Papa, we've all grown up a lot faster than you and Uncle Richard did, just as you say yourself, times are harder. Why, she's sixteen, she's a strong girl – not given to the vapours and any fancies like that. Only last week I heard Job say she had to help him with one of the ewes, and he considered her as handy as any of the shepherds. Maybe she's got her share of fancies and high falutin' ideas but that girl's got her feet on the ground. He just needs someone who'll travel with him, keep him company and in good spirits and we know she does that alright. She's always been his favourite. Mary Ann's the one to go."

"Such a long journey! Oh, if only he hadn't had that fall. Why didn't he listen to us. Old folks get too stiff for the saddle. If only Sydney wasn't so far away."

"We all know that, Papa, but if Dr Morton can't undertake surgery of that kind then there's nothing we can do about it. He's got to take that journey. Mary Ann'll look after him."

"It's dangerous, remember that. If the rain comes then it's the swollen creeks. Or what if the old coach meets a calamity - that coach wasn't new when we got it and it's done us proud, what if we lose a wheel on that road? You can be held up for days. And then of course there's always the bushrangers. If her dear mamma was still alive I'm sure she'd forbid it."

"Well, she isn't, is she?" Elizabeth muttered. Why was it

always the women who had to make the decisions? Men were alright for matters on the property but they never seemed to get their thoughts straight when it came to the everyday things. "We have to do what's best for the family and getting Grand-père to that surgeon's the most important thing at the moment. And I say Mary Ann can well be spared. She'll be beside him to fetch and carry and if he has a fall she can call on Job. She's the obvious one. She's got a good head on her shoulders. She'll not be plagued with fancies or suffer from migraines or think every moving shadow's a bushranger or a wild black! Let's waste no more time. I'll send a letter by the next mail."

"Well, I suppose if Job's with her nothing much can go wrong."

For more years than the family could remember, Job had worked for the family. Everyone knew he'd lay down his life for them.

He had been assigned to Richard Guise as a lad of seventeen, newly arrived in the Colony and wishing he were dead every minute of the day.

Each night, lying amongst his fellows in the barracks, he tried to shut out the terrible new world where he found himself. Some said that when night blanketed the land in this awful place then it was daytime back in the old country, so he'd lie there screwing up his eyes and willing himself back amongst the spinneys and the hedgerows or on the banks of the stream which flowed through his valley far away in Dorset.

That was exactly where he'd been taken, on the banks of the Tarrant, caught one moonlit night by squire's gamekeeper, tickling a trout for Old Ma's supper.

All that had kept him sane was the remembrance of the fields, the cottages, the beechwoods and the river as it flowed past the villages in the valley on its way to the sea. His life had always been lived in the valley.

Unschooled and untaught, Job had learnt all he knew from the old'uns, and what else did he need? A strong frame and willing hands which worked their way from year to year following the calendar of the seasons. Spring brought the wood anemones and the first fluttering of the birds from their nests. Summer was ushered in by the lambs skipping along the time-honoured chalk trails cut into the side of the hills by generations of sheep stretching back beyond the Magna Carta. Chestnuts and mushrooms heralded in the coming of autumn, with the apples to pick and the last of the potatoes to dig up, but you had to be quick or Jack Frost would start painting his pictures on the window, the only glazed one in the cottage.

Job had not realised there could be any other world. The horror nearly sent him out of his mind. How would he survive? Where would he find a place in this cursing, bullying, toadying world of thieves, murderers, cutthroats and just the plain shifting mass of unfortunates who'd taken to the wrong side of the law to survive. For he was sharp; he soon realised that many a soldier and sailor had been spewed out when they were no longer needed for good King George's battles, then added to the huge mass of those who were being put out of their traditional work by machines. Dorchester gaol was overflowing and he was lucky not to have been executed. He'd shivered through many a night as he'd lain in his cell, listening to the whispered stories. Boys as young as fourteen were hanged, even if the gaoler had to tie bricks on their feet for the drop.

Perhaps some kind angel watched out for Job because he weathered the gaol, the hulks and nearly six months crammed below decks,

When Richard Guise came searching for a farm hand and stood in the barracks at Sydney looking at the human debris sent over from the old country he didn't expect much success and was particularly despondent. Ambitious, strong and forever increasing his acreages, he'd become completely despairing of the labour on offer. Free settlers weren't prepared to give their time to such as him and the assigned labour often proved little better than a horde of cutthroats and thieves. And if they weren't criminal in themselves they certainly weren't versed in the ways of farming life. Petty criminals, miscreants from the city, soldiers and sailors thrown out on the streets. Men who had no idea that cows must be milked on time, sheds cleaned out, hay cut and stooked and all animals fed and watched.

"*Mon dieu*," he'd complained to Elizabeth, "half of them don't know one end of a cow from the other. You could tell, they'd be more trouble than they were worth."

"So your journey was fruitless?"

"Well, I suppose I just have to settle for what I can get. Finally took this young fellow, I'd trust too young to have learnt any real vice but that's a vain hope, I daresay."

"You have to have someone."

"Well I took a chance. This one was up for poaching, as I said, they're all thieves. He looks young enough to learn some sense. But he'll be like the rest, I wager, give satisfaction for a few weeks then lining his pockets whenever he can."

And there, for once, Richard Guise was completely wrong. And Job never ceased to bless the day that his master took that chance. All the skills of farm life were at his fingertips: milking, shepherding, digging, planting, and everything vital to a property. He began his seven years labour on Richard Guise's property out at Parramatta and his master soon learnt that Job could be trusted to milk the cows, shut up the fowls at night, watch out for straying sheep, and went about it willingly too. He needed no second bidding, animals had always been part of his life, their routines were as important to him as those of humankind.

And Job in his turn learnt even more. In this contrary new world the trees dropped their bark but not their leaves, huge birds screeched their way amongst the branches and streams dried up and disappeared, nothing like the Tarrant which flowed without ceasing between its grassy banks where old white shells of snails brought over by the Romans could still be found deep amongst the clumps of comfrey.

Quickly he learnt the ways of this new world and when his seven years of servitude were up and the time came for freedom Job could think of no other life than sharing the fortunes of the Guise family. He'd seen the births of so many children, the steady advancement of the family's fortunes, he'd laboured through flood and fire and he trusted his master as much as Richard, in his turn, relied upon him. He considered himself fortunate and intended to stay with the Guise's for the rest of his mortal span.

When the old coach rumbled out through the gates of Bywong and started on its long journey to the city, Job held the reins as usual.

Bags and boxes, rugs and canvas were piled up to such an extent that Mary Ann had to be squeezed into a corner so her grandfather could stretch his throbbing leg out to its full extent.

A tediously long journey lay ahead, the roads barely more than beaten tracks. Added to that, who was watching, who was lying in wait to rob and possibly even worse? But when there was no choice in the matter, what could be done? Never once did Job take his eyes off the road. Hawk-like, he noted every hillock and rock, every corner and every clump of trees, and once out on the open road he cracked the whip and they set off at a spanking pace.

Briefly they called at a wayside inn. The old man insisted on getting out for his own comfort and to see if the accommodation was acceptable but he limped back to the coach shaking his head.

"One of those bloodhouses. We'll not spend a night under *that* woman's roof, my oath we'll not."

"What's a bloodhouse, Grand-père?" Mary Ann asked as she propped a cushion under his painful leg.

"Place where you'd wake up covered in blood. I can tell, I know, I can smell 'em. Remind me to tell you a story about that sometime... saved a man's life that night... never forget it. Get eaten alive by bugs you can be, eaten alive. Soon as I put my nose inside that door I smelt 'em. Anyhow, we're not sleeping anywhere like that. We're better under the stars."

"But what if it's raining?" She regarded him with a questioning look.

"But what if you stopped quizzing me?" he snapped. His leg hurt and he dreaded five days of jolting and jarring. He secretly wondered if he'd have been better accepting that he might be lame for the rest of his life and not started on this painful journey. "Confounded horse, confounded rock... everything's a confounded mess," he groused as he shifted and tried to make himself comfortable.

Mary Ann said no more but contented herself with looking at the passing scenery. Everything was so new, so different from Bywong. In all her life she'd never once been beyond Goulburn, now every inch of the way enticed her as they creaked and lurched on towards that far off enchanted place called Sydney.

Even if she had never been there she knew all about it.

Sydney had cobbled streets and fashionable carriages spinning along the highways and byways. Afternoon teas and evening *conversaziones*, balls and race meetings filled the days of all who lived in that far-off city. Though whether her sister might consider her old enough to attend any of those wonderful events remained another matter. Poor Grand-père's predicament had been a blessing for her. Not many girls of her age would be taking the road to Sydney.

Camping out under the stars proved to be yet another enchantment, in spite of Job's grumbles as he hobbled the horses and set up the tent, dragged the tarpaulin out and made the fire. "There you are Missy, I'll see to yer grandpa. Now the fire's sparked up real nice, them chops'll be real good if you don't let 'em burn."

The novelty of cooking over the campfire, boiling the billy and mixing up damper preluded a night when the world changed from a hot, dusty succession of forest and plain to a mysterious place filled with the cries of the owl, the rustle of possums above them and the distant howl of the hunting dingo. Not for one moment was Mary Ann apprehensive as she lay looking up at the myriad stars gleaming through the branches of the gum trees; instead her whole being rejoiced that she'd been allowed to make such a journey. Travellers often spoke of the magic of sleeping under the stars. Well it was more than magic. It was a revelation.

But banks of storm clouds ushered in the next day, and as she helped Job pack up the camp and listened to his grumbles the first hint of concern about the journey niggled at her.

"Change in the weather." Job took up the reins and urged the horses back onto the road. Little more than a potholed track, in some places so narrow the trees brushed the windows, in others widening out enough for two carts or coaches to pass.

On the next occasion when they stopped, his pessimism had increased as he complained about his rheumaticky joints.

"Rain's not far off, me screws tell me that. Mark my words we'll have rain before long."

All day they travelled under an overcast sky, the first drops of rain falling before light began to fade from above. Soon it slid like teardrops down the windows. Mary Ann stared out at the darkening landscape and the teeming downpour.

"What's he stopped for now?" Grand-père demanded.

"P'haps we've shed a shoe?"

"What we gonna do, sir?" Job's face appeared at the door. "Can't see no sense in setting up our camp tonight."

"We've the tent and the tarpaulin."

"And what we do for kindling, eh? Bin raining hereabouts all day, I'd say. Ground's soaked and that last creek we passed is rising fast."

"Haven't you ever camped in the rain before, man?" Grand-père snapped.

"Not with a young lady in the party and a gent as ain't in the best of health…not ever." Job replied with the familiarity of a long-time retainer. "We'll be soaked to the skin afore we get's anything up. There'll be no meal tonight, only what's left of last night's damper. It may be alright for some," and he sniffed loudly, "some as may be sittin' up inside like, but for others… well it'll be the worst. Gotta take a look at what's troublin' the mare. She's made heavy weather of that last mile or more…"

Grand-père stared obstinately out of the window. All his life he had travelled this road up to the city. Whenever business demanded his presence or family matters needed attention he'd saddle up and take off. How easy everything had been when strength and health were on his side. Reluctantly he admitted to himself that now there were other considerations.

"There's an inn, near the Bogong Rock," he grudgingly admitted.

"Is that the place where the bogong moths come from?"

He smiled at his granddaughter. "Bogong moths are everywhere in their millions. The Bogong Rock's not where they come from, it's just one of the places where they settle on their journey and where they go to, no one knows. Most of all they are found up in the mountains about now, in fact, that's why you'll not have seen any blackfellows at all. They're all up there."

"You mean they've all moved off?"

"Only for now; they follow the food. It's said that when the snow melts on the lower ranges of the great mountains, and that's now, early October, then the first of the men start for the foothills. Then more follow, soon whole families make the journey in search of the moths."

"But what do they want with moths? Moths are just like butterflies. Just flutter about." Grand-père was sure to have a story to tell.

"You've seen the bogongs. They're big moths, about an inch long. 'tis said they're good eating."

"Eat moths! Ugh…how revolting."

"They tell me the Bogong moth is so important to them that they gladly make these great journeys. After the bitter winters of the plains they can feast on those fat bodies and when they return from the mountains their skin is glossy and they are sleek with the nourishment."

"I cannot see how eating moths can even keep a person alive, let alone make them sleek and glossy! What goodness would there be in a moth to feed a person?"

"Not a bit of it. It's the quantity that does the trick. Thousands and thousands of moths breed up in the mountains.

They hang in great clumps inside caverns and amongst the rocks. The natives creep in with burning switches and smoke them out so they tumble down into the waiting nets, then they cook them in the hot ashes of their fires."

"Ugh! How disgusting!"

"Not at all. I've tasted them, they are quite sweet...like nuts."

"But to go to all that effort for a few meals seems strange to me."

"They last for longer than that. The moths' bodies are fatty and any not eaten then and there are pounded with seeds and made into cakes that can be kept for weeks. These cakes are smoked so they last even longer."

"Well, I still can't see why, with so much around in the way of kangaroo and lizards and birds anyone should bother with moths."

"It is a way of life. You've got to take my word for it."

"It must be miserable up there amongst all those rocks."

"Not so. There are many caves...good shelter for everyone." He paused and stared out at the sodden landscape.

Job's rain streaked face was at the door again. "She's right,' he nodded towards the mare, "just a pebble in her shoe, that was all... have you made your mind up, sir?"

"Perhaps one night in an inn would be acceptable. This weather's not going on for ever. It'll probably only last one night."

An inn! Mary Ann had never set foot in such a place. A hint of wild goings-on, drinking and carousing hung about the mere mention of those establishments. There was an inn at Collegdar but even her brother avoided the place, and the only other inn near Gundaroo was owned by a French man rumoured to be in league with the bushrangers. He'd give his accomplices the nod if anyone of substance stopped by. Word travelled fast, there were no secrets on the Wool Road down to the coast or the highway to Sydney.

Disappointment tweaked at her when Job reined in the horses outside the Bogong Inn. Such an ordinary place! Almost snug as it nestled under a forested hill. A horseman must have just arrived as the ostler had started to lead a handsome bay gelding round to the stables.

"I'll look at the place first." Pain contorted Grand-père's features as he struggled to pick up his stick which had fallen to the floor.

"Let me go." Mary Ann put a hand on his arm. "If it's really nasty and dirty you'll have had all the trouble for nothing. Let me go."

"What could you tell about a place?" retorted her grandfather.

"Papa told me to be a help. How can I help if you won't let me!"

Her quick reply brought a smile to the old man's lips. You'd not keep a Guise down, that was for sure. Blood counts.

Mary Ann brushed down her bodice, smoothed her dark curls and motioned Job to follow her. In truth she felt quite nervous, inns on the whole having unsavoury reputations. But now was not the time to be timid. Holding her head up high she nodded to the servant by the door as though visiting wayside inns, and far more salubrious establishments, was an everyday event for her.

This inn proved indeed as snug as its appearance had promised. A fire crackled in the large room serving as entrance, parlour and dining room. From the rear of the building the sound of male voices came loud and clear. That would be the bar, Mary Ann decided. She stood at the table and waited.

She sniffed the air. Wood smoke, lavender and a tantalising hint of roast meat. "That's nice, Job," she said over her shoulder without looking round. "I can't smell a single bug here."

"And I am sure Mrs McCready, will be most flattered by your recommendation."

She spun round and found herself facing a tall, broad-shouldered man with a saddlebag clutched in one hand and a pair of boots in the other.

"Sir!" Momentarily shaken from her confident poise she glanced around the room but could see no servant or even any other person than Job who remained respectfully in the background, perhaps the words must have come from him.

"May I introduce myself, Frank de Rossi," he put down the boots, but not the saddlebag, and gave a slight bow.

"I was looking for the landlady."

"Ah, the admirable Mrs McCready, our hostess, she's busy in the kitchen, I believe." Picking up his boots he smiled at Mary Ann, "I'll ask one of the maids to send her to you…and may I assure you, this is a most excellent inn. You will not find better this side of the city and you can be assured not a single bedbug has ever crossed its portals."

"I doubt there's a better inn this side of Sydney," observed Grand-père later that evening as he sipped at his port and for a few moments forgot the throbbing pain in his knee.

"Just my very words to your daughter earlier this evening," Frank de Rossi raised his glass and looked across at Mary Ann who had left the table and now sat with her crochet by the fire.

"My granddaughter, sir, granddaughter. My son William's girl. Not that he doesn't have plenty of girls. Giddy things that they are…all married off now, excepting young Mary Ann of course. She's got a head on her shoulders, she's accompanying me to the city…a trifling operation's needed…a trifle…then we'll be home. Tell me, how's your father…haven't seen hide nor hair of him in years."

"Father's in the best of health. Busy as the day is long. I have had to make the journey home, Corsica that is, as you know, and he says he scarcely missed me! He says his own travelling days are over so I have to attend to matters over there. He's starting to build our new house at Rossiville."

"Yes, I've heard of that. Talk of the countryside. They say he's even putting in a ballroom!"

"That's right, sir. Father's got an eye for the future. He says one day the Limestone Plains'll have a society like Sydney. That ballroom's taking all his time and attention at the moment. Hardly started the house yet, but one day it'll be there."

"Can't see the sense of that. Where are all the people coming from?

"He'll be hard pressed getting enough for a ball! Half the ladies never live down on our properties they prefer to spend their days in Sydney or Melbourne… like my daughter Hannah where we're bound. Couldn't wait to follow her husband to the city life."

"Ah, times are changing, sir. This is such a new country, give it time."

"Well, I doubt I'll see much alter in my lifetime, different for you young'uns. I've seen enough changes already in my day. When we first came to this country this was still a wilderness. Who'd have imagined I could ever travel in my own coach from Gundaroo to Sydney. 'Twas horseback for us and naught else. First sight of the Lake I ever had was from the saddle. Now here we are, spending a night under a decent roof and ready to be on the road again, first thing."

"And no bedbugs I assure you," Frank de Rossi glanced

across at Mary Ann with the hint of a smile.

She sniffed. He didn't need to remind her!

"There's inns and then there are inns!" muttered Grand-père. "You said you'd tell me that story about a man being nearly murdered at an inn. What happened, Grand-père?"

"Oh, another time, remind me again."

"The evening stretches before us, sir… what better way to spend it than listening to an interesting tale." Frank de Rossi leant over and filled the old man's glass.

"Just an incident, something that happened when I was new to the Colony, something which made a great difference to me at the time, but that's all in the past."

"Go on, Grand-père, tell us." Mary Ann put down her crochet hook and joined them at the table. "Grand-père's stories are famous. No one can tell a story like him and he remembers just about everything."

Frank topped up his own glass. A log crackled in the fireplace as a piece of wood flared sending a shaft of light across the girl's face. Her dark curls cascaded over her features as she leant her elbows on the table. Her face was hidden but to Frank it seemed he had known every feature for ever. For the first time in many years his heart beat to a quickening pace. Had they ever met before. Certainly not, but perhaps in another life, another time, another world their paths had crossed. He shook his head at the absurdity of his thoughts… and yet he savoured for a moment the happiness of a lonely man who has wandered and searched and finally stumbled upon all that he had ever longed for.

"New to the Colony, I was. New and green but I soon learnt, same as we all do. Every man for himself. It's always been so, then sometimes a chance comes that you can't ignore."

"Just as my father said, almost the same words," Frank muttered.

"But old Francis came with a silver spoon in his mouth, didn't he. Your father had a Government, position, all the rest of it. I came as a private in the New South Wales Corps. At fourteen pounds a year and me and my lovely Elizabeth sleeping twelve families to a room. A pretty big room, but one room all the same with just hessian curtains between us all.

"The New South Wales Corps... surely not. The scum of the land! Why, I heard that in England they took the men from the condemned cell gave them a second chance of life if they would join the Corps."

"You don't need to look so shocked, young Frank. Those were hard times. I had served in Flanders before I went to the court of Versailles, all I knew was court life and soldiering. Getting across the Channel to London was the luckiest day of my life. Meeting your grandmother, that was the second most fortunate."

He paused and sipped at his port. "The king and queen had been taken from Versailles, taken up to the Temple prison in the city and do you know what that mob did? They paraded outside their prison with the head of the Princesse de Lamballes upon a pike. The Queen had to look upon her dearest friend's white face, that beautiful hair caked with blood. Think of that! I was lucky to escape with my life."

"Fortunate to have a haven, fortunate to have friends."

"Friends! I had no friends. I knew no one in that cold unfriendly city... that London. No money, no one to assist... I'd not wish such a predicament on any man. But then Fate smiled... that was then I met your grandmother," he leant across and patted Mary Ann's hand..."met her at a wine trader's house...only person I knew in the whole of London, had once shipped cognac over from the de Guise estates. Only there because of some hope the fellow could find employment for me…and of course some of those English liked to feel they helped the *émigrés,* as they called us. Ha! *Emigrés.* Outcasts more likely. I'd been invited for dinner and when I walked into the room – there she was."

"Grand-mère's never told me this."

"Perhaps one day she would have done, if she'd been spared long enough. There's tales you don't tell children," he paused and smiled to himself. "Well, I'm telling you now. Seems you are ready for it."

"Ready for it?"

"It was love my girl. Love at first sight. You aren't the age to know about love…but when you do then you'll understand. Love at first sight they call it and there is no going back, not in a lifetime."

Amazed, Mary Ann stared at her grandfather. Never before had she heard him speak so intimately of his past.

Surprisingly confused she gave a laugh. "Oh Grand-père , such things only happen in stories!"

"One smile, one look and that's enough. Sometimes you look straight into another's soul."

"Sir…you are quite the poet." Frank de Rossi stared down at the table, his expression shielded by shadow.

"But then those were hard times…my dear Elizabeth preferred not to remember the hardship but believe me she went through the mill… we both did."

"You had a long and happy life together." Frank leant over and refilled the other man's glass.

"The best. The very best. You hear about such things but you don't believe them do you? One look, one glance and you know that you have found all you ever need in life."

"Yes, that can happen, indeed it can." Frank suddenly found a thread unravelling on his sleeve and doggedly set about tucking it in and smoothing the stitches.

"You were going to tell us about the inn Grand-père."

"Indeed. The inn which changed my life! All things happen in threes don't they, think of the fairy tales. The princess has three wishes, the king has three sons, the suitor has to perform three tasks. Well going to that inn was the third thing for me, it changed my life. My first piece of luck was escaping across the Channel, my second was meeting dear Elizabeth, the third was walking into that inn." Sipping his port the old man's gaze drifted into that middle distance when memory picks up the brush and paints once again those enduring pictures of the past.

"We were stationed up beyond Parramatta, a wild and lonely place but travellers passed that way on many occasions and Seamus O'Reilly's inn was all they could hope for. You could smell the bugs the moment you stepped over the threshold, that's what brought it to mind. Bless me I'd nearly forgotten about that inn, and the captain, and those murderin' Irish and what happened."

"Was he murdered then, was that what you meant."

"He came as close as any man, the knife was on his throat."

"And what happened?"

"I'm telling you, child… stop being so impatient, listen for once, Always skimming around, wanting to know this or that or hurry folk along. Listen."

Frank de Rossi smiled. "Your grandfather is right, he'll tell the story in his own time."

Not another person telling her what to do! Mary Ann scornfully half turned her back on him. What was the matter with old people. First grandfather never seemed to keep up with things. And now this man, old enough to be her father trying, to tell her what to do.

"Our Captain Corrigan had been visiting a young woman

for quite some time. She was the daughter of this inn keeper, Seamus O'Reilly. Now his inn was not a place you'd want to spend the night in, I can tell you that.

"That Seamus was a good enough fellow but like all the Irish he couldn't keep his inn clean, neither did he keep his nose clean. Got himself mixed up with every shady deal in the place and in particular he'd taken to helping out many another Irishman. You know the Irish, forever rebelling or escaping. Well his inn was a haven for anyone on the run from the road gangs and such.

"Of course we didn't know what was going on under our noses, typical of the military I'd say, and certainly Captain Corrigan didn't realise he was keeping company with the daughter of a traitor.

"That evening a messenger had galloped over from Parramatta with a message, an order more likely. Governor Hunter would be arriving that night. Quite unexpected, I might say. Well, if the governor arrived and our commanding officer was nowhere in sight there would be hell to pay. I knew very well where he would be.

The door of the inn was unlocked and as I stood there that stink of bugs made my guts heave. A filthy place, and that smell! Well, I've spoken about the smell of bugs before. I might have shouted out for the landlord or a maid, I could have called out for the potboy or anyone but I didn't want to set foot in the place. Could not face the stink of those bugs. So I walked round to the kitchen, which as you know, would be quite separate as they always were for fear of fire. It lay out the back behind that establishment. Unexpected, unannounced, I got the shock of my life.

"I'll never forget the sight of those men, and our poor Captain lying, spread eagled on the floor. Later he told me he'd never suspected there were any such goings-on. Usually he visited his lady-love late at night, this time he arrived unusually early, no one expected him at the inn. When he went round to the kitchen and walked in as usual six desperate men confronted him. They never meant him to get away and tell the tale.

"As I said when I came looking in that kitchen, the knife was already at his throat and it didn't take much to make me realise they'd do for me next. No one must know and believe me there's miles and miles of wild country stretching on for ever. Two bodies could be disposed of in a trice.

"'Let the captain go lads, let him go. No more will be spoken of this.' I knew how weak that sounded as I mouthed those words, 'This began as a matter of the heart, let's not make more of it.'

"That's all fine speaking, sorr', said Seamus 'but I've a livin' to make. One word blabbed and I'll be hanging from that tree outside. Never trust an Englishman.'"

"That single word saved my life I am sure. 'I am not an Englishman,' I said. "I am a Frenchman, baptized in the faith, and in the name of the Holy Mother I swear this shall be the end of the matter. Have you thought what will happen if an officer of King George disappears? The country hereabouts will be turned upside down and even if they have no evidence, plenty could be found about your other activities…" I gestured to the ragged men who watched every movement I made.

I took another step forward and leant over the captain whose eyes rolled with fear. "No more will be spoken of this. Will it?" I repeated and he just shook his head. He was so scared he couldn't even speak.

"So that night when the governor arrived at the post he found his captain and everything as it should be." Grand-père sat back and closed his eyes for a moment.

"How could that change your life, Grand-père? You haven't explained that."

"As I've said before, the pay of a private in the New South Wales Corps was fourteen pounds a year but grants were often made for services rendered. You could be rewarded by money or land. The very next day the good Major made it clear that my lips must be sealed and I'd not go unrewarded. Well, I was wise enough to have understood that. He was as good as his word. A grant of land came my way, my first piece of property, those acres out beyond Liverpool, we still have them in the family. And now so much besides sir. The Guise lands stretch for thousands of acres, Up to the mountains and down to the lake. The holdings around Sydney are well known, too."

"And it all happened because of that night at the inn and your going round to the kitchen because of the stink of the bugs!"

"Well, that was the beginning: a piece of land, cattle, some good years when you sell at a good price, bad years when drought stifles you… good… bad. "The old man's head nodded upon his chest.

"Your grandfather's very tired."

"I'll ask them to find Job to help him to his room."

"Let me do that, Miss Mary Ann."

"We have our servant with us Sir."

"Perhaps for one moment I can be your servant?"

Mary Ann busied herself winding up her wool and putting her work away in her tapestry bag. She did not look up. So much that was new had happened in the last twenty-four hours, not least the uneasy sensation of treading upon completely unknown territory when she caught Frank's glance.

CHAPTER 4

M ary Ann stepped from the carriage and looked up and down the street.

Catching her breath she gazed at the sandstone facades, all uniformly handsome and imposing. The city at last! An elegant street in an elegant city just as imagined. What a relief to be finally free of that lurching coach. To be able to stand upright once more! Taking a deep breath she hurried up the path to her sister's front door.

Everything became better and better. In those few moments she moved from everyday life into a dream, and when dreams become the new reality then anyone's life is transformed.

Greeted by the scent of pot-pourri and beeswax, hugged and kissed and hugged yet again, Mary Ann immediately felt at home. Her height, her hair, her complexion, in fact everything about her person became the subject of amazement and admiration for the elder sister. And soon it was her own turn to wonder and exclaim as Hannah finally led the way up the hall. The delicate plasterwork in the cornices, the archway above their heads and the soft carpet under their feet! The floorboards and planks of Bywong were a whole world away.

Briefly Mary Ann felt like a wild creature which had

strayed out of the forest into one of the paddocks, one of the brumbies from the mountain slopes rubbing shoulders with the thoroughbreds. Silly, she shook herself, a home is just a home, after all. Certainly her grandfather did not appear to be overawed.

Grand-père, supported by Job, hobbled behind them.

"Dear Grand-père, I'll take you to your room at once. The girl can bring you some tea and…"

"Tea! Haven't you anything stronger than that?"

"Dear Grand-père, I forget your country ways," Hannah inclined her head and pursed her lips. "Oh, the doormat's back there," she pointedly frowned at his boots. "Well it doesn't really matter, not raining today…yes, of course you can have anything you want. I'll speak to them in the kitchen. Let us settle you down and make you comfortable after that great journey. First things first."

First things first. She lived by popular maxim. A stitch in time saves nine, do unto others etc. Life was easiest when lived according to convention in Hannah's view. Her shrewd grey eyes saw what they wanted, nothing else existed in her world. The first of the Guise girls to marry, she had long forgotten the easy life of Bywong and happily embraced the formality of city living. Standards must be maintained, obligations met and time needed to be spent ensuring daily routines were correctly observed. Neat ringlets framed a face which was beginning to owe just a little more to artifice than nature. Time marched on and Hannah intended to remain at the forefront. Brisk, kindly, without a trace of any disturbing fancy in her head, Hannah welcomed her visitors…but she did not expect her life to suffer too many disruptions.

"We can't have the place turned upside down," she'd shared her opinions with her husband earlier that day. "I hope he's not going to expect everyone to wait hand and foot on him. And Mary Ann will need to change her ways too. None of that racing off doing her own thing all the time, life is different here. She'll have to mind her manners. There's so much I'll need to show her." Hannah allowed herself a heartfelt sigh. "But I hope I know my duty, I've always known my duty." And her husband nodded, dutifully.

"It's most gratifying to have my family under our roof, but I hope they haven't brought their country ways with them. We don't want any nonsense. No nonsense, I say." He had nodded again.

Settling Grand-père took up to the best part of an hour. Hannah made it clear to her young sister that looking after all his needs remained firmly within Mary Ann's domain. "He's such a demanding old man, isn't he? Seems to think he is the centre of the universe."

By the time his face and hands were sponged, a pillow propping up his back, another under his knee and a glass of wine in his hand Mary Ann had learnt the layout of the bedrooms and the kitchen and the washhouse.

"Let me show you the parlour." Taking her arm, Hannah led her sister down the hall. The rich colours of a Kidderminster carpet glowed on the polished wooden floor whilst on each side pictures covered the walls and a French clock ticked the hours away upon a mahogany card table.

"Oh, so elegant," exclaimed Mary Ann as she rested her hand on the Turkey-style sofa which had no ends or pillows. "I've never seen a sofa like this… and how beautifully those crystals reflect the sunshine." On a small table between two red morocco armchairs a large candlestick with lustre drops caught the last rays of the afternoon sun.

"Newly arrived in the Colony my dear, the latest in fact."

The dining room proved no less stylish but as Hannah ran her finger along the back of one of the eight rosewood chairs she frowned. "These servants, no better than Gundaroo, I'll be bound, you'd think they could at least manage the dusting. Oh, mind that vase!" She frowned as Mary Ann brushed against the sideboard. "Wedgwood, of course, not that ordinary blue stuff, black jasper it's called."

Wedgewood, Hepplewhite, *soirées, tête a têtes* as quickly as the words tripped from Hannah's lips Mary Ann squirreled them away, an exclusive vocabulary of delicacy and pleasure.

Harvesting, haymaking, footrot and the myriad ills of livestock and crop had always dominated the conversation at home, now the arrival of the latest ship, the date of the next ball at Government House or the beginning of the Races were on everyone's lips.

Over the next weeks, as Grand-père underwent his operation and began the slow business of recovery, Mary Ann's head echoed with words she had never heard before. *Chinoiserie, deshabillée, boudoir, pot pourri* and of course the necessity for the careful observance of etiquette. Sometimes she seemed to be learning another language. But she found little time to ponder that, Grand-père's needs filled up most of the day. Sitting reading to him or listening to his chatter took up a lot of time and when she wasn't expected to be at his side then Hannah whisked her off on shopping expeditions and visits to friends.

Mary Ann found the latter quite daunting. They were very fine ladies indeed. Hannah took her out paying visits nearly every day, the strict etiquette demanded that calls were made and returned with almost military precision, especially in the afternoon when Grand-père snoozed. On the days when they did not go out ladies came calling round to become acquainted with this newly arrived relative of dear Hannah's from the country. Smiling and nodding they plied her with endless discreet questions as they sat perched upon the rosewood chairs sipping tea.

As soon as polite enquiries about events in the country flagged, because of course everyone knew nothing of importance ever happened away from the city…they fell back on their usual exchanges.

"Sixpence! Can you imagine, sixpence to be rowed just across the Harbour. And then the lazy fellow shipped the oars before we got to land. The gentlemen in our party had to take turns. Exhausted they were! That fellow declared he had the cramp and could go no further. I ask you, sixpence!"

The disgraceful lack of respect, the idleness and the sheer frustration of dealing with the lower orders came continually to the fore in their conversations.

The evenings proved no different. When guests arrived for dinner - whilst the Sauternes, the claret and the brandy lightened the conversation - the deplorable fecklessness of the working class remained the overriding topic.

The upper echelons of Sydney obviously had very hard burdens to shoulder. Only when talk turned to gold discoveries, and the new wealth that would follow on a good investment, did the mood lighten. When the port circulated and the ladies retired to the drawing room each sex could talk about matters that really interested them. Money and sport for the men. Marriage and fashion for the ladies.

As she listened Mary Ann was surprised to find she increasingly yearned for the old parlour, with the flames licking up the sides of the stones in the fireplace, the familiar smell of tallow candles.

"…and don't you agree?" one of the ladies turned to Mary Ann for an answer but Mary Ann had never heard the question. Her thoughts had been back at Bywong and she stuttered out some hastily composed reply. With slightly raised eyebrows the ladies exchanged glances – these country folk!

It's the newness of it all, she kept telling herself as Hannah's housemaid fussed and tidied and dusted and polished every surface even though it already gleamed like glass. As she dutifully followed her sister into the parlour and waited for the ringing of the front doorbell to herald yet another caller she told herself not to be such a dullard. This was how ladies spent their days, after all. The only change in their routine occurred when they themselves went out visiting and invariably another orderly, prosperous establishment presented itself.

"And did you prefer Maritana to Satanella?" the ladies were sitting on the verandah at the rear of the house belonging to Hannah's bosom friend Mrs McAllister. Mrs McAllister gleaned the gossip and ground it down to the tiniest particle, only then did it waft around the city's tea tables.

"I felt the story of Maritana was a little…well, you know, a trifle risqué and I certainly preferred the singing in Satanella."

"Ah, wait till you've seen Farouita," chimed in another lady.

"I can assure you, Mr.McAllister would never suggest such a performance to me. No respectable person would be seen in the audience."

The other lady was momentarily chastened, but only momentarily. "I certainly saw the Governor's lady in a box and her friend Mrs. Wentworth was there, too."

"We all know the company Mrs Wentworth keeps. Enough said."

"While I think of it," Hannah was adept at changing the

subject if it became controversial." That new dressmaker, the one who made up that lovely yellow taffeta of yours, where does she live?"

"Ah, Madame Duval. I'll find her address later, my dear." Mrs McAllister turned to her guest, "do you find the city very tiring, that is, after your life at…where is it…yes, of course… Gun… Gundarry…no, I remember… Gundaroo?" Before Mary Ann could reply another question followed.

"It must be wearisome, so far away from town. Do you have any society in that part of the world…does anyone actually live there?"

"There are several very large properties in the area…"

"But I don't suppose anyone actually lives there more than a few months of the year, do they? The men would go down for a hunt now and then and see how matters are progressing but beyond that…what is there for them to do?"

"Many certainly prefer city life. Strangely, our mother seemed to favour the country. I can't tell you the relief for me when dear Edward agreed to us moving up here. We've a very good overseer on the property. We only go back when I need to visit my family."

"I have a cousin near Goulburn. That isn't far from Gundaroo I believe?" Mrs McAllister gave Mary Ann a pitying glance. "She's frantic, absolutely frantic to get back to the city. Not a soul lives down there, she tells me. There's nobody living down there at all."

Nobody? Uneasily Mary Ann shifted in her chair but she did not want to speak out in such sophisticated company.

Nobody? What about the schoolteacher and the blacksmith and the new store in Gundaroo where you could buy anything from cough linctus to a blade for the harrow. What about the hunting parties of the Canberri and the smoke rising from the fires of the Ngunawal? Then there were all the newcomers to the district, for people were always on the lookout for land. And round about seethed that underbelly of life, the runaways and the ne'er-do-wells, those who'd lost all they possessed and existed in the bush since they had nowhere else to go.

But of course they were all nobodies! Annoyance surged through Mary Ann as she listened to the desultory exchange.

"Everyone works very hard in Gundaroo," she blurted out.

"Works?" muttered Mrs McAllister, rolling the word distastefully round her tongue. "Oh, really. How interesting. Surely there are picnics and the occasional races and perhaps a ball?"

Mary Ann shook her head. "Sometimes Ashton's Circus comes, then just sometimes we have a ball. The Count de Rossi is going to give a ball one day. His father is building a ballroom."

"Count de Rossi...doesn't the family live at Rossiville?" a lady asked.

"The very same," Mrs McAllister was quick to show off her knowledge.

"You know it's said the old man gave up his title, but his son has reclaimed it," another lady chimed in and others followed.

"Why would he do that?"

"Who knows with people of that ilk."

"What do you mean?"

"Well, it's common knowledge. The family come from Corsica."

"Like Bonaparte?"

Mrs McAllister nodded. "But not of the same persuasion. The old count had been a spy in the pay of good King George."

A hush had fallen round the table. "Of course he was well rewarded, that's where their fortune came from. Perhaps that's when he gave up his title. But his son has certainly taken it back, always over there attending to their property. You say he is giving a ball?"

Mary Ann nodded. "Yes, it will be a great occasion. We've never had a really grand ball before."

"There! It's as I said. Just one ball! So remote. You poor girl." Her hostess added the last remark with a doleful shake of the head. "Ah! Out here, my love, we are taking advantage of the clement weather."

Mrs McAllister raised her hand majestically as they heard a footstep inside the house.

The little man who tentatively put his head round the door and just as cautiously advanced across the verandah reminded Mary Ann of the doomed male spider in the clutches of the murderous female golden orb.

Lateish in the summer these spiders weave multi-layered webs stretching between bushes and plants and trees. Not a flat web such as spiders usually spin, but a great trap which stretches in three levels and snares a multitude of flies.

The fat, striped female spider waits complacently in the centre for her next victim, and further out the single, tiny male clings to a strand and awaits the remnants of her meals. Wing of wasp and leg of beetle are his lot while his mate gorges on fat bodies. Not wanting to be her next repast he keeps to the furthest edges of the web.

Mary Ann had always marvelled that birds did not swoop down and gobble up the fat spider waiting in the middle but Grand-père had explained the spreading gossamer confounded them. Not one web but several confronted them, so they kept away.

Mrs McAllister extracted yet another piece of Turkish Delight from its box and discreetly brushed the icing sugar moustache from her upper lip. Her mate hovered just out of reach.

Two more weeks of this? Mary Ann picked at her cake and wished herself many miles away. How much she had looked forward to the visit and now her thoughts were entirely of Bywong, the space and silence of the farm. Away from this place where heavy sandstone and brick and cobbles crushed and covered the earth.

As the ladies clucked and commiserated the hours away Mary Ann thought longingly of just such a mellow afternoon back at Bywong. The air would be filled with busy calls from the chickens as they wallowed and fluffed the afternoon away in their dust baths. From the fowl run would come those deep contented exchanges the birds made as the soft sand slipped through their feathers and between their claws. Living so close to Nature she'd observed that hens had different calls for different times of the day. In the morning an urgency marked their exchanges, sometimes the triumphant cackle for a newly laid egg, but, in the afternoon contentment softened their songs, bringing forth deep caws of pleasure, sounds redolent of full gizzards and fat worms and all the things that made a chicken's life a delight.

Just like the hens in their run Hannah and her friends filled each day with routine; a visit to the dressmaker, a pianoforte concert at a neighbour's house, an afternoon at the races, a conversazione, or maybe an opera. Soon Mary Ann had no heart for all these entertainments, so intriguing at first, now she could think of nothing except Bywong.

She yearned for the fresh wind from the ranges touching her cheeks. She pined for the soft touch of the grass under her feet as she made her way down to the orchard.

"When are we going home?" complained Grand-père,

"Can't stand much more of this. House full of clacking women and that Edward! Fellow's got nothing to talk about. I asked him for the price of this season's ewes and he just stared at me! Got the conversation of a counter jumper."

"Another week the surgeon says, and remember, Dr Morton said you mustn't attempt the journey home until you can walk up and down the steps on your own. Remember what he said?"

"All I do is listen to what people say these days! No one listens to what I have to say any more, do they? It's 'do this' or 'go there' and..."

"Grand-père!" Hannah's head came round the door. "You have a visitor. Mary Ann, take that bowl away. Brush your grandfather down, he's got crumbs all over his waistcoat...I'll give you a minute."

"Who can be visiting us?" Mary Ann puzzled, no one of their aquaintance would be in Sydney...

When Frank de Rossi came into the room she was still tidying up her grandfather.

Something in his confident stride, his polite bow and warm smile made Bywong feel a little closer. No mincing city fellow, a real man. Someone from home, what a pleasure!

Smiles wreathed her features as she grasped his hand, definitely not a ladylike greeting, but all thought of those stiff circumspect bows and proffered fingertips that Hannah had inculcated was swept aside.

"Excuse us, sir, we had no idea you were still in town."

"Delighted. Delighted." A rare smile wreathed Grand-père's features, for so many months pain and irritability had been the order of the day. "Now I can have a decent conversation for once. All they talk of hereabouts is politicking and prices. Sick to death of it all, I am. What's happening down at the lake these days?"

"No rain for one thing. We badly need a drop and some are talking about a drought."

Mary Ann picked up her embroidery. She might have left the men chatting but could not bring herself to leave the room. Just like her grandfather she yearned for news of home.

"Help me, Mary Ann," Hannah snapped, "We need to bring in the wine and biscuits." Soon they were back in the room again, the younger sister hanging on every word.

Swiftly Frank de Rossi moved from details of the latest sales in Goulburn to the worrying lack of labour on the properties. Granpère had so many questions; so much can happen on the land in a matter of weeks. Then there was the flight from the countryside of so many in search of gold, and the burden which fell heavily on the squatters. Of course the harvest prospects proved the most important topic but what about that mysterious blight that had taken the crops further out on the Limestone Plains? And what about those new-fangled butter churns everyone was talking about, and was that Murray going to stand again and, and, and…

Then all too soon the visitor was making his adieux, thanking his hostess and bowing before Mary Ann.

Hannah could scarcely wait till the door shut behind him before she launched a barrage of questions.

"Why didn't you tell me you knew he was coming up to town? I could have asked him to dinner." She frowned as she looked at them. "I don't know, what is wrong with country people. They don't seem to know how to make a life for themselves. How long have you known the Count de Rossi?"

"How long?" Grand-père scoffed. "I knew his father before you were born, my girl. He came to the Colony a few years later than me. Just had the two boys, his wife had died… died young. The old man gave up his title, wanted none of it, but young Frank always had a liking for his birthplace, Corsica that is, he took up the title."

"A real count!" Hannah shook her head in wonderment.

"Oh they're a noble family alright. Old Rossi told me once they can trace their ancestors back to Charlemagne. Mind you, he was possibly trying to go one better than the de Guises." He chuckled to himself.

Even Edward was impressed when he returned that night. "Ah, the de Rossis, yes, clients of a chap I know, most dependable family. Of course many notable families settled on the Limestone Plains. End of the War and all that, all those officers from the army and the navy looking for good land. Yes, some fine people down there."

"The back of beyond," sniffed Hannah, "but he was a charming man, wasn't he, Mary Ann?"

Surprised at the question being addressed to her, Mary Ann felt her cheeks burning. "Nice enough."

"I'm surprised he's not wed, such a handsome man with such a great inheritance coming to him."

"Oh he's been sought after. I've heard that. More than once a lady's set her cap at him but seems he didn't find any to his fancy," the old man answered.

"Well, Grand-père, he's too old now," Mary Ann shrugged.

"Too old! Too old! Why my girl, he not much older than I am. That's not too old for anyone to marry," her sister spoke up.

"Who'd want him anyhow? Nice enough, but he can be a bit stuck up too."

"I'd prefer you didn't speak so disrespectfully, Mary Ann," her grandfather regarded her sternly. "I've invited him to dinner before we leave town. I trust that is alright with you, Hannah?"

His eldest daughter beamed at him and clapped her hands with delight.. "Oh Papa, how thoughtful of you."

She ticked off her potential guests one by one on the fingers of both hands. "I'll ask Mr and Mrs McAllister, and the Frobishers and that pretty daughter of theirs. And Dr Kennedy…oh, it will be such a gathering, and I'll see if the McMahons are in town."

Dismayed, her grandfather glanced at Mary Ann. "I didn't expect half the Colony to be present. I'd just thought we'd give the poor chap a decent meal and have a few laughs, even." For Hannah's establishment tended to be too correct and reserved for his taste.

"That may be the way you entertain at Bywong, Grand-père, but here we do things in a proper style, a style as would befit a count, I might say."

Indeed, the style which Hannah favoured differed in every aspect imaginable from the usual hospitality at Bywong.

When the great day came the leaves of the dining table were pulled out to their fullest extent and from the épergne in the centre of the damask-covered expanse to the rosewood chairs flanking its entire length, the table was the epitome of excellence.

The glow from four silver candlesticks highlighted the silver, the crystal and the brilliant white table napkins. Hannah had hired a butler for the occasion and even two waiters from a nearby, more opulent home.

Mary Ann shifted uncomfortably as she tried to adjust her neckline. Too low for her taste, too revealing. On first hearing of the count's coming visit Hannah had demanded to see Mary Ann's 'best dress'. Her dismay was immediate and intense. "My heavens girl, what are you thinking of? A positive hayseed you'll look, for goodness sake. I'll have you with Madame Duval first thing tomorrow."

Now, Mary Ann squirmed every time she needed to bend forward, uncomfortably aware of her breasts and her almost naked shoulders.

Fortunately no one seemed to even notice her, all eyes were on Frank de Rossi. A real count! Sitting down to dine with a real, live count brought quite a flush to the cheeks of the ladies and a respectful hum to the gentlemen's conversation.

Frank de Rossi had been delighted to accept the old man's invitation but he had no idea that such a banquet was about to be spread before him and equally sure old Richard and Mary Ann hadn't guessed either.

Certainly he had always been regularly invited out and wined and dined by many a hopeful mamma. Sometimes even a papa might suggest a dinner or a picnic or even, daringly, a ball. Of latter years the invitations had dropped away. Overseeing his father's properties took up so much time, journeying to and from Corsica to watch over family interests and a general contentment with his solitary life had deflected the world's interest in his matrimonial future.

He had walked in to Mrs McReady's inn that evening a few weeks ago with not a care in the world, but when he left he knew that a part of him was lost for ever. What could he say? What could he do? Usually young women were only too pleased to make his aquaintance, far more pleased than he was to make theirs. What was he going to do about a girl who mostly turned her gaze away and whom he sensed regarded him as one of her father's generation.

"Couldn't you be a little more attentive to our guest, Mary Ann," hissed Hannah as the ladies later made their way to the drawing room, "After all, it was on account of Grand-père, and you, of course, that the gentleman is here. There's Amelia Frobisher making sheep's eyes at him from the far end of the table and all you can do is scowl and look as if you don't want to be here."

"Oh, Hannah. He's just a neighbour, and what can I say to someone as old as him anyhow, he'd be bored stiff…even more bored stiff than me!"

When the gentlemen joined them Mary Ann retreated to the alcove at the far end of the room and stared out into the night. She had often dreamt of such an occasion as she sat by the light of a candle in the kitchen back home. What would it be like to exchange her cotton dress for a silk gown and spend the evening with fine company listening to sparkling conversation and eating exotic food? Now that she had obtained her heart's desire the reality proved quite different and only highlighted the beauty she had left behind.

Pushing open the window she gulped in a deep breath of the cool night air. Oh, for some fresh air! Instead she filled her lungs with the very lifeblood of the city. Smoke, a faintly metallic whiff from rattling carriage wheels on the cobbles outside, a telltale hint of something stale, a suggestion of decay…all these pervaded the atmosphere. Whilst far away in Bywong the night air would be sweetened with the scent of the gum trees and the perfume from roses as they cascaded along the window sills.

'You don't wish to sing for us?" Frank de Rossi had followed her across the room. "That other young lady is eager to oblige… in fact, I don't think she can be stopped." A ghost of a smile touched his face as he glanced across at Amelia Frobisher who sat at the piano, her mother turning the pages.

"I can't sing."

"So glad to hear that. She can't either, but it doesn't stop her."

Mary Ann did not reply, but he did not go away.

"Have you enjoyed your visit here, Miss Mary Ann?"

She looked at him. What did it matter… might as well tell the truth. "It's not what I expected," she blurted out, then lowered her voice. "All they do is chatter… on and on. No one talks about anything important at all."

"And what do you consider important?"

"Well," she paused, then went on, "all the things we talk about at Bywong, the weather, and if there are going to be any more frosts, and oh, you know, all those important things."

"Everyone has their own world, you know. That's your world and it's mine to some extent, but their world is quite different, and just as important to them as ours is to us."

"I think I'll be quite satisfied with my world from now on."

CHAPTER 5

Job cracked the whip as they rumbled out of Sydney.

Home! All Mary Ann could think about was walking up the steps of the verandah and throwing her arms around her father. Every mile added to her excitement. The city had been all she had imagined, but also a lot of other things. Noise, dirt, the unconcerned glances of strangers, the pettiness of those who live too close to each other and see too much.

The image of Bywong filled every waking thought. Even the weather welcomed them home, not a drop of rain, four nights of sleeping under the Milky Way. And by the time the coach approached Goulburn she could scarcely contain her impatience. How many hours before they rumbled up the track beneath the swaying elms?

"Night's falling fast. We've come off the main road, Job knows he won't make home tonight. We'll have to stop soon and set ourselves up for the night." Gingerly Grand-père shifted his knee. He still could not quite get used to the lack of pain but now the whole limb had stiffened up from the operation. Successful as the surgeon had been, the upheaval of the visit to Sydney, combined with the nagging discomfort and the sheer worry of it all had tipped him from a contented old age into a less-than-happy frame of mind. The body which had served him so well for all those years no longer moved with ease.

"What is that?"

"Where… what… what are you looking at?"

"Look! Look!" Mary Ann cried out.

Breasting a hill they had turned to the right past a tall clump of trees and were at a crossroads.

From a gibbet, at this place of eminence, hung a terrible reminder of justice meted out.

Two bodies in their chains dangled from the gallows. Wind-burnt and shrivelled, they would no longer have been recognisable as humans if their hair hadn't fluttered and the bones of their fingers had not showed white and fleshless.

"Oh my God," Mary Ann covered her eyes. "Oh, we must go on. Grand-père, don't let Job stop! We must go on. Stay on the road, we don't stop in this place!"

"An example, that's why it's done. There, there!" He reached across and patted her hand. "Don't take on so my girl. Whoever they are, they must have deserved it. They're left up there for weeks, months, sometimes a year or more, as an example to others. They'd have deserved it."

"Deserved it! Deserved to be left up there for the world to gape at!"

An omen! Bile rose in her throat as her heart throbbed. A terrible omen. *Go on! Go on! Whip them up! Hurry, hurry!* In her mind's eye she could see those bodies as once they'd been, clothed in flesh with stout limbs and desperate eyes, taking their last look at the world. *Hurry, hurry,* the words went round and round in her brain but not a sound came out of her lips. Just as in a nightmare when disaster looms and you try to cry out and you can't even escape as your legs won't move. Transfixed, you cringe before that terrible Thing which pursues.

The panic and the pain of those men's last moments were as real as the thudding in her chest.

"Good heavens girl, you're white as a sheet! Close your eyes, sit back. You have no part in these matters. Don't be frightened."

Mere words, feeble phrases to combat the overwhelming reality of sheer dread. Mary Ann gasped and squeezed her eyes tight shut. For a tortured moment in time she was no longer inside the familiar old coach. Instead she swung high in the bitter wind of the plains, the noose cut into her neck as her body floundered at the end of the rope.

"Don't stop Grand-père, don't let him stop. We must get home, oh, let's get home! It's a wicked place. Wicked, wicked!"

At a snail's pace now Job made his way back to the highway and continued their journey. By the light of the moon he carefully guided the horses across the Breadalbane Plains. Every rut could have claimed a wheel, every rocky outcrop might be harbouring some desperate bushranger.

The landscape which had been so exciting now became a place of threat and for every inch of the way Mary Ann clutched at the leather of the seat and stared into the night whilst Grand-père snored amongst his cushions.

Mary Ann's heart was still heavy when, many hours later, she finally walked up the steps to the verandah at Bywong. She could not shake off the memory of those two men hanging and twisting and turning in the wind. Once upon a time they'd been someone's son or husband or brother, a caring hand had stroked and comforted them, their thoughts had been respected, their bodies loved. Now their souls were banished and every piece of the fabric that had made up their bodies was hideously displayed for all the world to see.

❀

Within a few weeks the journey to Sydney and their time in the city became no more than a memory. The worsening drought, the loss of several men from the farm as they disappeared to the goldfields and, overshadowing all, Grand-père's slow recovery, all conspired to turn everyone's thoughts to the present and the future. Who had time to dwell on the past?

Weeks trailed into months as the old man gradually regained his strength. The injury had healed but in spite of the surgery his nimbleness never returned and, not being able to ride or even walk for very long, he began to lose interest in much of their day to day life. Meals became tasteless, the usual gossip had lost its piquancy as, without an active role in the running of the farm, he found little to enjoy in life.

"The Devil's playing with his marbles again," he muttered one day as he sat staring out at the parched acreages.

"Come, come, Papa. I've not felt a thing." William looked up from the Herald.

"You don't have to feel. Look at the clock!"

The old man pointed at the grandfather clock. Silent, with its hands motionless, the handsome oak timepiece loomed from its place of honour opposite the front door.

Very few homes possessed such a magnificent grandfather. Once his new venture prospered and the construction of his home been completed entirely to his wife's satisfaction, Richard had made the possession of a really fine clock one of his priorities. Ordered from the old country, brought out in pieces wrapped in rags, hessian and straw and secured in a stout wooden box, the handsome grandfather had survived the rolling of the ship and the jolting of the cart and proved none the worse for its journey. Painstakingly reassembled the clock was soon towering over even the tallest visitor to Bywong and its hearty chimes causing some to block their ears.

The brass face glowed in the light of day and the soft beams of candlelight gave a gleam to the delicately carved hands as its steady note ticked and tocked their lives away.

Though sturdy and solid the clock had to be kept delicately balanced. Tiny slivers of wood wedged under the base corrected any fault in the uneven floor. Only a sudden movement could put the pendulum out of kilter and stop the hands.

"How long have we lived in Bywong? Nearly forty years... well, I've seen a few things in my time and I can tell you there's more that goes on around here than meets the eye."

"Oh, you're just imagining things, Grand-père!"

"That clock stopped at two in the morning! You wound it up three days ago, I saw you do it, William. What else could cause the hands to stop?"

"Well, I suppose there could be some truth to it," his son conceded.

"The earth shifts. We all know that. In this place the earth shifts."

"Some say, some say." Even at nearly sixty he did not like contradicting his father, outlandish as some of the old man's notions might be.

"Some say!" mercilessly Grand-père mimicked him. "There's more to this land than meets the eye, just as I've always said. I've lived in this house for too many years now and I've seen things I can hardly credit. Why is the water going down in the lake? Why are there dead fish floating on the surface? It's a devious place."

"What do you mean? Devious?" Mary Ann asked.

"Underhand perhaps, would be better to say, underground. Where is the water going to? Who knows what happens when the earth shifts, it's common knowledge we get these movements here. Nothing like this happened in Sydney, or Parramatta or

Liverpool, come to that. Why else is our lake draining away?"

"Why? Papa, have a care. Don't tempt the gods with all this despondency. We are in drought once more. No rain's fallen on the ranges for months. The level could be expected to drop."

"Drop! Haven't you seen how far out from the shore we can walk? The mud's baked solid. Mark my words, with the earth shifting there's a mighty crack out there in the middle beneath the waters. Deep, deep down in the earth anything might be happening. Remember the old legends of the gods and the forge in the centre of the earth? Well, we do know such people never existed but these things happen all the same. What can it be but a crack letting the waters drain away?"

"Next thing you'll be telling me we are living on top of a volcano," laughed William.

"Not such a joke after all my son. Didn't Frank de Rossi's father show me those white stones he found? Not real stones but what he called pumice, such as are found on the slopes of the volcanoes in Italy. A wise man, Captain de Rossi. He said that ages and ages ago a river flowed through here and he believed something like one of our shakings of the earth, something like a volcano or a calamity, closed off the valley and that's why we have this lake. Tell me how it is no river flows in or out of Lake George. Contrary to nature itself."

William sighed with resignation. He knew better than to cut him off in full flood before he had finished whatever he wanted to say.

Nowadays, with just Job for help, William was hard put to keep up with work in the paddocks as well as the tasks around the yard. Now that young Elizabeth was married and over at Woodbury and Charles so often away overseeing other family properties William was worn out from the never ending routine of the property. Only Mary Ann, of all the family, remained to see to the chickens, make the butter and the cheese and ride out with the rations to the shepherds in their lonely huts. Let alone look after the home.

"Dunno what we'd do without you," William said one evening, as he sat back and pushed away his empty plate. "Meal and a half that was. Your mother certainly taught you how to cook." Praise did not come readily from her father's lips. Her heart swelled with pride as she looked around the kitchen which had become her domain. The crockery gleamed on the dresser shelves, the embers glowed in the fireplace and dried bunches of basil, thyme and rosemary hung from the rafters, softening the air with the scent of summertime.

"Daresay you'd rather be up in town with your sister. Going to all those balls and spending time at the races, but it'll happen one day my girl, it'll happen."

"Not for me, Papa, I'm happy. Never think otherwise."

"When this confounded drought ends there'll be money in the bank again, there'll be enough of that alright. First off we'll have one of those gigs, those really smart turnouts from America, think they call them buggies. You'll be the talk of the countryside in your buggy. You will." He laughed.

Mary Ann smiled. "Never you worry, Papa, I'm happy. Just wish we could have some rain. The paddocks are crying out for a real downpour."

The relentless sun had desiccated every blade of grass. Four weeks before Christmas her father sent the last of the Bywong sheep to be boiled down. Only a shilling a beast they fetched; now the pastures lay empty. Due to his foresight the flocks up in the mountains survived, scrawny and scraggy and so dusty as to be almost undistinguishable from the rocks, but they certainly survived. Every time Mary Ann rode up with rations for the shepherds she marvelled that the flocks still increased, in spite of the dry conditions and the dingoes.

There was no doubt the Guises knew how to manage when the hard times came. But others did not fare so well and within the first year of the drought several neighbouring families had packed up and moved back to the city.

"Mary Ann should go up to Hannah's, you know." Sister Elizabeth, visiting for a few days, gave her opinion freely. "What is there here for a young girl? Mary Ann must go to the city, Hannah will look after her. She can go back with Charles, he'll be coming down soon. He can take her next time he goes up north."

"It's all very well for you to say that but I don't see how we could manage without her these days."

"Manage! It's no place for a young girl, there's not another single lady hereabouts, not another one anywhere. The Mitchells have gone, the Barrys have gone. Even the Coulthards have left. Only the men remain."

"There's the women down by the river!"

"Women! That's a kindly term for them. Sluts, more likely. Our Mary Ann needs proper company. She's burned brown and her hair's in rats-tails half the time. There's not a spare bit of flesh on her, out all hours with Job, and if she's not in the paddocks she's in the dairy. And if that's not enough – there's the kitchen. Spick and span, I admit, but the girl's never free of chores."

"And how would we manage without Mary Ann in the kitchen? If it weren't for Mary Ann we'd be in a sorry state."

"If you didn't have her to run around after you then you could manage like all the others do. Men on their own can cope, just like the shepherds. There's always meat and then there's damper. What more do you want. No, I tell you, this is no life for a young girl."

"No, Papa. No! I can't go. I won't go!" Mary Ann had her own views on the matter when it was raised. "Bywong's too important. Much more important than all that folderol in the city. You need the help. Who'll tend the dairy? Who'll take out the rations? There's too much to do, and with Grand-père not his usual self too."

"He'll be alright after Christmas, he just needs time. Even if he can't get about much, this long rest probably's all for the best, he needed to slow down, the older folks get, the longer it takes them to recover. This rest is doing him the world of good." All the problems in William's world had silver linings and if he could not find one he kept his own counsel. Certainly no good would come trying to persuade Mary Ann against her will and secretly he did not want her to leave.

Time was needed, just time.

The whole countryside needed time. Time to revive from the suffocating heat which poured down from the sky day after day, time to pay off the debts relentlessly piling up.

"Even the blackfellers are leaving," William muttered. "That camp down near the river's deserted and some say they're all heading for the Monaro."

Only very rarely now did Grand-père get Job to saddle up for him, and venture across the paddocks but even if he spent increasing hours sitting on the verandah, his very presence kept their spirits up.

He'd seen hard times, he'd lived through good and bad. With his memory undimmed he made light of every fresh setback.

"Look, Grand-père, some plovers' eggs! I found them over past the dam, such a treat!" Carefully Mary Ann unwrapped the speckled eggs. Surely they would tempt her grandfather's failing appetite?

A faint smile touched his lips. "Plovers' eggs? Well, that's a delicacy now."

He picked one up and looked at it. "Food fit for a queen."

"Well, no queens round here and…"

"Perhaps not. But blood counts, Mary Ann. Do you know why you were called Mary Ann?"

Sensing a story in the air she gathered her skirts about her and sat on the stool at his feet. "Tell me."

"Because of the queen, Queen Marie Antoinette. Marie Antoinette, Mary Ann… do you see now? Marie Antoinette belonged to the House of Lorraine, so did the de Guises. Something to be proud of. A kinswoman – think of that. Noble blood flows in your veins, Mary Ann."

"Isn't much help now, is it?"

"That's rather an impertinent remark to make. Remember where we came from, remember I came to this Colony as a common soldier."

Immediately sorry she'd offended the old man, she pulled the stool closer and took his hand. Over the last months he no longer mentioned his early life. The times when she had listened spellbound had disappeared and now she realised how those reminiscences had been lost amongst a welter of hauling buckets of water to the orchard, searching for lost animals, carrying the hay into the stables, cleaning up the dairy and fetching and carrying in the house.

"Did you ever think you'd one day be sitting in your home, at the other end of the world?"

He sighed. "As one door closes, another opens."

"Tell me, Grand-père."

"It's so long ago."

"You've never forgotten, have you?"

How could he forget that screaming mob that had surged

out of Paris and struggled through the rain and mud for the fifteen miles that divided the capital from Versailles? The air had been filled with curses and demands that the king return to the country's rightful capital and not waste his time amongst the pleasures of the countryside. How could he forget the shrieks of the crowd and the frantic panic of the courtiers as they tried to escape from the palace before the mob arrived? There was no hope of securing Versailles against them for no door or gate could be locked or bolted as none had been secured since the days of the great Sun King. Louis XIV. Rusty and open the mob poured through the portals as the nobles took flight as best they could, dressed as servants, grooms, lady's maids… anyone of humble appearance. Disguised as the poorest of the poor they made their escape. The words poured out as Mary Ann listened.

"But not a de Guise, we would not desert our queen. A de Guise never turns his back on the enemy."

"But you did escape. How did you get away?"

"The King and Queen knew they would have to follow the crowd's bidding and return to the capital. Her Majesty told me I was not to come with them, she knew only too well the fate that awaited all who were faithful to the monarchy. But I would never leave them unguarded." For a moment he shut his eyes as he saw the scene once more. The white- faced woman with her children, her husband standing, silent and defeated staring down into the courtyard where the blood of their bodyguard crimsoned the cobbles.

" 'Go,' she said. I did go, but only to my room to fetch my sword and pistol. A tiny room too, do you know, Mary Ann, that to live at Versailles conferred such an honour, many of us would make do with a cupboard!" He laughed." A cupboard! Well, mine may have been a little larger than that, but it was smaller than our smallest room at Bywong! I can tell you.   I knew I must follow the king and the queen but my servant thought otherwise."

"Your servant? How could a servant alter things?"

"Jerome had been with my father, then he came to serve me. I've often marvelled when I've thought of him. It would have been so easy for him to have joined the crowd and washed his hands of his master, but he didn't."

"Did he stand up for you?"

"Stand up for me! They'd have put a pike through him in no time at all. No, he argued with me, told me that Queen Marie Antoinette and King Louis had no chance at all. He begged me not to return to them, it would be my death warrant if I followed them to Paris. The guillotine awaited, we would all die."

"So you listened to him. That was…"

"Of course I listened but I'd never have deserted my masters and my kin."

"Were you caught?"

"Patience, child. I told Jerome to hold his tongue and help me prepare, help me put everything needed in my saddlebag, call the groom and have my horse saddled. I needed to be off and follow them on their journey, not a second must be lost. A shriek came from the courtyard below where a guard had always stood at the entrance and a scream of triumph followed, then the thunder of footsteps as a horde of people came hurtling up the stairs. I was kneeling by my chest, rummaging for my pistols when suddenly everything went black."

"Black? How do you mean, Grand-père?"

"Jerome must have hit me on the head, picked up a chair, I daresay. He'd knocked me out. Not clean out, but the shock sent me spinning across the room and next thing I was staring up at him. He stood over me with a knife in his hand."

"Oh, Grand-père! He was going to kill you!"

"Certainly looked like that. I could just see a crowd of faces at the door. Fresh bright red blood spattered their shirts. Funny how things cross your mind when there is panic all round. That's Pierre's blood. Or perhaps it's the blood of one of the Swiss Guards, I remember thinking as they stood there, their eyes so keen and excited, waiting for my blood. But Jerome knew what he was doing. He threw himself on me with the knife in his hand. Don't know where it went, suppose it slid down the side of me. Then he got up and faced those rogues."

"What did he say?"

" 'Leave him to me, citizens,' he said, 'leave him to me. Too long I've been waiting for this moment.' And they cheered him and went off without another glance."

"You mean they thought he'd killed you himself?"

"Exactly so. Groggy I might have been but finally I managed to struggle up. The footsteps were thundering away and in the distance came terrible screams. Others had not been as fortunate as I. I cursed him though, still nothing could wipe that satisfied grin off his face. By the time I was *compos mentis* the king and queen had been bundled away in their carriage and where their guard had stood there was just a pool of blood. Old Jerome didn't say much, gave me my saddlebag and said I'd best make good use of the time and get to Calais…"

"Pity our Mary Ann hasn't more company her own age nowadays," Elizabeth observed yet again to her father on another of her quite frequent visits from Woodbury. "When it was the two of us that wasn't so bad but nowadays all she has is men! And old men too! Grand-père forever filling her head with those ancient tales, Job grousing away out in the yard spouting parables at the poor girl. "T'isn't natural for a young girl."

Momentarily William felt a twinge of amusement. Where did he fit in agewise?

"Think how she enjoyed herself when she was up at Barrack Street, think of the different things she could do."

"I seem to remember she was very thankful to be home again, though."

"Oh Papa, of course anyone likes being home again but I'd say the city is the place for her at her age."

"Well, you speak to her then." The running of the property posed enough responsibility for William. Having to concern himself over the womenfolk was a burden he did not want to shoulder. "Perhaps she should go up to Hannah after all. Just as you said way back, this is no place for a girl, no life at all. We could manage, Grand-père and me, no doubt about that. Just get in a woman to clean up once in a while. There's always women down in the village needing a shilling or two these times."

"Reliable decent women? I doubt it. Every wife and mother worth her salt is hard put to it keeping their own homes and family together."

"Well, there's the Irish family. Down near the river."

"Certainly not reliable or decent! They're not setting foot inside this house and that's an end of it. Neither Mama nor Grand-mère would have had them coming within a mile of Bywong."

"Never fear, we could find someone."

"And I'll speak to her again."

But speaking to Mary Ann brought no more success than the last time it had been suggested she might go up to the city.

Never, never would she leave her home! Mary Ann was

not naïve. Whenever Papa and Charles met she'd noticed they immediately fell into deep conversation. Overseeing the distant properties, making decisions about their lands around the lake, their property up in Sydney and leased holdings elsewhere around New South Wales, all required care and attention. Always so much to talk about, so many decisions to make.

Who would be left to care for the Guise property? Two sons already lay in the family at St Johns, only Charles remained. And his life was spent riding out to the other holdings, up to Parramatta, over to Macquarie Fields, then off to the mountains. Maybe she could not pass on the Guise name but she could make sure the property was never neglected. Amongst all the other properties, Bywong was their home and through good times and bad it was going to be looked after.

This is where I belong, Mary Ann muttered to herself, *I'll not go up to the city, never again. No, this is where I'm staying.* "One day the rain will come. The drought can't get any worse. It can't get any worse!"

"Don't tempt the dark gods, my girl. Don't say such things," her father warned.

The dark gods must have heard for, bad as times had been, they soon became even more desperate. Burnt to a cinder by the pitiless sun and chilled by icy nights, the heavens looked down on a ravaged countryside. The last willow sacrificed for fodder, the surviving beasts driven up to the mountains and even the water in the well turned dark and brackish. The sun beat down mercilessly on that expanse which had once been Lake George.

Dust now rose where water had glinted in the sunshine. Cattle, sheep, kangaroos, wild turkeys, wallabies, pigs, goats – a whole mixture of creatures scavenged over the acres and many left their bones bleaching in the sun. Where yabby and eel and cod had multiplied in the depths not a single puddle remained.

Then a fresh disaster gripped the land, a plague of grasshoppers descended. They devoured any remaining patch of greenery and, worse still, the carefully tended vegetables in the backyards disappeared under the relentless tide of insects devouring, breeding and dying. In some places their dead bodies piled up two feet deep around the dried-out lake, and the stink that filled the air made Lake George a place to be shunned.

No sooner had the grasshoppers ravaged all that remained than sickness followed. Measles, scarlet fever and whooping cough swept through the tiny communities all around. Already decimated, the numbers of Canberri and Nunghawal who had remained were cut down even further.

Gaunt cattle on the properties huddled in any patch of shade, mere shadows besmirched with brown dust. Skeletal, dirty, desperate-their only value lay in being boiled down at a shilling a time for glue or tallow.

The daily round for the beleaguered settler centred around saving their water supplies. Many of those without wells had already taken the road to the city, braving heat, fearsome potholes and clouds of dust as they took their chance with any bushranger who might bail them up. Turning their faces away from the lake, they deserted those cruel acreages.

Those who could do so left the land, but some had invested all they possessed and had no choice but to stay and husband any remaining resources. Fricasseed possum and quail on toast became a luxury and any creature fair game, even the bony crows weren't shunned.

"Reckon them over there'd be dead and gone but for they crows!" Job pointed to the Irishwoman's hut across the river. "I seen 'em with me very own eyes, out with the nets, find some rotting carcass and fix them nets in position and next to no time they've got their dinner hopping straight in after the bait."

"Well, all power to them, Job. They'd never have the wherewithal to leave that hovel. 'Needs go when the devil drives'. There's plenty of hungry mouths under that roof. All those young lads and no work."

"And that there girl taking after her ma, 'tis said. Like as not no better than she ought to be."

"Desperate times, Job!"

"Like 'tis said in the good book," muttered Job.

William made no reply. Over the months his oldest hand was becoming more and more morose.

"You can't read; how do you know, eh, Job?" Mary Ann spoke up. She was holding the twine as he tied up some sacks in the barn.

"Don't need to. Mr Sowerby said…"

"Hurry up, Job," William snapped. He didn't feel in the mood for any more dire predictions.

"What did Mr Sowerby say?" Mary Ann persisted. William Sowerby being such a powerful preacher, his words universally respected. Whenever he journeyed from Goulburn to the outlying villages his sermons drew crowds eager for comfort.

"He said we're all sinners. Says so in the good book. And the Lord sends the plagues on the sinners, and it's all just as he said."

"That was a whole world away, in Egypt, wasn't it Father?"

William nodded. "Hurry up Job. We don't want to be here all night."

"Praise the Lord!" Job refused to be silenced. "We've had the first plague when the fishes come up dead and floated and we've had a plague of flies alright."

"If I'm right," William put in drily, "the next plague warns of boils and blains though I'm not sure what a blain is. Well, you can't say we had that!"

"Oh, can't I? What about all the sickness that's keeping the blackfellows in their camps and the fever's goin' through the properties. They reckon all the littl'uns in Gundaroo is comin' down with it. And haven't we had them grasshoppers?"

"It says locusts in the Scriptures."

"Near as no difference. I tell you we'll have the darkness before we're finished and then the worst of all."

"What's that?" Mary Ann asked.

"Last plague's the death of the firstborn. Firstborn calves, firstborn lambs, firstborn sons."

"Come father, we need some help with those buckets." One glance at her father had been enough. Over the years he depended more and more upon his eldest son. Now his other sons had gone, only Charles remained. Watching over the scattered properties of the family had become Charles' occupation and William Guise fretted at the young man's long absences from home.

She cursed the old man under her breath. Why couldn't he keep his mouth shut.

As William wearily followed her up to the house he tried to shake off his servant's prediction. Why had such disaster overtaken the land? Never before had he connected the events of the last years with any such pattern as Divine Providence. Could it be? His spirits were still at a low ebb the next day when Charles returned on one of his brief visits.

"Mary Ann'll have to go up to the city. I'll take her up to Hannah," Charles urged his father. "How many months have we endured this? The house is a burden. You've enough to do keeping the horses and the pigs and the chickens watered. All the rest, the orchard and the garden. It's nothing but a burden Father. What is the point of running the pair of you into the ground? You can camp out alright, you'd be fine here with Grand-père and Job to fetch and carry, but Mary Ann's a different kettle of fish. She must leave, this is just not right for her."

But that was not to be.

"I'm not leaving Bywong, Papa. I'm staying and that's the end of it." Mary Ann stalked out of the room, leaving them nonplussed. Then she put her head round the door, determined to make her point. "Leave so much to die in the drought? The orchard would be the first to go, then there would be the vegetables and Grand-mère's roses. And the chickens? Who'd make sure they were shut up? Job's got a head like a sieve. Then there's the calves, would he remember to shut them away before milking? Leave all that to fall into nothingness?"

Mary Ann wagged her finger at them, a broad smile on her face. "Remember what you always say, Grand-père? A de Guise never goes back on his word? Well, you've heard my last word."

CHAPTER 6

"'Tis said over Bungendore way, land'll never recover from this 'ere drought," Job muttered as he filled up a bucket from the well. "They says there's cracks opened up that big you'd never believe. Forty sheep was lost down one of 'em. Here, Miss Mary Ann, gimme me that pail, and sit yerself down for a spell."

"I heard that too," William stepped off the verandah and picked up a bucket.

"'Tis said old Cap'n Rossi's sent the last of his sheep to be boiled down."

"Oh. Speaking of the Rossis, they are going to give a ball for the whole neighbourhood. I met Frank yesterday coming back from Bungendore, he said he hoped we'd all be there."

"A ball!" Mary Ann exclaimed. "A ball! Yes, he talked about that when we met him ages ago. When Grand-père and I went up to Hannah's."

"Time flies, Mary Ann, that was nearly two years ago," her father reminded her. "Seems the work on that ballroom got held up due to our drought, only just finished now."

"A real ball! How wonderful! But who'll be going? There's hardly anyone left round here."

"Such a deal of money in new pockets these days. There's newcomers buying up the properties cheap, always hoping the drought will end. There's plenty of folk around still. Gold, that's what it is. People say it's the making of the country now. I wonder. Gold's the new wealth of this country, not wool. Some say there's new chums down in Melbourne lighting their cigars with pound notes. But even so, there's always people hereabouts. There's plenty come down for the hunting this time of year, like they often do. People like to get out of the city once in a while."

"Just think. A real ball!"

"Not, I trust, like the one they held in Gundaroo a few years back?" William frowned to himself. He'd only been there as young Elizabeth had some fancy to listen to the fiddler and watch the dancing. Children, old men, anyone who could stand on their two feet after all that drinking. What a shocking night! They'd not stayed long.

That country ball scarcely deserved the name – a noisy mass of people throwing themselves about as the lone fiddler scraped away. Children leaping around with their relatives, the usual young men eyeing the girls and couples shyly taking to the floor.

A very old man had walked around the room asking anyone who cared to dance with him. The trill of the fiddle had kindled a long dormant spark in his ancient frame. His eyes shone and his feet tapped as he held out his hand time after time for a partner. No one followed him on to the floor. He didn't give up though, didn't retreat to his wrinkled isolation; instead with a rueful shrug danced out across the room all on his own. Time rolled back for him, with the stiff elegance of many years he spun out the measures and whirled his solitary way around the room. With flushed cheeks and smiling lips, his face glowed as the music took him back to his youth, to a time when he held his love close to him once again. Surely someone would be brave enough to take to the floor and keep him company in his dreams.

William for a moment knew how empty those arms must feel. He'd turned away and sighed. In the end we are, each and every one of us, on our own.

Balls nowadays weren't worthy of the name. Mary Ann was far too young for the mixed sort of gathering this might be. She'd soon see for herself.

"No, Papa, I'm sure it would be nothing like that. The Count would never let such things happen under his roof. A real ball!"

"Of course you are right." Her father could not help but smile. Who could grudge her such delight? "This will be a great occasion. An orchestra from Melbourne and all the ladies remaining in the neighbourhood have been invited and asked to bring parties. Naturally Elizabeth and Henry'll come over and stay."

Mary Ann's excitement steadily mounted until by the time her sister arrived she could barely contain herself.

"Do you think they'll have ices? They have ices in Sydney these days, Hannah told me, though I never saw any. A real ball! What did you wear to your first real ball?"

"I had a respectable frock for the first thing, none of this silly nonsense you brought back from the city." Mary Ann was twirling around in front of her sister. "Can't imagine what Hannah was thinking of letting you go out into company dressed like that. Perhaps she thought it suitable for Barrack Street but you certainly can't wear it here. It's quite shocking, and what's more I was a mite older than you."

"I know, I know, but naught can be done about that, can it? Still we can do something about my dress, some lace'll fix all that up. Won't take a minute to make it quite respectable."

"And that hem can come down, just a smidgin," Elizabeth observed. "It's quite a pretty dress, I grant you that, but it certainly needs to be toned down a little bit. Keep still a moment, I'll fetch the pins."

"I can't wait, I just can't wait. But what if no one asks me to dance? What shall I do Elizabeth? What if I just sit there the whole evening?   Oh the shame of it!"

"Come now, my Henry'll take you round the floor and I daresay Dr Morton and his wife will be there too. We'll all be round you. You'll find most of the neighbours as well I've no doubt. What a shame Charles won't be home in time but I'm sure Papa will oblige with a couple of turns too."

"Oh, Papa! He wouldn't even know how to dance."

"Don't you be so certain. I can remember when Mama was still with us they cut a fine pair at any party. You'd be too young to remember. Your papa could probably still dance you off your feet."

"And will there be those little cards for people to write in, you know, you read about them in the journals, just to make sure you get the right dance? And what do you think the Palmer ladies will wear? They can afford anything they want. They'll be there won't they."

A ball, Grand-père mused as he listened to his granddaughters. The mere mention of a ball in days gone by had sent his dear departed wife fluttering off to the dressmaker. Once their first struggles were over and prosperity came to the Guise family there had been many a dinner and a ball. Satin slippers, feathery fans, velvet wraps and white gloves. Those were the days he sighed to himself, that first flush of success and their years in

Barrack Street. How different life had been once they moved away from the city.

Balls and picnics and race meetings had been part of their lives once upon a time. They had worked hard and played hard. Close on the heels of all those memories came a chance remark which still resounded down the years. A girl never forgets her first ball'. Perhaps Frank's ball would mark the beginning of a new era for everyone, maybe it would be a landmark.

He could only hope it would be nothing like some of the country balls he'd seen. Why give them the name of a ball at all? Merely a bacchanalia of bumpkins eagerly eyeing the drink, sweating in their Sunday best and huddling together until one or the other summoned up enough courage to take to the floor.

At least Frank de Rossi was a man of breeding. His generosity and hospitality were legendary in the region. He would never tolerate rowdy behaviour, decorum would be observed.

Even if times had not been so hard, the ball at Frank de Rossi's would have been the talk of the neighbourhood. Many fine stone houses had been built when times were good but none of them boasted a ballroom.

Although ladies of quality mostly did not choose to dwell permanently in the country they had always spent part of the year on their properties, moving down from Sydney or up from Melbourne to join their husbands in the new land of promise when the season and the weather suited them. But when the fortunes of those who settled in the area changed many no longer bothered with the journey.

Numbers of properties went on the market, some weren't sold but left in the hands of an overseer, some just left untended. After all, if things picked up the land would still be there. Fences could fall down, huts could crumble and roofs could leak but the land remained. Land was where the value lay. They had their options.

Options to suit many a settler, but not the Guises, they were a tenacious family. The Guises had always stayed together. Perhaps it was the closeness of the migrant, the obstinate determination to succeed and their dependence on each other, perhaps it was the great love which had bonded Grand-père and Grand-mère. Whatever the reason the Guises held on to their properties and certainly held on to each other.

Mary Ann clutched at her father's arm as they mounted the flight of steps leading up to the de Rossi's verandah. A servant waited to usher in the guests. A servant who moved awkwardly and stepped carefully as he'd been temporarily relieved of his flannel shirt and moleskins and boots and was now splendidly arrayed in a white jacket with big brass buttons and everything to match.

Out of the corner of her eye Mary Ann caught sight of women laying out supper in the dining room. Their flustered faces glowed in the candlelight as they arranged the platters and tossed the lily-white throwovers across the table, over the expanse of silver and crockery. Beeswax sweetened the air in the hallway and swags of gum leaves added a pungency all their own.

"Slow down, slow down," muttered Grand-père as he hurried to keep up with the others. "We'll get there soon enough."

"Wait for your grandfather," admonished William as he hesitated and grasped the verandah rail.

Not for the first time William felt a twinge of discomfort.

For the last few months a heaviness had gripped his chest on occasions. Now he had to stand still and catch his breath.

"Take my arm, Papa, just mind your step!"

Common sense told him that he should sit down, tell the others to go and let him be for a moment, sit down with the old man and take the weight off his feet, but rational thought does not rule when uncertainty surfaces. William frowned. How could he, the head of the family, admit to any infirmity?

It must be all that worry over the drought, the debts or maybe a twinge of one of those ailments of later years which so soon become chronic. Nothing to worry about!

"It's certainly a magnificent place. Right down the back, sir, that's where the ballroom is. What a construction!" Henry called over his shoulder.

"Come on, Papa, come on!" Mary Ann turned back and took his hand.

"Let Gran'père catch his breath," but in truth it was he, himself, who took a few quick gasps.

Momentarily they paused. A passage stretched in front of them and through an archway at the far end the bright lights of the ballroom beckoned. They could only wonder at the magnificence displayed before them when they finally stood on the polished boards. Pillars cunningly painted to resemble marble stretched up to the high ceiling where silver stars and a fat, white Man in the Moon gleamed down from a midnight sky.

At a loss for words, the party stood and stared. The burnished wood of the floor shone like glass, reflecting candle sconces set every few feet along all four walls. A small group of musicians tuned their instruments upon a raised stage, against a backdrop of apricot velvet drapery. Chairs lined the walls, not the square wooden chairs which everyone used each day but neatly upholstered articles of furniture with curved backs and graceful legs and seats of the same glowing velvet. All around, from picture rail to skirting, the walls were painted a delicate cream and garlands of greenery framed each window and doorway.

For in that alone Frank de Rossi had been unable to fulfil his dreams. No flowers bloomed at this time of year so he'd had to make do with the branches of gum and fronds of she-oaks.

"The Ball of the Yew Trees. Oh! Grand-père. Remember you told me all about it. This is just the same, except here we have the gum trees."

The old man smiled as he gazed upon the scene and his smile broadened even further as he as he watched the rapt expression spreading across his granddaughter's face. "Who'd have thought it?" he muttered, "Who'd have thought anyone could have constructed all of this?"

"It's how they must have lived once, over there in Corsica and such places. They're a deep lot, the de Rossis. Look at Mary Ann. You'd think she'd walked into Government House ballroom." Elizabeth nudged her grandfather. Mary Ann held her head high and glanced around with perfect composure.

For Mary Ann had stepped into her dreams. That sturdy reality which ruled her days counted for nothing compared with the shimmering reveries of her nights, and now she had walked straight into that hidden world. Leaving behind everyday life; the pinafores, the pipkins, the bowls of settling cream, the clucking of the hens and the plop, plop, plop of fruit boiling away into jam - she had crossed the boundary between reality and dreams.

Here perfection lay, all around her. Just as she'd learnt from her grandfather's stories: the satin and brocade, the lilting music, fluttering fans and polite conversation. It really did exist!

She gave a deep sigh of contentment.

As the countryfolk entered the ballroom and hovered a trifle awkwardly by the door their loud voices and pushy ways gave way to a whispered hum of conversation. The ballroom set its own standards and in the space of a few moments the visitors had to adjust to a different world.

The guests stared and whispered amongst themselves, some shifted uncomfortably from one foot to the other and everyone glanced around in search of familiar faces. Most of them knew each other. If they did not at first comprehend the etiquette of the ballroom they could still chat to their neighbours until, with nods and greetings, the atmosphere eased, and warmed as Frank moved among them setting the tone of the evening.

Greeting the Guise family with a broad smile, he bent low over Elizabeth's hand. "You must take a seat. The dancing will begin in a short while, you'll be parched from that long drive, a glass of wine or perhaps a cordial for you ladies…"

William hesitated. What he really wanted was a draught of ale and something warned him such refreshment would not be available on this particular evening. But he was wrong. Frank immediately discerned his hesitation. "There is plenty of home brew. Ask one of my men to show you the way, perhaps later? For the moment a glass of wine?" He did not intend that his ballroom became filled with beer swillers.

"Come, Miss Mary Ann," Frank offered her his arm, then he held out his other arm to Elizabeth. "I'll find seats for you close to the orchestra. I am sure you'll enjoy their music. And I'll take your grandfather away for a chat with my father later in the evening."

A trifle overcome, Mary Ann hesitantly took one arm, but her sister grasped the other with a confident flourish of her fan as she sailed down the ballroom at his side. The fan fluttered expertly and her eyes glanced to right and left as she acknowledged those all about her. Then, gathering her shawl about her shoulders with one hand, she swept her silk skirts expertly to one side with the other and took her seat as though balls were commonplace and her days were spent in the most select of company.

"I can see you've been a very fortunate young lady to have such sisters. I've never forgotten that evening at your sister Hannah's, such a gracious lady." Frank de Rossi smiled down at Mary Ann. "Pardon me, are you feeling quite well?" Her spellbound face highlighted the brilliance of her eyes. She no longer inhabited a country where the kangaroos grazed outside, the hooting owls swooped from tree to tree and possums scurried along the branches, instead, she'd been transported to a place where carriages clattered across the cobbles and footmen ushered guests into the throng. In that world the men bowed in a courtly fashion to the ladies and swanlike necks were bent and hands kissed.

Speechless she could only nod her head and smile. Frank de Rossi had to look away. He'd counted the months till the completion of this grand venture over and over again; and he'd stifled all those memories of Mary Ann, or tried to put them out of his mind. Yet still they'd surfaced in his dreams. Countless times he'd imagined her walking into his home. He'd tried to arm himself against the wave of emotion he knew would surge through him when he saw her once more. Now, despite himself, he sensed the muscles of his face spreading in a smile. A great glorious smile. One glance from her would reveal the depth of his emotion. He must restrain himself, the time had not yet come. He looked again at her soft cheeks, the delicate arch of her brow and those eyes which sparkled with excitement. Then he tightened his lips and looked away. Time was needed, time to get to know each other. He'd not go overseas again, he'd be the constant neighbour and then, who knows?

William smiled at his daughter. With great satisfaction he observed the different side now revealed. Forget the sun bonnets, aprons, sensible boots. The Mary Ann smiling up at the tall, distinguished, slightly grizzled man glowed with a new elegance. That priceless possession of a young girl, the bloom of a perfect complexion, gave her face a rare radiance. From the tip of silk-shod dancing slippers to the dark curls about her forehead, she was a picture of anticipation.

Frank de Rossi inclined his head gravely. "So long since I had the pleasure of making your acquaintance, Miss Mary Ann. Perhaps later in the evening I'll have the honour of a dance?"

"Mary Ann will be delighted," William spoke up. "Of course you'll have to make allowances for our rustic ways. But I am sure she'll find her dancing feet before too long."

"They'll bring round some refreshments soon, sir. Will you excuse me while I greet my guests?" He hurried away. A moment longer and he'd have lost his tongue. He knew it. He'd just have stared into those dark eyes and stammered like a schoolboy.

At that instant the leading fiddler struck up.

Mary Ann had barely settled herself on a chair, carefully placed not too close to the musicians, not too far from a window and the cool breezes of the evening, when a commotion heralded the arrival of a much larger party.

Two ladies who flounced past them sat themselves down even closer to the orchestra. Once settled their eyes raked the room and behind their fans they giggled to each other. Ringlets of an unlikely golden hue bobbed around their sharp features as their eyes narrowed with disdain. Their pointed toes tapped in time to the music and one of them called out to an escort to hurry up with a glass of wine. "Or something stronger if you can get it!" The egret feather in her hair nodding in time to the melody.

Elizabeth sniffed and looked the other way. "Don't stare, Mary Ann, you don't know those people." But when the men returned with their drinks she couldn't control her own curiosity. "Who are they? I'm sure I've never laid eyes on any of them before."

William laid a finger on his lips. "Careful, Elizabeth, they're our new neighbours. Bought that property on the way to Bungendore. Old Furness was lucky to sell in these hard times, but land's changing hands as quickly as the gold's coming out of the earth. He was lucky to find a buyer like Patterson, petty cash for the likes of him!"

"Ah, the goldfields. Fortunes made in a day and lost just as soon."

"Not for folk like these. Heads screwed on, I'd say. Struck lucky and putting their cash in the land. City folk they are, city folk struck it rich. Soon they'll be back in Melbourne. They'll leave their overseer in charge."

"There seem to be a large number of gentlemen in their party. Look! That man over there's wanting to speak to you."

Several men had followed the ladies into the room and Frank moved across to the party to welcome them.

The woman who addressed him had a loud voice which carried across the room. "Such a first rate place, Mr de Rossi, such a delightful orchestra. You've really done us proud."

"Ugh! 'Done us proud'!" Elizabeth muttered distastefully. One of the men in that party detached himself and came across to William, a stocky man whose sunburnt face contrasted sharply with his white shirt. Everything about him appeared brand-new; shiny dancing pumps, well-fitting suit and a waistcoat which stretched just a shade too tightly across his chest.

"George Brownlow. May I introduce myself. Mr Patterson's overseer."

"Heard tell he'd taken someone on. Good reports, word gets round." William smiled as he shook the man's hand.

George Brownlow bent low over Elizabeth's hand and then stepped back with a slight bow as he acknowledged Mary Ann. "We can't get over it. Mrs Patterson and her friends had no idea what to expect. They'd imagined it would be just some pleasant gathering for all the neighbours. Not a great ball like this."

"Some of the balls in this part of the world are scarcely worth the name, sir." Elizabeth agreed, "but the de Rossis are a very old family, certainly not strangers to the ways of the world. They'd have their own ideas about how to go about things. Though society is certainly changing." Her eyes lingered on the lady of the egret feathers. "Nothing surprises me these days."

George Brownlow hastily turned away and continued in conversation with William for a few minutes, then bowed politely to Mary Ann. "Might I ask for the pleasure of a dance, Miss Guise?"

Mary Ann couldn't believe her ears. She'd expected to sit for half the evening listening to the chatter of her elders. Living on such large properties, seeing others only occasionally, when people met they just talked and talked. The weather, the crops, the prices, the machinations of the middle men who cheated the squatters and led the markets up in the city astray, an endless litany of complaints.

"Thank you." She smiled as she rose to her feet.

First on the floor! The words whirled round in her head as they spun around. She hadn't had to sit there and wait for her father to take her round the room. What a wonderful evening this was going to be, she'd never feel like this again. A first ball, a first partner, a first dance.

As he had led her onto the gleaming boards and held out his arms, Mary Ann knew without a shadow of doubt that she had walked into another world. Never before had a man held her so close. Brothers and her father and uncle didn't really count; they belonged in their male world of wood smoke and the reassuring whiff of tobacco. This man was different. His hands were just as rough as theirs, his face as weatherbeaten, but he moved with a certain resolution, a confidence that belied his position in life.

He said nothing as he guided her into the dance with an animal grace which completely swept her off her feet. With his arm pressing into the small of her back and his hand holding hers she forgot that her knowledge of the steps was not very good, that she had never been to a dance before.

George Brownlow made it all so easy. His arms enfolded her, his sturdy body led the way and words were not needed.

When he escorted Mary Ann back to the Guise party he bowed low over her hand. "May I expect a second dance a little later, Miss Mary Ann?"

"Please don't let us keep you from your friends, Mr Brownlow!" Grand-père interjected firmly before she had a chance to reply.

"Oh, Grand-père, what's the matter?" Mary Ann settled herself down again. The old man's features were cast in a severe mould.

"Birds of a feather stick together, don't they? Look at them, I swear that's rouge on that woman's cheeks. She's getting quite warm and it's making her look like a turkeycock. And anyhow, you don't want to be seen dancing with a man who's not much above a servant."

"Oh, Father, a little charity, please. I know he's an overseer but Brownlow's a first-rate fellow. Best overseer this side of Goulburn I've heard tell. You need to be pretty highly skilled to be left in charge of a property that size!" William remonstrated. "Life's different these days. Time marches on, you know. There's plenty of money around, you've only got to look at them. The Pattersons, well there's hundreds of folk like them around these days but at same time there's precious little skill. Many an able man makes his living by managing the property of others."

"Grand-mère would certainly never have invited any overseer of ours as a guest to a neighbour's house. Let me tell you that."

"Well, I'll give Mary Ann a spin. Care to come, my dear?" William knew the best way to divert his father was to put a full stop to the conversation.

"Does he think Mr Brownlow's not a suitable person to talk to?" Mary Ann asked as she followed the slow, wooden footsteps of her father.

"You know your grandfather. Always feels no one comes up to the standard of the Guises. Blame Grand-mère for that really, she was very particular… oh sorry, my fault," he muttered as he stood on her toe.

Mary Ann caught the hint of a smile on the face of George Brownlow when they danced past. He was speaking to one of the women of the party, intent in conversation, but his eyes followed Mary Ann.

"Gran'pere would much rather you danced with Frank de Rossi."

"Frank de Rossi! He's such an old stick."

"Now, now Mary Ann. He's a proper gentleman. That's the difference. At least in Grand-père's eyes. There. Had enough? Shall we sit down for a bit?"

The orchestra played a mazurka but no one dared take the floor. As if they were nailed to their seats the assembled company looked sideways at each other or else appeared to be deeply absorbed in conversation. Such a dance had not yet become commonly known.

Another waltz followed and out of the corner of her eye Mary Ann saw Frank de Rossi weaving his way towards them through the guests. Then he was stopped, buttonholed in conversation by the brassy lady with the egret's feather. Suddenly George Brownlow was at her side.

"May we repeat the pleasure? Miss Mary Ann?" Once again his arms held her close. The whole room dissolved into a lilting, swaying, clinging firmament where lesser mortals spun around them and they, alone, existed.

Whether it was George Brownlow's words, or the orchestra's music, Mary Ann did not know, but her whole body melted into his arms. They circled the room almost as one being, the broad-shouldered man and the slender girl.

"We are all very surprised. No one had expected such an event. The count has certainly given everyone a magnificent evening, don't you agree, Miss Guise?"

"I've never been to a ball before," she blurted out. "All I know is, it's just magic."

"Magic! That is the word I've been searching for. The whole evening is magic, is it not?"

Unusually for Mary Ann she found herself tongue-tied. Her partner chatted on as he guided her through the dance, but she could only half listen as her whole being exalted in the excitement of the moment. Never before had she felt such pleasure, such certainty and such an abiding sensation of sheer joy.

Confused by the sudden intensity of her feelings she barely thanked him as he led her back to her seat. Elizabeth frowned as he went back to his party.

"Surely he should be dancing with those ladies," Elizabeth

observed as Mary Ann sat down again. "A gentleman should be attending to his own party. They don't seem to have left their seats."

"Perhaps they aren't quite able to. I think that lady on the left has just consumed her third glass of wine." A wry smile touched William's lips.

Another neighbour's husband politely took Mary Ann around the floor, then a spotty grandson of Dr Morton summoned up enough courage to lead her into the shottische. Mary Ann smiled politely though all she could think of was George Brownlow's arms enfolding her once more.

By the time the supper interval arrived the Guise party had danced their way round most of the other families of note. Mary Ann had been partnered through one half of her dance card and finally managed a stately mazurka, at the urging of Frank who had learnt the dance when in Italy.

"He's got absolutely nothing to say, Elizabeth," she grumbled when Frank had led her back to their party. "I think Papa dances better than he does."

Nothing to say. But everything to feel, as he had held her in his arms for those precious moments. Light as a feather, her dark hair contrasting so vividly with that peach bloom complexion, with every step she danced more deeply into his heart.

Tongue-tied he could find no words to bandy about. Instead, his heart swelled with all he would have liked to say. The sheer pleasure of seeing her again, the wonderful completeness of holding her in his arms and the vain hope that she might look at him as a man, not as a rather dull neighbour, all conspired to leave him speechless.

He would have liked to spend longer with their party but the demands on a host were great. Every time he saw Mary Ann upon the floor she was dancing with a different partner, many seeming mere striplings to him.

"Supper is served!" In Mary Ann's estimation this amounted to a tiresome intrusion into an evening of delight. Who wanted to stop and eat?

The throwovers had been lifted, revealing the feast. Vol-au-vents filled with delicate concoctions of chicken and mushrooms, slices of pale pink beef, and in spite of the drought, Frank had managed to run down a few bush turkeys so now these were carved and set out on platters and decorated with parsley. Raised pies and ducks with forcemeat, rissoles and smoked trout, all garnished with chopped egg and mint, whilst hearts of lettuce and tiny tomatoes glowed like rubies in the candlelight.

"Look, Elizabeth, look at that fish! It's covered in jelly, and look at the leaves and the peppercorns all over it. Fancy serving a fish in jelly!"

"Hush! That's not the sort of jelly you're used to. It's aspic, fish in aspic. Put that plate down, come outside, we'll find a table, you don't serve yourself! The men'll help us to it."

Tables had been laid upon the verandah and further out under the trees. Cut glass and silver gleamed upon the damask cloths.

"Sit down, child, sit down. Wait for the men to come." Her sister patted the chair near her with her fan.

By the time the meal finished, when the last piece of tipsy cake, and the last spoonful of trifle had disappeared from the serving dishes, the company had lost any hint of their earlier awkwardness. Faces shone with pleasure, the air was full of the laughter of good fellowship, drink had loosened many a tongue and the succession of tantalising dishes had brought to the evening a touch of the banquet, the feast, the celebration. A celebration of their way of life in spite of the drought.

But Mary Ann had to force the smiles to her lips. What a waste of time, when they could be dancing! Not a soul would have guessed as she sat dutifully with her family, that all she could think of was being in George Brownlow's arms once more. She could see him chatting and joking and handing platters and plates to his party, she could almost hear him above the noise, at least she thought she could. Why didn't he turn once in her direction? How could he spend his time with those two blousy women? Of course they belonged to his employer's family, but even so, hadn't he felt the magic of those moments together?

Stubbornly she set her lips in a smile, obstinately she nodded and agreed and listened to all the conversation around her. Catching sight of the steps leading up to the verandah she caught her breath. She had come up those steps as simple Mary Ann from Bywong, now she knew herself to be a completely different person. Something had happened to her and she did not understand.

After supper the evening dragged on for her. Everyone else had been invigorated but she had been disappointed. George Brownlow's back seemed always turned towards her. Occasionally she caught sight of him in the throng of dancers as she allowed herself to be steered around by one elderly neighbour after the other. Almost in tears with disappointment she did not at first feel the tentative touch upon her shoulder. "Miss Mary Ann… you promised me another dance, remember?"

There he was, smiling down at her. As if he knew how her heart had leapt he grasped her hand tightly then pulled her to him.

If this wasn't Heaven then no such place existed.

As she lay in bed in the small hours Mary Ann relived every minute of the ball. Even when the magpies were chortling and the clanking of Job's milking pails came from the cowshed she still lay there dreamily conjuring up every moment of the night before.

The music went round and round in her head, the lilt of the violin, the melodies which came one after the other from the pianist. The sound, the scent and the sight of all that had taken place sent her spinning from the awaiting domain of household chores, calico skirts and eternal pinafores to another place, a place where, instead of scurrying about endless tasks, people would sit and exchange pleasantries, they'd nod and greet and compliment each other.

She experienced once again the pleasure of being held in George Brownlow's arms, the completeness of looking up and seeing eyes that held only her reflection.

How could Mary Ann understand what had happened? That she had chanced upon that unique moment in a lifetime when you look into another's soul and your destiny is clear? Those strong arms had enfolded and for the first time in her life she had been the focus of a man - and she could feel his longing. She still could not believe the sensations that had flooded through her. Happier than she had ever been in her life, smiles wreathed her face as she burrowed deeper and deeper into the pillows and danced once more to the memories of waltz and mazurka.

She was in his arms again, she had reached that place where you swim in the enchantment of another's gaze, experiencing the ecstasy of swimming on and on, buoyant, weightless, ethereal. A cobweb on those deep waters of desire where you scarcely care if you drown.

CHAPTER 7

Two weeks later George Brownlow came calling. He did not come as a suitor, instead managed to find quite another reason for visiting William Guise. The whereabouts of some missing steers, he maintained, had brought him over to Bywong.

"Thieving blackfellows!"

"The camp's empty. I thought they'd moved off because of..."

"It'll be them, mark my words, there's always a few around and when I catch up with them they'll wish they'd been long gone. Sooner we're shot of the lot of them, the better."

But quick-witted and observant, he immediately noticed the flicker of disapproval on the older man's face. "Things aren't getting any better," he swiftly changed the subject. 'They say folks are even eating quails and the little bears. Anything to keep going now there's hardly any stock left. I'm putting a padlock on the chicken run. That's for sure."

"People are becoming desperate."

"And the lake's disappeared before our eyes. You'd not credit it. Someone told me they recalled a time when five men drowned out there, difficult to accept. Their boat turned over in a storm and no one worried much as they were near enough to land and reckoned they'd wade ashore. But the bottom was just a thick layer of mud! Sucked down they were, not one managed to escape. Difficult to believe it nowadays. Mrs Patterson drove her curricle right across it the other week. Speaking of the Pattersons. There'll be hell to pay when they come back from Melbourne. So I'll trouble you to keep your ear to the ground, sir, if you hear anything about those steers."

"I'll speak up for you," William offered. Friendly as George seemed to be with his employers, losing stock would be regarded with severity. "'Tis more likely to be some of the riff-raff over Bungendore way. 'Tis said, not a dray's safe, they sneak the bales of wool off the back when it's on the road. Else there's that Frenchman, one with the inn, he's in with every cattle duffer in the place, keeps his ears open – and in their cups quite a few tongues wag – then he passes it on. We're surrounded by thieves and been cursed with the drought. It'll be a marvel if we're still here this time next year."

Drought, bushranging, cattle duffing, the perils of the Wool Road? The two men mulled over a multitude of events as George skilfully steered the older man towards the real object of his visit.

"You enjoyed yourself the other night? Trust old Mr Guise did not find the evening too tiring – wonderful man for his age. Trust Miss Mary Ann enjoyed herself of course?"

William smiled to himself, at last they'd got to the real reason for the younger man's visit. "Passing fair, passing fair. You'd best call in at the house on your way back."

George eagerly accepted the tacit invitation of welcome, certainly not repeated later by the irate grandfather. Grand-père was sitting on the verandah as he watched their visitor approach the house, all the time regarding him with even greater suspicion than he had in the de Rossi ballroom.

"Thank you, I'm very well, Mr Brownlow. And yes, I certainly did enjoy the ball."

In the silence that followed George shifted nervously from foot to foot.

"And I trust Miss Mary Ann is keeping well?"

"Well enough, sir. She's occupied at the moment but I'm sure would like me to give you her kind regards." With that he picked up the Herald which lay beside his chair and flipped it open decisively.

"That ignorant fellow!" Grand-père exploded as William came up the steps a while later. "I'll not have him set foot in this house."

"Come now, Father. You can't keep our Mary Ann wrapped up like a precious china ornament all her life. He's a perfectly decent chap."

"There I beg to differ. I've kept my ear to the ground since that ball, heard a thing or two, it's said the company he keeps is not to be recommended. Weakness for the horses too. Four-score years and fifteen I've lived, don't forget that, my son. And I've kept my wits about me. Very rarely misjudged a man, all those years. Known who could be trusted and who could not," he eyed his son sternly, "and he's not welcome under our roof."

"Oh really, Father, any man making his way in the Colony has to rub shoulders with all and sundry."

'Making his way! Don't presume to talk to me about making a way in the Colony," snorted Granpère as he struggled to get out of the chair. "I certainly didn't like the way he had his eyes on our Mary Ann."

"Maybe like any other single man? Seeing a pretty girl and a smiling face? Think back, Father, think of when you first laid eyes on Mamma."

"And that's what I'm doing, son. The moment I laid eyes

on her I can tell you I knew she was the one for me but 'twas weeks before I even spoke with her. Never walked up, straight up I might say, bold as brass, and asked for a dance!"

"Times are changing, Father."

"You can say that, alright. But human nature's always been the same, hasn't it? And always will be. Hard times we're having but I can tell you they're nothing compared with the hard times we had back then."

William sighed, he'd heard it all before.

"I had nothing to offer my dear Elizabeth and she had less than that! Running away under her family's nose. What was I? A rank and file soldier with the Corps. When we came out here back in '96 we were sleeping with twelve other families, twelve to a room in the barracks. And here we are now, with more property than we can even manage, land up in the Monaro, land at Liverpool, land at Macquarie Fields, and more besides. We made our life, didn't go round toadying up to any folk better off than ourselves. We made our way fair and square. This George Brownlow's nothing but a piece of flotsam on the surface of life."

"And how'd you know that?"

"I know, I know, alright. I haven't lived over ninety years without being able to see beyond my own nose! Our Mary Ann's young, she needs to meet the right sort of people. There's bigger fish in the sea than ever came out of it."

"You are referring to Frank de Rossi I suppose?"

"Anyone marrying into the Rossi family would be most fortunate. Frank's a true gentleman through and through. I won't deny a match with him would be a wonderful thing, but I daresay he's a confirmed bachelor by now. He's not a young man any more."

"And what's more, he's so occupied with his father's estates.

So often having to go back to Corsica for the old man, old Rossi must have matters of great importance over there still. The city's the place for a young girl, Father, girls need to be up in the city. Who would they ever meet round here? Going to flower shows and bazaars should be the order of the day, dancing around with their friends and taking part in charades, that's what Hannah tells me anyhow, when she writes. If we want better things for our Mary Ann, that's where she should be."

"The de Rossis are a good family."

The mention of Frank had came closer to his secret ambition than he would ever admit. Alone, amongst their scattered neighbours, the de Rossis had style. Who knew what the future might bring? Where people lived remote lives, death coming early in some families, loneliness stalking so many, then May-September marriages were quite common in the Colony.

"Perhaps a few months up in the city might be just what is needed." The old man smiled, half to himself. "Absence makes the heart grow fonder, they say."

"But which heart, Father? Frank de Rossi's or George Brownlow's?"

"I'm not thinking of that chap. It'll be 'out of sight out of mind' for the likes of him. No, certainly not George Brownlow."

But now nature took a hand. Even if Mary Ann had finally agreed to sample the delights of the city it would have been impossible.

The drought broke.

Far away up north of the continent storm clouds sweeping in from across the ocean saturated mountain, forest and plain. The land was inundated with deluges so heavy that every channel and creek overflowed and soon floods swept their way down south Blankets of grey rolling clouds swallowed up the blue skies. Rain lashed down. First of all it ran off the baked earth but very slowly even that softened and then sopped up every drop. Journeying any distance on the muddy roads became nigh impossible.

Walls of water surged along dried-out creek beds, sweeping before it mud, twigs and every little creature that had nested and burrowed along the banks. Sticks and stones swirled and eddied in the dance of death which in a short while would bring back a celebration of life to those deceptive waterways. Anything which had been left down near the banks of the river whirled away. The Irishwoman lost her pails and wash boiler, stock-in-trade for the dirty linen she took in. The torrent snatched them up and spun them into oblivion.

Being the focus for three hundred and sixty square miles of the Great Dividing Range and over two thousand feet above sea level the lake surface at first merely dampened but then it, too, began to fill. Soon every nearby creek surged into the rising waters. Roads became impassable and any stock wandering too close to the water risked being swept away. Four pigs' carcases lay bloated at the bend in the river.

"Pigs can't swim," muttered Job as he set off to drag away the remains and cut them up for the dogs.

"Every animal can swim if it has to," proclaimed Mary Ann. What did he know?

"'Tis the way God made 'em. If they tries to swim, their trotters slits their throats."

"Well, they look just plain drowned dead to me."

"Washed down from upstream they be. And from the look of the sky we'll have a sight more surprises before a few days is out."

The rain kept falling.

"Won't it ever stop, Grand-père?" Day after day the rain battered down on the shingles. Every time she darted out to the dairy or the henhouse she stumbled back soaked to the skin. Water streamed down the walls and some even splashed into the bowls of milk, the sodden chickens clustered in a corner of their run to peck at the grain thrown to them, then disappeared into the henhouse. No happy clucking or scratching or dust baths in the earth; instead, their legs were black with mud.

Several weeks later the same question was still being asked. When would the rain ever stop? True everyone had yearned for the end of the drought, but the pendulum now swung completely in the opposite direction. At midday a candle had to be lit in the kitchen.

"When will it ever stop?"

"Stop? You'll never have seen rain like this in your life, my girl. There's something strange about our weather in this part of the world. We'll get years and years of everything just ordinary, then of course we had that terrible drought, but then sometimes we get this. I've seen this before. Seen years and years of drought, folk thinking this is the way of the world and building sheds and homes in beautiful places, settling on plains and river banks. Then the heavens open. Up on the Hawkesbury I've seen ninety-foot floods sweep whole towns away. Could be much the same down here. I've seen haystacks bobbing around like tennis balls. You are lulled into security and then once in a while the hand of Fate turns against you. You'll never have seen rain like this in your lifetime."

"Better than the poor animals dying in the drought."

"Soon they'll be scouring. We've had the scab and the footrot. The scouring will be the next," muttered William.

"Better than dying of thirst," Mary Ann persisted.

"Better maybe, but not good. Mark my words, we are in for months of rain, maybe a year or two to come. My joints tell me this, my back's playing up. I'm going to ask your father to bring my bed in to the little parlour. I can't manage those steps out the back."

Mary Ann glanced at the old man. Never before had he asked for help. Till now he could manage to walk slowly beyond the back paddock and down to the dam, most days he was able to make his way across the yard and fetch in the kindling box.

The ferocity of the rain eased off, but not the frequency. Day after day dawned to a leaden sky, the showers falling relentlessly. For a while the blue skies might open up again, perhaps for a few weeks the sun shone weakly onto the sodden land, then the rain returned. In the vegetable garden weeds sprouted between the lines of carrots, and runner beans climbed so quickly up their poles that the tops had to be pinched out. Phalanxes of snails streaked out from the undergrowth and slugs slimed their way amongst the vegetables.

"Want to take a look at those shorthorns," William announced.

"You go with your father," Grand-père glanced across at Mary Ann.

"I want to prune those young pears today. It's the first fine day in weeks," grumbled Mary Ann.

"Never mind what you want to do, young Miss, you go with your father. He's not to ride out on his own and it's a fair step over to Geary's Gap. Didn't you see him last evening, when he came back from the village. White as a sheet he was."

"Papa's alright, he just gets out of breath at times."

"He's not well."

"He's not told me that."

"And neither would he, your father would keep it to himself."

Over the last few months he'd noticed his son's increasing breathlessness. A frightening spectacle indeed to watch the mainstay of the family begin to fail, especially when he knew that his own body could not last much longer.

"Job can go with him. I want to get on with those pears."

"Job's close on being an old dodderer. He'd be no help. No, you do as I say, Mary Ann, you go with your father."

She urged her pony into a trot as they left the yard, all the time complaining to herself. George Brownlow might call by. He'd found the opportunity to ride over on several occasions and if she was lucky she'd been able to exchange a few words before Grand-père beckoned her indoors.

George had not called in yesterday. Surely he'd ride by today? And she'd be out!

Apart from that, this would be a whole day wasted. Too few days were without rain and now that the sun shone briefly she could have spent the time in the orchard. And such a fuss too. As if her father was really ill! Grand-père worried too much.

Optimism laced with the headiness of youth makes for a powerful combination. In her eyes her father was mantled with that enduring cloak of invulnerability. He could ride, shoot, track through the bush, swim across flooded creeks, round up cattle and keep the men in order just as expertly as he could add up all the debits and credits in the big ledger and work out the cost of every single item on their property.

Any thought of that strong body failing or that mind failing to grasp the last tiny detail was unbelievable. So why did she have to spend her day trailing behind her father when so much needed to be done at home?

It wasn't till they sat upon the rocks near the bridle path below Geary's Gap that the first hint that Grand-père might have been right became apparent. Mopping his brow William took a deep draught from his water bottle. A cool wind tempered the sun's unaccustomed heat day and the ride had not been arduous.

Even so the lines etched upon his face deepened as his eyes took in the great expanse before him.

Once again water gleamed in the lake, not very deep, but whilst upon his last visit some of the steers had been browsing a couple of miles out on the green expanse, now they were up nearer the Cullarin range. Further out where they had grazed a couple of months ago the sheet of water reflected clouds from on high.

"It doesn't seem possible, does, it Papa?"

"Anything's possible in this place. Admittedly the lake has always had its times. Sometimes fuller than others. But never before have we seen such a disaster as we've just had.

"When I first laid eyes on Lake George back in '33, musk duck, swans and herons were in their thousands. There were spoonbills and pelicans and we'd even see the brolgas doing their mad dances. The Canberri and the Ngunawal hunted along the shores. Now the blackfellows are just called the Lake George tribe, what's left of them, poor devils."

"Were they hunted too, Papa?"

"Not so around these parts. They sickened with the white mens' ills, they lost their hunting grounds, many moved away. If anyone had listened, if anyone had even asked we surely would have learnt the lake's secret, for they must have lived with it for generations and generations."

"What is its secret then?"

"Ah," he laughed, "that is its secret. The fact is that no one knows the truth about the lake, a true mystery. Some say there's a great cleft at the bottom and the water drains away, some say it just dissolves into the air in drought years. No one knows, but at least all those old people would have been privy to it. What's just happened is enough to shatter your faith in nature herself. But now it's filling again, just look. I wouldn't be surprised if we don't see water right up to the base of the hills soon."

"And then we'll have birds and fish again, and will the reeds all come back?"

"They'll come and the land that's almost worthless now will yield a good return once more. We live with a riddle on our very doorstep, Mary Ann. We must learn to build up our fortunes during the good years to see us through the lean ones. Like it says in the Bible."

She looked at him sharply. Papa never mentioned the Bible. A listless quality flattened his voice and he stared across the lake with lacklustre eyes.

He'd seen a true disaster. Nothing equals the dismay of humankind when faced with the betrayal of Nature. How can this happen? The framework of life should remain constant; rivers should flow, the sun should shine and lakes remain filled to their shores. How could the largesse of the land be offered one year and denied the next?

He'd watched the struggles of the poorer settlers and followed the waning fortunes of the more wealthy ones. True, the Guise family kept afloat, didn't they still have their lands at Liverpool, Macquarie Fields, the Monaro and up in the mountains. Admittedly, mostly mortgaged to the hilt, but they still owned them on paper. But his heart had always been at Bywong. On this property his mother and father had been happiest and he'd married and raised his own brood of children.

Who would have guessed nature could be so fickle? Fear tugged at him, was it the eternal insecurity of the migrant? Born and bred as he might have been in this vast country, the stories of his father still remained with him. The home you had taken for granted could suddenly become a place of uncertainty. Danger snapped at your heels and sent you off far away. His father had been born and bred into prosperity and privilege.

He would never have foreseen a time when the guillotine threatened and the mob howled for the blood of kith and kin.

Admittedly here there'd never be the screaming mobs and the impassive faces of those who sat in judgement, but here there could be unbelievable changes in the world around you. Droughts, floods, lakes that filled and emptied on a whim leaving the dried bones of cattle bleaching in the sun. Then, that awful spectacle - financial ruin, and the stony faces of your creditors.

William pondered as he watched Mary Ann walking along the new margin of the lake, pausing every so often to pick up a stone or examine a plant. Having been a child born and bred in this country, he understood her feelings. She had been eleven when her mother died and, being so close to her grandparents, had grown up with the ways of that generation. What would happen when he died? Grand-père wouldn't live for ever. What then for Mary Ann? Three sons he'd fathered, and two in their graves, Charles forever occupied with the affairs of the family. Well at least he'd keep an eye on Bywong. If she wasn't wed by then she'd have a home.

He could not deny the evidence of his own body. One moment his whole frame shuddered with the cold, then next moment a sudden heat surged through him and his heart began to pound. During many a sleepless night he tossed and turned trying to come to a decision. Sell up? Who'd buy after those years of disaster which had left depleted flocks and empty pastures? If only Mary Ann was a few years older. She understood the running of the property like the back of her hand, but she'd never be able to manage on her own.

Marriage! Marriage would settle so much, but on the other hand it could stir up a hornet's nest. George Brownlow had become a constant visitor and Frank de Rossi's intentions were obvious too. Of the two, his choice, and certainly Grand-père's, would be Frank. They knew each other's families and they understood the ups and downs of a squatter's life. Mary Ann wasn't seventeen yet, she had a few years to go before worrying about a husband. Perhaps by then she'd be wise enough to look on Frank with favour.

With a sigh William rose and called to his daughter. Never the right time to make decisions, always the need for waiting and planning - but time was running out for him. More out of breath than usual he clutched at a nearby branch, cursing the sudden weakness in his legs. If he'd been in the city a physician could have been called. Some physick and a few days rest might settle the matter, for a while at least. But here? No time to take to his bed. Here he was the focus of everyone's needs. The ministrations of Dr Morton had to suffice, good enough for infant sicknesses and childbirth, but now he could only smile and nod and hand out doses and pills.

William sensed the shortening of his days, thank God he still had Charles, though it would be a heavy burden for a young man and so much would be left undecided. Impatient with himself he tried not to let them see the occasional tremor which took hold of his body. He knew he was failing. Grand-père looked the other way. There was no answer as he faced up to each day with every appearance of vigour but absenting himself at times for a doze and going to bed as soon as darkness fell.

In the end you are on your own.

And here was Mary Ann. With all the energy that the others had lost, and steadily gaining the knowledge that he himself had gathered over the years, would she be able to manage? It would be true to say she knew every hillock on the property, she certainly knew every tree and wombat hole. Would that knowledge be enough in this harsh world to enable her to manage the farm?

"Storm's coming, Papa," Mary Ann interrupted his reverie. "Look at that lightning down south."

"Well, we'll be home before it breaks. Can you hold the mare a moment."

Not a necessary request as his faithful old mare stood like a rock, but nowadays it took several attempts before he was comfortably in the saddle.

"We'll have stew tonight, Papa, I made some dumplings, just like Grand-mère used to do. We'll have stew and dumplings."

"A good evening then, eh, Mary Ann?"

Later that night the three of them were sitting by the fire. The storm had peaked and subsided but then gathered strength again; once more rain lashed down upon the shingles of the roof. A wind had risen and howled round the brick chimney and when the old clock began to strike nine o'clock Mary Ann gathered up her sewing. "It's time you went too, both of you, don't sit…"

"Hush! What's that?"

Cutting through the moan of the wind and the chimes of the clock came the sound of horse's hooves.

"What's that? Who can be calling at this hour?"

Grand-père shifted uneasily as he looked across when his son jumped up and stood by the door. Several properties had been raided in the area, in the bad times those who had not been able to keep themselves and their families afloat had taken to the highways and byways with their rifles. Many a family had been relieved of all they owned in their own home. A solitary dwelling, the candlelight shining from the window, a family gathered together around the fireside were bait enough to tempt any prowling bushranger.

William stood alert, someone shouted from the yard.

"I know that voice!" He took the chain off the door.

"Have a care, son," his father warned. "Have a care. Put that chain back."

"Mr Guise! Mr Guise! I must speak!"

"Bless me. It's Frank de Rossi." William threw open the door.

Saturated and streaked with mud Frank grabbed the lintel to steady himself.

"For heaven's sake, man, out in this deluge! Were you caught on the road. How long have you been travelling? Come in, come in." William half caught the other man as he stumbled over the threshold.

"I have to speak." Frank's gaze met Mary Ann's. "Yes, I was on the road. I was coming to speak on such a different subject. Later perhaps, but now is not the time." Still his eyes held Mary Ann's. Suddenly she understood. Knowing how she herself felt about George Brownlow, she recognised the longing in the man's eyes.

"Speak then, but sit down. Here, by the fire. I'll fetch some dry things in a moment. What do you have to tell us?"

Frank lowered his head, he did not want to see the pain he knew he was about to cause that family. "Your son."

"My son? Charles? What of him? He's not home, he's been away several weeks, he'd down at our property on the Murrimbidgee."

"Sir, the great river's burst its banks. It's roaring down in flood. There's whole herds of cattle carried off in the torrent, there's huge trees bobbing about like twigs and cottages and barns washed away and lost for ever."

"What?" William shouted. "What? What are you telling me?"

"It's said he left the party he was travelling with and went upstream in search of some straying cattle. He is lost."

Grand-père clutched his son's arm, Mary Ann stood transfixed for one moment staring at her father. "Papa, oh Papa," she gripped William's other arm but her eyes were on Frank de Rossi. "How can you be so sure? How can you know?"

"Those who understand the river better than I have told me this. I came as I did not want you to hear rumours and careless chatter."

"But this is only a rumour! This is just hearsay. Oh, dear Papa," she guided him to his old armchair and then knelt with his hand in hers.

Frank stared at them both.

"The Murrumbidgee! Broke its banks!" No more needed to be said.

In times of drought the mighty river might narrow down to a peaceful stream but when the rain came it swelled and roared and swept through the land with a vengeance all its own. Swirling muddy water would sweep away all that lay on either side in a vast moving maelstrom of destruction. Animals, haystacks, barns and the debris of forest, farm and plain that had lain upon its banks would be torn away and tossed into the flood. The monstrous flood of brown heaving water swept all before it.

"But no one has seen him? Seen the... seen any sign of poor Charles?" Mary Ann had to speak for the others. Her father sat silent, her grandfather's face veiled in shadow. "Then how could you, sir? How could you come with this news when no one knows for a fact, no one knows!" Her anger began to rise. In fact the anger was rooted in their terrible loss. Something inside her told her that she had heard the truth.

A flash of memory. Job's prediction. The death of the firstborn. Rage throbbed through her. Rage and frustration that screamed out to be vented but it was her father's stricken face which really gripped her.

Shock stripped his features down to the bone. His eyes glittered with the intensity of emotion welling up as his lips mouthed words that would never be said, words too desperate for any ears to hear. He had lost his last son.

"How could you come like this! How could you know?"

"Those who were with him saw him ride away. Miss Mary Ann, that was two days ago and no more has been heard."

"People are found days after a flood. You know that, sir. A woman was caught in the Yass river. She hung on amongst the boughs of a tree for over three days."

"The river's a raging torrent, Miss Mary Ann. You've never seen anything like it in your life. Boiling, swirling, brown with mud, branches, trees. The whole world's on the move. No one would stand a chance."

"I don't believe it. Charles is so used to the river and everything thereabouts, he's seen floods before, he'd not put himself in danger like that."

"No one has seen a flood like this one."

"I think you are wrong. Wrong! Wrong! Wrong!" She flew from the room.

But the next weeks proved that Frank de Rossi had not made a mistake. Although the body of Charles Guise was never found, neither did the living man ever appear again and with the loss of his last son the father turned his face to the wall.

CHAPTER 8

The making of a will is an undertaking of no mean importance. It can be the testator's last chance to turn the tables on those left behind or an opportunity to set matters straight within a family.

Seen from any angle it is a human being's final act to leave their mark on the world.

Fighting back the pain William forced himself to consider how his properties must be divided. How straightforward the task had been only weeks before! He could have trusted his son with all that belonged to the Guise family: Grand-père, daughters, nephews, nieces, all would have been watched over and cared for.

Now he shied away from the considerations. His chest ached, his eyes were tired and he longed for sleep and forgetfulness. The task was too great - but he could not turn his back. How much longer did he have? Shaken to his very core by the terrible loss, he noticed with distaste how his hand shook as time and again he took up the pen, then put it down from sheer exhaustion.

Constantly the temptation to confide in Grand-père nagged at him. Throughout his life his father had advised and guided, but now? Only Dr Morton knew his secret.

Time and again the words almost came to him as now more than ever he needed that sage advice, but he was determined with his last breath to save the old man such a worry. William could not bring those terrible fears into the light of day. Whatever was ailing him might possibly pass, Dr Morton seemed to think an old inflammation of the lung persisting from the winter caused the breathlessness. "Time, sir, time, that is what we need. The current damp is not helping. Our constitutions suffer with these violent changes of atmosphere, believe me. The mind plays a sovereign part in our health too, and you've had such tragedy, such blows as might fell a lesser man."

As William sat with his papers his old father shook his head.

"Why burden yourself now. Wait a while, son. 'Tis too soon. Granted, none of us could have foreseen… well, even imagined such a terrible thing. But don't burden yourself further just at this moment. I know 'tis a job that must be done. Though, God willing, there'll be many more years before we need to worry about all this."

"Father! How easy it should have been. Only weeks ago there'd have been no two ways about it. Matters must be settled, our family must be protected. Protected against accident or anything else. I must have a Will."

"The good Lord gives and he takes away. Remember. You've got sensible daughters and their husbands are fine men. No need to worry. Be grateful for what you've got, my son, with Mary Ann being such a help."

"If only she was a boy."

"Now that's a silly sort of thing to say. That girl, well provided for, is the equal of many a man, I'd say."

His father watched on as William procrastinated and silently mourned the losses which had reduced their family circle to a mere echo of the past.

Sticks and stones, chattels, stock on the hoof and crops in the ground can all be disposed of in a neat orderly fashion but there is that other factor, that essential vagary of human nature, which no one can foresee. That unknown quantity - those who become allied by marriage - certainly not strangers, often much loved, but all the same they are not of your flesh and loyalties can be fickle.

Due consideration must be given to those in-laws, that unknown band of half-relatives which slowly collects around a family. Those accommodating human beings who chatter like a flock of starlings at marriages and christenings but descend like vultures when death intervenes.

They are wary, always watching that others do not overstep their mark and curry too much favour. Nearly everyone has a selection of in-laws but those who gather about a man of wealth become more evident as the years roll by.

Sons! Without a son and heir William sighed over the complexity of making his final testament. To have even one son to take over the reins would have been a blessing. So he apportioned his land as best he could, knowing he would leave them very well endowed. But much depended upon the families into whom they married. Well he had a pretty good idea of his elder daughters' circumstances, but what of the marriage yet to be made? How to secure his last daughter's inheritance against any unscrupulous fortune-hunter?

He sighed again and fumbled with the pen, sharp enough with figures but lacking an easy hand when it came to words. Not always sure of the size of his flocks, not always able to describe the boundaries of his property accurately. Nine pages were completed before he sat back with satisfaction.

William would have no favouritism. He had many debts and there remained a legion of mortgages to be settled. The holdings of his nephews and nieces were inextricably woven into his own estate for his only brother had died some years earlier. The two brothers had agreed that the Guise properties should remain intact so now there would have to be careful division if he was no longer there to watch over the holdings. All of that had to be detailed and made clear. Even so the amount he'd leave should be enough to repay all and provide handsomely for his children. Land, effects and livestock would meet with everyone's satisfaction and, now the pastures had begun to flourish once more, the old prosperity was returning.

Finally he set his mind to the task. *This is the last Will and Testament of me William Guise of Gundaroo in the County of MURRAY in the COLONY of NEW SOUTH WALES Grazier. I hereby revoke and make…*

But even as he penned their names he wondered again about the inheritance each of his daughters would receive. Whatever fine words he might use, however carefully phrased his bequests, the fact remained that the real owner of any property belonging to a woman was her husband. Hannah and Elizabeth had already married. Edward Cantor and Henry Lintott were reliable chaps. Never set the pond afire, but reliable, so he felt no concern over them. Certainly they were both cautious, dependable men and there need be no worries for the future.

But what of Mary Ann's portion? Young and single, such an inheritance weighed heavily – and whoever she married might not have the stability of Henry or Edward.

Pondering over this for many hours, he puzzled over how to keep the Guise property in Guise hands. Finally coming up with a carefully worded formula which he used for each of his daughters.

Meticulous and fair, he left each girl the same. What Hannah and Elizabeth did with it depended on them. If they did not care to live on the land he gifted to them then they could sell it or put in an overseer. He knew which course Mary Ann would take.

Each bequest in turn had the same careful wording and when he came to disposing of the old Bywong property, the core of the Guise holdings, he left it to Mary Ann and breathed a silent prayer that she would not sell up or hand over control to any other…

1920 acres to the use of my daughter Mary Ann Guise during her natural life for her sole and separate use independently of and without being subject to the debts control or engagements of any husband with whom she may intermarry…

To each of the daughters he also gave three hundred head of cattle and ten mares.

Nearly two thousand acres constituted a large farm. Combined with the livestock she'd be the owner of a fine property.

Sitting at the table by the window he pondered yet again over his decisions. Fine words but everyone knew that it was the husband who had the say in all matters financial. Crows circled in the sky, swooped down to earth and perched for a moment on the branches of the gum trees near the dam, then finally flew off in search of food.

How many times he'd watched those birds as they squabbled over anything they'd been so fortunate as to find. The corpse of a ewe, a dying lamb or even an exhausted heifer struggling in the mud at the half-empty dam was food for their rapacious appetites. Fiercely the birds tore at the flesh, old ones squawked and hopped away from the jabbing beaks of the young bloods, several birds bunched together and waited their turn while the strongest gorged and gobbled with lordly indifference – just so, he mused, there would be many who might make a claim on the Guise estate.

Waiting for a will to be read was one of the eternal guessing games of life and well before the last breath left there would be many who had added up time and again what they might expect. Grimly William smiled to himself as he contemplated the questions which would go through the minds of all those related to the family.

Much would be gained from the breaking up of the Guise estates, the land at Macquarie Fields, the property beyond Liverpool, acreages in the Monaro, many a mile round Gearys Gap and up at Bywong. Rich pickings indeed.

Mary Ann never spared herself as she watched her father fading away before their eyes. She politely declined Hannah's invitation and, when Frank de Rossi called one day, regarded him with chilly indifference.

Unfair, she admitted to herself, but she could not detach him from that moment when he had stood dishevelled before them and told them what had happened.

"Thank you for calling, Mr de Rossi," she smiled vaguely in his direction. "Grand-père is resting and… and Papa is down at the washing pen," she added a white lie. Her father lay upon his bed staring into space.

"I can send over some fellows. You probably could do with some extra hands at shearing."

"Thank you. Mr Brownlow has kindly offered help. He rides over frequently and Father wouldn't know what to do without him."

After a few banal exchanges she watched him ride away. His shoulders were broad and strong but if she had seen the pain on his face she might have regretted her words. Each day she rode out to check on the stock and galloped home to spend the rest of the time helping Job in the yard and working in the orchard or the vegetable garden. Mary Ann was on her feet from sun up to sundown. When another invitation came from Hannah to spend a few weeks in the city she politely declined again. And secretly William rejoiced; as he admitted to himself, he had come to rely on Mary Ann more and more. Her knowledge of the farm was now nearly as good as his own.

"Well, I'll ride over and have a look at those ewes, Papa. If I can't make up my mind we'll ask George, shall we?" Ever more frequently she'd defer to George Brownlow. Her father always nodded and agreed and had to admit to himself that he felt easier with the other man's practised judgement. After all, the younger ones kept up with the times, he had to admit to himself.

Scouring sheep, pink eye and beasts with the fluke were all in a day's work and he knew he could rely on Mary Ann's calculating eye to single out any ailing animal. And she, in her turn, when in need of practical advice, felt more secure when she received George's verdict.

The rains had eased, leaving burgeoning pastures. Now water splashed within twenty feet of Geary's Gap. Flotillas of black swans circled the water, swimmers, waders and flocks of seagulls had returned and once again the familiar sound of the Lake filled the ears. The heavy beat of the waves and the persistent splashes as ducks alighted on the waters and pelicans skimmed the surface filled the air with that uplifting chorus of hope and vitality. The Lake was alive again.

Familiar with every creek and waterhole, Mary Ann knew where stray cattle could be found or if the dreaded abortion had taken hold in the herd. Had the moment come to move them to fresh pastures? Time to cut out the weaklings? "Plenty of years ahead for the city," she repeated yet again. "We're just getting back on our feet. Look at that barley, doesn't it do your heart good to see it? After all those months and months when we only had dust blowing about?"

Her father smiled. A true farmer's daughter.

"If I went now, who'd finish that work in the orchard? Next year I'll have those pear trees espaliered, you wait and see. Grand-père's always wanted that and he can't manage it, can barely manage getting down the path any more."

Of course another reason ruled paramount but with her grandfather's disapproving glances those thoughts were kept to herself. Hardly a day went by when George Brownlow did not call at Bywong. Sometimes to offer some help, other times just for a chat with her father, but always making sure he paid his respects to her grandfather and managing a few moments conversation. She looked forward to those visits more than she'd ever admit.

As she stood beside him, looking across the pastures, or listening to him talking, she could barely manage not to reach out and take his hand. She yearned to feel if the reality of his body matched the perfection of the man she embraced in her dreams each night. His weatherbeaten hands, his sinewy arms, as strong and purposeful when he helped her father throw a beast as they had been when they'd encircled her waist upon the ballroom floor, would she ever feel their touch again? What she would not give to have his face close to hers once more, his eyes looking down with that softness which was only for her.

Mary Ann ached for George to turn, just once, and look at her and say the words her fantasies dreamt up each night.

If George had any inkling of her feelings he did not make it obvious. He had remained aloof from serious matters of the heart. All his life he had given his labour and been rewarded, never ventured into the mainstream of life which swept so many along on tides of passion and love, but sometimes stranded them in the backwaters. No, George bided his time, he intended to make something of himself.

Endowed with good looks and a shrewd personality he stood out amongst the local men like a racehorse amongst the hacks. Not a tall man but stocky and nimble and spectacular in the saddle.

Mary Ann was alert for the first clatter of hooves as he rode into the yard, smiles wreathed her face at the sound of his voice. She'd hurry to her room and hastily brush her hair, twisting the long dark ringlets ever more tightly then tracing the outline of eyebrow and lip with her fingers, biting her lips to redden them and slapping her cheeks in the hope of bringing more colour into them. For she had the olive complexion of her grandfather. 'One of the de Guises, alright,' her grandfather always maintained. His Elizabeth had passed on the fair haired English heritage of her own family to all her other grandchildren. Golden hair and hazel eyes, the bloom of a peach until the harsh winds of the Colony roughened it. Mary Ann alone had the aquiline features, the glossy dark hair, the deepset eyes and the stately carriage of her grandfather.

A natural aristocrat, Grand-père sighed, dragging his thoughts back from those far-off days in France. Surely someone better than George Brownlow could be found? Immediately he pulled himself up. This was a new country, a different society; wasn't his son forever telling him this? Values were not the same. Success with your own two hands had become the order of the day. The refined ways he remembered so lovingly would be regarded more with suspicion than admiration.

There was no doubt Mary Ann was in love with the man.

Love is not so much blind as completely blinkered. Only the central vision is intact. You look at the person and see the façade of that other human being, the eyes, the mouth, the entrancing whole of that intensely desirable person. Behind that façade you create your own vision of perfection and soon your Pygmalion stands before you. Nothing can match the exhilaration of this vision. You have found love. Love is beautiful, exciting, enticing and totally absorbing.

Those who can remove the blinkers and glimpse the uncertain edges of their creation may be wiser, but are they happier?

Who was he to stand in the girl's way? So few men left in the family, such a responsibility to fall upon her shoulders in only a few years. Perhaps he was wrong, Grand-père puzzled, perhaps he'd misjudged the man. Perhaps he should take heed of William's words; the world was changing. Anyhow, no time remained to alter the way events were unfolding. At his great age he had little energy to change anything at all. Wisdom dictated that the moment had come to sit by the fire and accept the remnants that life had to offer.

Age brings its own kind of loneliness. There may be people around, children nearby, but no longer can you share the memory of the past for it is better not to reminisce too often for fear of becoming an object of amusement.

Your world is still peopled with those you loved and lost. Those around have busy lives full of birthdays, daily tasks, arguments, making up, making do and listening to the latest piece of gossip. There is no one to share your memories. Who sang that song? Who wrote that piece? Was it a christening or a funeral when we met those people last?

As the wrinkles grow deeper the memories are buried even more profoundly, no one really cares. The conscious, polite expressions on your children's faces are even more hurtful than the disinterest of the outside world.

When the body begins to fail the mind enters that no-man's-land between reality and dreams. In his mind's eye Richard still saw Elizabeth's face opposite him at that dining table of long ago when she first walked into his life.

The sparkle of the cut glass decanters, the glint of the nutcracker in the bowl of walnuts – all that had marked the beginning of their great adventure. Now he was at the end but when he looked across the scrubbed table, past the guttering candle with its winding sheets of clinging wax he watched Mary Ann – at the beginning of her own journey in life. So like himself, such a de Guise, with her sombre dark eyes and lean features, the same dark hair and fine arched nose, the same impetuous movements and quick resolve.

For once, old Richard found himself at a loss, whether he should speak up or not? Whether to continue expressing his doubts and urge caution, perhaps suggest his granddaughter wait a while longer.

For the magic was working. Before his very eyes he could see the beginning of that fascination which grips and takes hold and listens to no reason. Mary Ann's eyes sparkled whenever George Brownlow came to the house. The old man guessed that on those occasions she was no longer even aware of any other human being in the whole world.

George Brownlow certainly had captured Mary Ann, and Grand-père could not deny his glowing reputation amongst those who farmed around Bywong. Owned no property of course, but an able man. Gossip had it that his mother had been an easy woman who'd netted a husband late in life. Grand-père had shuddered when he heard this. Then he shook himself and thought again. No, this was what everyone admired in this new country—you put the past behind you and forged ahead to better things.

Since George Brownlow had become a frequent visitor at

Bywong, Richard sensed his son's growing reliance upon the man. A load of posts? Some extra hands for the haymaking? Help sorely needed, with the quest for gold. That word was still bandied about all over the land. 'Gold', and every able-bodied man dropped his tools and made for the diggings. Servants left their masters, soldiers deserted their posts and rumour had it that ships lay idle in the ports as all hands made for the goldfields.

Again and again he puzzled over the man. The heaven-sent answer to a family's prayer, or the adventurer he feared? Even if he spoke out no notice would be taken of his words. People hear what they want to hear. He could sense that William had begun to see the saviour of the Guise property in the attentive younger man.

As the trees blossomed once again and the grass grew back to such an extent that the cattle brought back from the mountains stood in pasture up to their hocks, as he watched prosperity returning to their acreages, the old man tried to quell his unease.

The land had deceived them once, it could happen again. If the very earth led them astray, then what might be expected of mere humans, how much more deceptive is fellow man?

"You'll see, Father. Good times are here again and if I'm not mistaken, our Mary Ann'll be a happy woman."

So he was surprised when William told him shortly afterwards that he had not immediately accepted George Brownlow's offer of marriage to Mary Ann.

"I thought you liked the man?"

"Well enough. Well enough. But I remembered your words, Father. You think no one listens to you but you're wrong. Mary Ann's only seventeen, plenty of time. Let's wait a little while."

"You'll do well to remember the three C's when it comes to considering a husband for our Mary Ann."

"The three C's?"

"Colour, creed and class. Well, colour doesn't come into it but class and creed certainly do. The Rossis are our class and their creed as near as makes no difference."

"And what have you against George Brownlow then?"

"Well, he's certainly not our class and as far as I can see he wouldn't even know what creed is."

"Times are changing, Father."

"And what does Mary Ann think? She's always got views of her own."

"Exactly. George brought up the subject yesterday, speaking to me first of course, which is very decent of him. She doesn't know. I prefer to wait a while and we'll see how the land lies. Plenty of time, plenty of time."

But William had very little time left. No one realised the effort he made when he rode around the property, or realised how frequently he sat in the shade and rested. The strange light-headedness and the fast beating of his heart were all indications but then – but then, wasn't that old age? *Look at Father,* he told himself. *Still getting down to the orchard, still poring over the Herald, still giving a hand in the dairy – and at well over ninety. Good stock,* he told himself. In fact he'd been rather foolish to bother so much over his will, plenty of time ahead.

In this William was wrong. One day too hot, one ride too far from home, a sudden dizziness and darkness engulfing him marked the end of his life. He went the way he'd have wanted to go, everyone agreed, he'd have wanted to end his life with the scent of the gum trees in his nostrils and the cry of the plover in his ears, rather than tossing and turning upon a sickbed.

As the family and friends stood around his graveside, Mary Ann shivered in spite of the hot January sun. Henry Lintott supported Grand-père who stoically watched the earth being shovelled upon his firstborn's coffin. Far away in Barrack Street Hannah would be going about her usual tasks, quite unaware of her father's death. "Poor Hannah," Mary Ann whispered, "all she ever hears is bad tidings from home. First Charles, then Papa. She must dread ever getting a letter these days."

The hot wind gusting across the Limestone Plains scorched the tips of white flowers in the wreaths and ruffled the veils of the ladies. Mary Ann did not weep loudly as her sister did, instead pulled her veil closer and stood straight, just like her grandfather. But beneath the black silk the tears coursed down her cheeks and she had to gulp for breath.

Among the crowd of mourners George Brownlow observed everyone carefully, and later mingled with the family and friends.

He watched the ham being sliced and the cheese being cut up, the tea poured and the beer drawn from its cask. As he offered his condolences he could not but hear some of the muttered comments.

"Reckon old William'll cut up real good," Constable Nugent speculated as he stood with others from Gundaroo, slightly apart from the mourning relatives. George edged closer.

"Them girls, tidy packet for them and no doubt about it," another chipped in with a knowing laugh.

"That Rossi won't know his luck, time he gets back."

Someone muttered, "Walk into a nice little fortune, I reckon. Sweet on that Mary Ann, some say. Who knows with them foreigners?"

Rossi! George's hand twitched.

"Steady on, mate!" Constable Nugent stepped back as some beer spilled over down his jacket.

Rossi! George had never thought the older man would ever be considered a suitable suitor for young Mary Ann. What a fool he'd been! So wrapped up in his visits, his frequent chats and the satisfaction that events were unfolding in a most rewarding manner that it had never occurred to him any larger scenario could exist.

He turned and regarded them closely. The old man leaning on his stick, the well-turned out couple standing close to Mary Ann, several cousins hovering around the teapot and cakes.

The family were busy with their own plans.

"Mary Ann can spend half the year with Henry and me and half the year with Edward and Hannah up in Barrack Street."

Grand-père listened politely to his elder granddaughter. "You'll come and live at Woodbury, of course, Grand-père. Henry says best to get an overseer for Bywong, someone to look after the property and then…"

"Thank you but Mary Ann and I are staying on the farm."

"But you'll be on your own, Grand-père. Who'll manage the farm? Dear sir, don't consider it," Henry Lintott insisted.

"Mary Ann and I will manage very nicely, thank you." He snapped his mouth shut and chewed discreetly.

No one was brave enough to ask the important question – for how long?

How much longer would the old man be in this world? And what then?

CHAPTER 9

"Pretty as a picture! Just shows what love can do." Hannah took her sister's arm as they settled themselves in the pew, flanked by their husbands. "I just wish she'd waited a bit longer, but would she listen?"

"That's our Mary Ann. Headstrong she is and always will be. But you've got to admit we need someone as'll take the place on. These days with half the properties going to the wall, hardly had the chance to get over the drought, then it's everyone off to the diggings. You can't deny George's an able man, and that's what this family needs. Can't credit our own family ending up like this. Charles going was the last straw and Papa well before his time too, and not to mention poor old Grand-père beginning to fail."

"He'll see a century yet, mark my words."

"I don't know Hannah, he can't go on for ever. Our Mary Ann needs all the help she can get. I reckon that George just stepped in at the right moment."

"I still think it's a bit soon to marry."

"She's that taken up with him, thinks the sun shines out of his eyes. Lovely to see really. She's never had much fun, has she? Still, I'd have been happier if she'd have waited a mite longer too. Mind you, there was no arguing with her. What do you think, Henry?"

'It's the French blood in her, that's what the trouble is. Always a contrary lot, the French. Headstrong, that girl is. Didn't your father want her to hold off getting wed, leastways till she had a few years more? But no, just like all them Frenchies, no patience at all. Can't even live together in peace. Look at what they did to their own king and queen. Hung, drawn and quartered they were." Henry Lintott had the same shadowy grasp of history that most of the Colony's home-educated population possessed.

"Sent to the guillotine, you mean. And people are hanged, not hung. Pictures are hung, people are hanged." Hannah Cantor was as pedantic as her brother-in-law was vague.

"Come to think of it," muttered Edward, "you've got the same blood in your veins. You are just as much a Guise as young Mary Ann, stands to reason."

She sighed to herself. Dear Edward, always going off at a tangent, never a quick thinker! "But I didn't listen to all those tales of old Grand-père, did I? Plenty of money in the bank those days, lake been full of water for as long as we knew. Times were very different. They sent me off for schooling, not left alone with an old man living off his memories most of the time putting all those strange fancies into her head. And look where it's led, can't see beyond her nose when it comes to George Brownlow. Her head's full of dreams."

"He's well spoken of. Turned round that property of the Pattersons, alright."

"She could do worse."

"Didn't I beg her to come to us, get an overseer, leave the place? Didn't I say, lease out the property, find a good tenant, come and live with us, or go up to Barrack Street? She'd have met more of her own kind, then she'd have had a choice and she'd have…"

"Her own kind! Where'd you find another like her? She's half wild that girl. She'd rather be out in the paddocks than sipping tea in a drawing room. Her own kind!"

"She'd never want to leave the farm, that's for sure. Loves every inch of it. Well, let's hope that fellow stands by her. Mind you, she'll always turn to us in the end I'd say. He's got no family…never mentions kith nor kin. Can't see any family here from his side, can you?"

"Maybe there's family alright, but maybe 't'ain't spoken of," muttered Henry.

"What do you mean?"

"Just what I says, word gets around," and Henry sagely tapped his nose, "but it don't mean a fellow's any the worse for it. Folks make their own way in life. Seein' as how her pa and brothers are gone… well, she'll be looked after at any rate."

"What you mean is, the Guise land'll be looked after. A windfall for a fellow like him."

"Ssh, here she comes."

Outlined in the doorway the bride paused for a moment before taking her first step up the aisle. Unlike her sisters, who tended towards a certain blowsiness, Mary Ann Guise moved with a stately grace, no way compromised by the simple lines of her wedding gown.

The congregation turned to look. Some smiled but some stifled a sigh. So young to be starting on life's great journey with so little support – mother, father, brothers, all gone. Admittedly her sisters remained but they were always busy with their own lives.

"Pretty as a picture, our Mary Ann's a credit." Hannah Cantor dug her sister in the ribs.

Elizabeth sniffed. Her own satin gown had been trimmed with Honiton lace, she'd worn a circlet of orange-blossom with a tulle veil. And the bridesmaids! Tarlatan and touches of Maltese lace with bouquets of white jessamine. Their elegance had been more than matched by the guests. Moiré, taffeta and grosgrain rustled in the pews whilst the scent or flowers, the subtle hint of eau-de-Cologne and the faintest whiff of papier poudre wafted over the bonnets and ringlets and corkscrew curls. Now that had been an elegant wedding, befitting a Guise girl.

No doubt about it, the dratted drought had brought them all down in the world. Where were the wealthy settlers of a few years ago? Up in the city, secure in their town houses. It would take years for land prices to recover.

Where once fine silks and taffetas had rustled in the pews, now stolid bombazine and printed cotton took their place. Lace-up boots scraped upon the floor and straw bonnets trimmed with paper flowers nodded to their neighbours.

"Everyone's pretty on their wedding day," snapped Elizabeth Lintott as she smoothed some wrinkles out of her gloves.

"Well, 'tis love, isn't it? You can see 'tis love."

"That's as may be."

Love is a habit. The words nearly tripped off the tip of Elizabeth's tongue but something held her back. Since there's only one true wedding day in a lifetime, best not spoil it with sour remarks. But what was love? Maybe it started with that radiance which engulfed a girl and wafted her across her first threshold, but soon the silk and the flowers had to be put aside for a gown of workaday stuff and the peeling of vegetables. And what of the other? Elizabeth sniffed to herself, she had no words to describe what happened to that! The soft warmth and escalating pleasure, the sheer delight of strong arms about you and a body given up to another. Well, nine months on soon told their own story. The agony, the hours of labour and the mewling, screeching creature laid in your arms.

No, if any vestige of love continued, then it had to become a habit like any other.

"Leastways she'll be looked after now. Won't have to leave the place," Henry muttered.

"Tied to the sink and the yard! That'll be her life from now on, I declare that's how it'll be. She's always been out in the paddocks!"

"She'll be mistress in her own home at least, 'specially since the old chap's coming to Woodbury with us."

Elizabeth caught the hint of resignation in his voice. Grand-père did not want to stay with the newly married couple. "Wouldn't do at all," he proclaimed and announced he'd move over to the Lintott's house.

"Typical of your old pa, typical," Henry had grumbled at the time. "That's the Guises for you. One word is his command. He never thought to ask if it's convenient." For Richard had simply announced that he had made up his mind and life at Woodbury was his intention.

"He'll be perfectly happy with us."

"He's going to miss Bywong that bad."

"Grand-père's coming to live with us, Henry." A certain doggedness had crept into Elizabeth's voice. "It's decided. Makes sense."

"Oh I know that alright, and I'm not saying nay to it, but that's the trouble with your family. Want their own way and never stop to think that others may look at matters differently."

"Ssh, Henry… ssh!"

Grand-père led Mary Ann up to where Mr Sowerby and George were waiting. He moved very slowly but every step was certain and sure and he held himself perfectly erect. As they came to a halt he turned his head and looked for the last time at his granddaughter, for every ancient tradition dictated that this was a parting of the ways. For all of her seventeen years she had belonged to them, the Guise family. Now her loyalties would be to another.

And yet... his keen old eyes searched her face, those dark eyes, that flawless complexion, the high cheek bones and the dark sweep of her hair beneath the simple circlet. Her face was raised and her gaze only for George. Her stance proud and so happy that the old man felt a tightening in his throat. His own dear bride had looked at him in just that way, so many years ago.

"Look, here they come." Less than thirty minutes later Mr Sowerby led the couple to the rails and they took their first steps as man and wife down the aisle.

"Well, all I can say is, I hope he looks after our Mary Ann. 'T'won't be no easy task neither, 'cause she's been used to having her head most times, not one to take to the bit nor the curb."

"Things'll be done her way or not at all, I reckon. She'll want that property to be just the same as her pa had it and her grandpa before him. Nothin'll change. Mark my words."

But in that the doubting relatives were proved surprisingly wrong. Something had come into Mary Ann's life that certainly did bring about changes. And that something was love.

CHAPTER 10

Imperceptibly Mary Ann's priorities began to shift, slowly at first and then with a gathering momentum which embraced all her thoughts. Her first care had always been for Bywong. Bywong meant the rolling paddocks, the dam, the clumps of gum trees, the riverbank and the tall elms along the driveway. Bywong and the family had made up her universe but as life with George settled into daily reality her concerns for the acreages took second place and her concern went ever more frequently to George's comfort, the house itself, the yard and the orchard. Mary Ann began to find all the satisfaction she needed in making the home a place of pleasure.

Time brought changes, and those changes mirrored the progression of her love. Her greatest joy lay in making a real home for him. She maintained that after a lifetime spent shifting for himself at the behest of others, the time had come for her George to have the pleasure of a proper home. Comfortless lodgings, lonely huts, draughty rooms would be but a memory.

By the time her firstborn arrived she had channelled all the energy she'd previously put into running the day-to-day work of the property into, first of all, making their daily life more convenient and comfortable, and then adding those touches of refinement which had been lost over the years as the Guise fortunes had dwindled. Glass for some of the windows which had only had shutters, then curtains to soften the glass. And the kitchen itself was not forgotten. Soon the flames glowed from behind the bars of a neat American stove - the latest.

By the time the Guise family gathered together again, this time for young Cathy's christening, Mary Ann's first care was for her daughter, husband and home. No longer did she ride out on the property and she even sometimes found herself leafing through the journals which Hannah sent down from Barrack Street, those long-ago despised publications full of hats and hairstyles and elegant gowns.

Every person experiences love in their own way - some dip their toes in the waters and hover at the edges, others immerse themselves and swim out into the depths. Mary Ann had never been one for caution so she gave herself completely. Love fulfilled her life. It became the sunshine that lit up the day, the moonbeam that glorified the darkness but, even more importantly, love became the staff on which she leant her whole weight.

How had she been so lucky? George took over the management of Bywong just as easily as he slipped into the saddle and guided his mare out of the yard and across the paddocks. He understood the land, he foresaw every change and dealt with every emergency.

"Well, Grand-père, seems our Mary Ann's settled down to married life alright. All those doubts of yours come to naught' eh?" Elizabeth Lintott whispered to the old man as she settled herself more comfortably in her chair beside him near the grandfather clock.

"Too many changes."

"Oh, come on Grand-père, of course everyone makes

changes. Trouble was, the old home'd been the same for too long."

"Why'd she have to put all that stuff on the walls? We never needed that."

"Come now, Grand-père, a picture or two makes a world of difference."

"Seemed all right the way it was," but he could not keep the trace of a smile touching the corners of his lips. Grudgingly he admitted to himself that the parlour had come up in the world. Quite handsome, was his verdict.

Sitting back on the settle he looked at his family scattered around the large room, and not for the first time wondered why he had been spared for so long, the last of his generation. The Lintotts and the Cantors, with some cousins, distant relatives and a few neighbours made up the gathering. Grand-père's gaze moved from face to face, all so happy and fulfilled. When glasses were raised in a toast he silently mouthed to himself those other names, those others who had gone, never to return, and to make a wish that soon he might join them. Dear Elizabeth, and both their sons, and then the last of his grandsons.

"Another jam tart?" Mary Ann bent over her grandfather, "No? Can I get you a slice of cake?"

The old man smiled up at her. The transformation in Mary Ann reminded him of those early days of his own marriage. For him it had been a new country, a new life entirely; for Mary Ann it might be said her life stayed the same except that nowadays she had a husband to manage the farm and had stepped into the role of a farmer's wife. Dairy, chicken, household, garden and orchard were her world and, circumscribed by love, contentment glowed in her face. Grand-père marvelled at the change, but then hadn't dear Elizabeth changed when she willingly gave up all she had ever known to share in his new world?

An overwhelming weariness enveloped him, so compelling that he almost dropped his cup of tea. The roomful of chattering relatives suddenly exhausted him.

So many years ahead for them, so many years behind for him.

Even as he looked at the walls, the pictures and the neat curtains he could still see the bark that had once made up the sides of the house and the golden light of early morning peeping through gaps in the shutters.

A tide of remembrance washed over him and pulled him back to that distant past when he'd ventured down south in search of new pastures.

To that time when he'd first ridden down from the city and seen the bounty of Lake George, when he had decided that this would be where they'd finally make their home. Besides abundant water for stock he rejoiced at the prospect of mile upon mile of open country stretching up into the foothills of the mountains where he'd be able to hunt and fish till the end of his days.

He'd already made their fortune, owned land and leases all over the Colony, but the country was becoming overcrowded in his view. Down here, on the Limestone Plains, space abounded and plenty of room remained to found a dynasty. His sons would one day build their own homes. Richard visualised all those Guise families spreading and prospering as generation followed generation. "Elizabeth, my love," he'd hurried home to tell his exciting news. "There's more land than you can imagine… a magnificent lake. No longer will we suffer the curse of this place. We'll never need to concern ourselves over water again."

"But so far away, my love?"

"Soon I'll have a home for you. You'll have the house of your dreams. This will be our last move." And wisely she held her tongue for she'd followed her husband for twenty years or more and he always moved on.

With his young sons working with him he was ready for the months and months of clearing. Then stocking the land and, after that, fencing. Then drafting, washing, scouring which had laid down the framework for Bywong, whilst Elizabeth and the younger children had remained in Sydney.

Living under canvas, spending the days with axe and shovel, riding for many miles, he returned to the city whenever he could but distances were great and there was always so much to do.

"You'll take us back next time," she'd finally insisted.

"One day, my love. Soon I shall have a roof to put over our heads, then we will talk about it some more. Till then you and the girls stay up here."

Just as with their other properties, land and livestock were their real asset. 'Put everything on four legs' was the advice for any man striving for his living. But, like so many successful squatters, the women remained in the city while the men worked on the property. Putting that roof over their heads came second in importance and many of the dwellings thereabouts were as simple as the gunyahs of the Canberri and Ngunawal.

Sheets of bark stripped from the trees and laced to the timber frame with greenhide straps formed the walls of that first Bywong. The woven lattice of wood strips was daubed with a sticky mixture of chopped-up straw, sand, and even dung. At one end of the hut a stout door opened to the outdoors and at the other end an enormous fireplace and chimney filled the whole wall.

'Too soon, far too soon," he grumbled when he finally brought them down from Sydney.

"No matter, we shall all be together." For Elizabeth had finally insisted that they travelled down to Bywong with him. "That is the most important thing. I've been living the life of a widow and the girls never see you and their brothers. What kind of an existence is that?"

"Well, I warned you, our home is not ready. All you'll have is a roof over your heads and draughts everywhere. The boys and I will manage under canvas again."

But Elizabeth cried out with delight when she saw the simple dwelling. "Put up a rail, Richard. We'll need to have some curtains round the beds, and look at that fireplace!"

That first night as the wind howled outside the entire family squeezed in around the great hearth for warmth. Richard had wedged a stout iron upright into the stones; from the equally stout welded arm that stretched out over the flames a chain hung down. Many a kettle and pan steamed above the fire during the oncoming months.

So began a makeshift period when, for the first time in many months, they shared their life and rejoiced at being together again.

Elizabeth never complained. She maintained that the gaps in the wall through which the wind whistled, the leaks in the roof and the beaten earth floor were scant price to pay for having her husband and family around her once more.

Even if visits to the privy proved an ordeal—spiders and lizards and once or twice even a snake sheltered under its roof—and hours spent over a hot tub in the wash house were almost too long and too hot to bear, Elizabeth delighted in her latest abode.

In this new Eden, she declared, they would construct their home together and it would be a haven for every one of them. The fortunes of the Guise family had prospered from their keeping together so far and that must continue until the youngest ones were ready to make their own way.

Next, Richard fenced off nearly half an acre around the home and under her discerning eye the planting began. Apples, pears, damsons, apricots, and then an experiment or two, an orange and a persimmon. As the saplings took root she and Job set about planting the vegetables. Strong and eager to please, he'd dug and furrowed and hammered in the stakes for the peas, the frames for the beans and when he'd finished that to her satisfaction, she was ready to make her secret dream come true.

Roses! She brought back some climbers on one of her rare visits to Goulburn and soon had them trained up against the walls of the kitchen.

Once the paddocks were fenced and the flocks thriving and the men had some time to spare the final Bywong could be constructed.

The old daub and wattle home became the kitchen for the new house which very slowly emerged nearby. A path connected the kitchen to the home. Cooking was kept at a distance, for fire remained the most serious threat to those living in remote places.

This new Bywong had a verandah six foot wide all round. They'd dug the post holes two foot deep for the outside and for the inside too, marking off the rooms. Battens still held down the bark roof, but boards an inch thick had taken the place of the mud flooring. A house built to last! A home as sturdy as its owners, a dwelling which looked to the future, with shuttered windows and two fireplaces and chimneys. Later, when times changed, the house changed too, with a glazed window or two and then a shingle roof.

All the while the life of the property accumulated around the ever-growing house. The dairy, the store and stables, all gradually made up the home that was Bywong.

Change became the order of the day as the years rolled by and time transformed the new dwelling into a rambling homestead. Lathe and plaster now covered the inside walls, all was rendered and whitewashed. Calico lined the ceiling and daylight twinkled in through the window glass. Now an outhouse-roof extended on all four sides to shelter the verandah hugging the house. Visitors slept there, plants and settles lined the walls. A herbaceous border, just as spoken of in the ladies' journals from across the sea, bloomed all the way to the gate. And roses, cuttings struck from the twining mass around the old kitchen, rambled on to the verandah and trailed along the windowsills, filling the night air with their scent.

Blinds excluded the western sun, old barrels and boxes were transformed into chairs, and every item that could be made was quickly put into use. With the passageway between kitchen and house covered against the elements, only the privy remained as it always had been - down near the orchard.

Grand-père's gaze followed the young woman as she moved about the room, exchanging a few words here, laughing with another one there, making sure everyone had all that they wanted. How true that love can transform. Mary Ann had grown from that leggy hoyden of a girl, impetuous and wild, to become this poised young woman. A perfect marriage, and yet… and yet Grand-père did not feel quite at ease. Never once had he exchanged more than a few pleasantries with George. This newcomer to the family was invariably smiling and polite but never joined in the easy chatter of the Guise clan. He kept his own counsel, did not take part in the cut and thrust of conversation or the occasional argument. Well, why should he, Grand-père asked himself - the Guise family have always stayed close to each other. Once that big family had argued, laughed, agreed, disagreed throughout the days, and even now, reduced as it was, everyone spoke up, said their piece and liked a good discussion. Perhaps being on his own, maybe an only child, would make such gatherings quite daunting for George.

Grand-père was wrong. Nothing daunted George. He did not care to join the family in their animated discussions because, even if he had gained entry to their world, he had no particular interest in it. George Brownlow lived in an animal world.

His entire working life had been spent amongst those who laboured on the land. Though not born to the countryside he'd passed so much time amongst shepherds, herdsmen and labourers that he knew no other way to earn his daily bread and preferred their company.

Grand-père and Elizabeth Lintott had been nearer the truth than they imagined when they'd speculated about his parentage. In this land of opposites, when a thief could become a landowner, a murderer a respected citizen and many a lady of loose morals find herself sought after for the marriage bed, in this mixing pot of 'class, colour and creed' there were in fact many fortunate turnarounds of fate that saved a poor soul from disaster.

Back in the old country, back in those cold northern cities crammed with the workless, homeless and hopeless tide of humanity swept up by the changing times, many a girl chose prostitution rather than starvation.

And what did it bring? Disgrace? Well, by then most were past bothering. The lively young face and body became ravaged with the effort of that lifestyle and the diseases brought with it, until the spectre of destitution beckoned the way to the workhouse.

Even in this new world the same obstacles littered the path of the unwary girl, but there were also opportunities which had been undreamt of in the backstreets of Seven Dials and the docklands of the Thames. Men outnumbered women by three to one and the possession of a female to keep the home fires burning, cook the food and mend the clothes was a luxury never to be attained by many.

Indeed George's mother had earned her living upon her back but that had not ruined her future. Those same talents could also bring security. An old husband, pockets adequately lined, vittles in the larder, a roof overhead proved a blessing. A home for herself and her baby son presented a life-saving option which no penniless girl would turn down.

And just as surely as apes evolved into human beings so, by slow steps up the ladder of opportunity, those humans could climb up and better themselves.

Untutored and unfettered by tradition, her son launched himself in his mid-teens into the ready market of this burgeoning world. A lively lad, full of strength and energy, he soon exchanged the city streets for sunburnt, windswept country inland where labour was always needed.

For twenty years he'd known no other existence. Twenty years is a long time in a man's life; by then many a man has a wife and children to support. Amid the demands of domestic life he'd lose his momentum and settle for the rented shack, the demanding landlord and mouths forever crying to be fed. But if George had inherited nothing else from his mother he had been endowed with a shrewd instinct for survival, and at over thirty remained unencumbered.

When he had first come to Gundaroo drought still desiccated the land. Tempted to move on, he looked again at the barren acres and shrewdly observed a greater opportunity by staying in the area. Many of the wealthier squatters faced a dilemma: should they leave their ruined properties or weather out the bad times, hope for the creeks to run and the lake to fill again?

George looked at the dead tree stumps in the expanse of dried-out lake bed, he took note of the middens and the rock paintings and realised this freak of nature must have happened before, and the old owners of the land had survived. Throughout history the lake would have filled and emptied. So, when bullock carts and drays headed back to the city, when carriages disappeared in a cloud of dust, George offered his services to a succession of dejected landowners. He would oversee their properties and they could depend upon him.

No longer quite a servant but certainly not one of the employer's class, he learnt to exist without companionship. Not accepted in the drawing room and regarded with suspicion amongst the labourers, he trod a lonely path.

George took his pleasure wherever it was offered, he made no promises and resolutely remained free of attachments. He realised a good reputation was worth more than any fleeting profit so eschewed all opportunities to gain by stealth and rendered to his employers their dues. His reputation as a trusted employee grew, in those remote acreages any man who could be relied upon to watch over a property being worth his weight in gold, so many a harassed squatter maintained. From sunup to sundown he laboured, his sole recreation being a visit to the racetrack.

From the dropping of the first lamb, to the stowing away of the last bale of hay, he lived by the rhythms of the land. Waking to the complaints of the wattle birds and the first seeping light of dawn, turning in at the end of each day to the last cries of the jackass and the wonga pigeon's lullaby.

Not for him the *fol-de-rol* of the parlour and the verandah. His possessions had been few: a horse, the clothes on his back, a few spare garments and a prized pair of Blucher boots, a couple of blankets, an almanack and a silver timepiece given by a grateful employer. No pies or pastry for his table; instead, the daily damper, a hunk of cheese, and meat whenever he killed a beast.

When a wealthy landowner invited him to hunt, to join the chase with the pack of newly imported hounds and run the dingoes to destruction, he declined. For a while they'd relish his company, he knew that too well, but after the hurly-burly of the hunt and the back-slapping and the camaraderie of equals came to pass, he would have to make his way back to his lonely hut.

Harrowing, sowing, reaping, shearing, fencing and a myriad of tasks made up the substance of his days, and his nights were untroubled by the luxury of dreams as he fell exhausted onto his mattress. Dreams were for weaklings and there was nothing weak about him. Anyone who considered he would always be a faithful servant would have made a great mistake because, if he did not have dreams, he had ambition.

He was determined one day to own a property of his own. Listening all the while to tales of disaster offset by success he watched as the acreages of men bankrupted by drought or death came up for sale. He weighed up the pros and cons of every property that came on the market. Did it have reliable water? Had the flocks suffered from the dreaded catarrh? Would the land be fertile or would it be barren?

Dingo-like he circled and watched and waited. Sensing the conditions around him, sniffing the air for that whiff of corruption or the healthy odour of success. For in all his years upon the land he'd learnt as much from animals as other human beings.

George Brownlow knew more about farming than many of the men he worked for. Perhaps that unknown man who'd lain one night with an easy woman had been a farmer, perhaps the genes had been passed on. Despite being born into a city slum he was a farmer through and through. A farmer without a farm.

But wealthy squatters ruled the day. Around the Limestone Plains and further afield men settled with their army and navy pensions, grants were given, mortgages freely extended to such upright citizens. He'd looked away when his employers' sons came down from the city and went out hunting and picnicking and sitting upon the verandah of the homestead supping their ale.

They had their lives, he had his. He was lucky to have his own horse, his hut and a steady wage. Enough for a man. But not quite. The years bring their own changes and as the decades started to add up he glimpsed the future, a trifle disquieting.

In another ten years would he still be sitting at his rough hewn table eating mutton and damper and drinking flat beer? On another property maybe, but his lot would be the same wherever he went.

One table, one chair, a narrow bunk, four walls enclosing silence.

Ten years after that infirmity might take hold. Would he end his days chopping wood, fetching and carrying and stumbling from one charitable handout to another?

That glimpse returned at random moments. Waking to the profound quiet of his hut, smelling the meat going off in the meatsafe, wondering whether he could be bothered to make some damper.

One of these moments of solitude had descended on him several years ago as he stood in the main street of Gundaroo.

He'd been a newcomer and as he watched old Job driving the Guise's trap down the main street with Mary Ann chattering beside him and bags and bundles of purchases stacked up around them he'd suddenly felt completely alone.

He knew nothing of the Guise family but what he saw was a comfortable, settled life and suddenly it became infinitely desirable.

As he watched he did not realise that he also was being watched.

CHAPTER 11

"The Good Lord helps them as helps themselves," Mary O'Rourke leant her elbows on the table. Her neck spilled out in a series of folds under the double chin resting on her ample hands.

"Ma!"

"Time was when I looked every bit like you does now. A man could put his two hands round me waist, he could, and many did. But time's runnin' out, it is. Half a dozen years'll make a mint of difference and then where'll you be? Takin' in the washing like me."

"Heard all this before, Ma." Brigid gathered her skirt as she rose to go.

"An' you'll hear it again, my girl. Maybe I ain't schooled, neither is you, but you've got a head on your shoulders and now's the time to use it, not going off in a huff 'cos he's wed another. What did you expect? Men looks after themselves, they do. Well, you only got to look at Mick and Seamus, selfish buggers, but then that's where we come in. We look after ourselves too, don't we. I always says, look after number one first."

"Well, it ain't done you too much good, has it, Ma?" Brigid glanced round at the beaten dirt floor, the rough table, two chairs, several wooden boxes serving as extra seats – and the torn curtain, separating the room from the sleeping area.

"Ain't done nothing for you, I'd say." She scoffed and got up to leave.

"Sit down, you silly little bitch. You ain't heard half yet. Mopin' away like a wet week."

Brigid sighed. Her mother had the latent power of a bushfire, consuming all that stood in its way. Her small eyes glittered and her lips were drawn thin and tight as she motioned the girl to sit down again.

"I'd not have been endin' me days down by this stinking creek if I'd played me cards right. That's what I'm telling you. You thought he'd ask you, didn't you? You reckon you'd a chance of a good match but you never listened to me, did you? He's looking after number one, that Brownlow. Looking after number one and doin' very nicely, thank you. And that's where you come in. 'Stead of flouncing off in a pet, 'tis time to make some plans."

Brigid regarded her mother with something akin to faint interest.

"We only got one thing on our side in this life, my girl. Others have property and families and all that sort of thing, but we only got one thing. We've got one thing in our favour, and it's the most important thing in all the world."

"What's that, Ma?"

"We're sittin' on it!" The woman leant back and laughed, her great hams of arms quivered and shook, her hair flopped over her face and she laughed till the tears ran down her cheeks.

"An' that's what I'm tellin' youse," finally managing to choke out the words. "You've fooled about with half the boys down the village, you think you've wasted yer time with that George. Mebbe you thought he wed yer, but believe me he's on to the real stuff now and if you've any sense in you, then you stick by 'im. He'll have that much cash in the bank as'd keep you comfortable for the rest of your natural." *And see me through me old age,* she smiled to herself.

"Ma, that's the whole point. When he wed that Guise girl that's the end, ain't it?"

"Not for men like George Brownlow. 'Tis the beginning, more like."

"The Guise family, think, Ma! Always so high and mighty."

"High and mighty they might always have been but they've had some mighty mishaps lately, haven't they? Losing them two boys was bad enough but when Charles went and the old man died, well, family's finished near enough, ain't it?

"Bywong's ripe for the picking. George Brownlow's sized it up, believe me, and this is when you sticks as close to 'is coat tails as possible. Second kiddy on the way, I've heard. Well, he'll have had enough of wedded bliss 'fore too long. He'll be looking for somethin' more tasty."

"How'd you know that?" Brigid stared glumly out of the window. "You don't know nothin' of George Brownlow."

"And there you're quite wrong, my bird. Quite wrong. First time I clapped eyes on him up in the village I said to myself, 'Mary, there's a likely lad. Him with his eyes all over the place, swallering up all the girls, lookin' all the so-called quality up and down. Mary, 'I said to meself, 'if I was twenty years younger I'd be lookin' to leave me boots under 'is bed.' You can tell, way he looks around him, smart turnout, decent horse, never a knock-kneed nag for him. Oh, it's easy to see those who are lookin' out for themselves. Anyone could see George Brownlow's on his way up in the world."

Brigid said nothing as she watched her mother's eyes narrow and a knowing smile spread across her features.

"But he always had one problem in life, hadn't he?"

"What's that, Ma?"

"Too fond of the horses! Like most of 'em it's either the liquor or the horses and our Mick reckons he'd 'ave made something of himself but for that. None of the ready, had he? Not till now, so he's had to spend his life looking after other folks' property."

"Well, he's always been an overseer. He told me that himself."

"Doesn't mean he wanted to end his days like that, does it? Bowing and scraping to someone who's just had a bit more luck than he has, bin born with a silver spoon in their mouths, or struck it rich on the goldfields. No, the way I sees it is that he's been very clever. He's got all that property and a good home now. I'll give it to him, from all accounts he's mightily respected and he's worked hard for it. He's laboured for others all his life, George Brownlow's worked alright. Perhaps now 'tis time for him to play!"

"Play! That's what you calls it?" Brigid sniffed loudly. She was rapidly reaching the conclusion that her days for playing would soon run out.

The first faint lines about the eyes confirmed the ravages of the sun and all too soon the wonderful bloom would be gone. Even if she could have taken her pick of the village lads once, now there were younger girls coming along and when it came to the serious business of marriage she shied away from the thought of hearth and home, screaming childen and a cradle always filled and another child on her knee.

"Yes, play. He's got cash in the bank now. He'll want to enjoy life. Always had a liking for the horses, he has, same as our Mick. Time's come for our families to get closer acquainted, I'd say. Play your cards right and he's yours – hook, line and sinker."

"Oh stop yer woolgathering, Ma! He's wed, he led me on and… "

Mary O'Rourke fixed her gaze on her daughter. "Stead of moping around like a wet week you'd be better getting in with them up at Bywong, if you see what I mean."

"All very well, Ma, but I ain't exactly brushing shoulders with them Guises, am I?"

"Use yer loaf. Go up and ask if Mrs Brownlow needs some help. You've worked in a kitchen before. If she is expectin' again so soon she might be glad of another pair of hands about the place. Another little'un on the way, well, yer never know yer luck!"

When Mary Ann opened the door to Brigid she did not at first recognise the girl who'd lived all her life in the hut by the river. Then she recalled that teeming family, the lanky lads all so alike and their little sister with her winning ways. Black curls framed a bright, heartshaped face, they highlighted the porcelain delicacy of her cheeks and the perfect Cupid's bow of her lips. The Irish colouring of dark hair and blue eyes had reached a peak of perfection and those deep indigo eyes gleamed with the joy of life.

Perhaps because the word 'gleamed' came to her mind too quickly, Mary Ann did not feel quite comfortable as she politely asked the girl to step inside.

"Our ma wondered if you was looking for a hand in the kitchen or out in the dairy. The boys is all workin' down Gundaroo. She thought you might have a place for me." As she spoke the words her eyes travelled round the room. The handsome clock, the long table with a bowl of fruit in the centre, the almanack, the stylish oil lamp – the very latest—and the half finished shawl and delicate white knitting wool. Hungrily she stared at the blue and red carpet and thought bitterly of their mud floor and the soft patches that oozed whenever it rained. A whiff of roses came in through the window and a hint of a baking cake wafted across from the kitchen. For a moment the bitter bile of envy almost sickened her as it rose in her throat, then she turned her brightest smile on Mary Ann and muttered something about being very used to general housework.

Mary Ann sat down at the table and gathered up her knitting. "It's really kind of your mother and so good of you to come over." She paused. Common sense told her that a helping hand would certainly not go astray, but something held her back. Brigid's covetous glances had not gone unnoticed. *Poor girl,* Mary Ann thought, *living in that pigsty of a place, all those rough brothers and just her mother…though gossip did hint the girl found plenty of amusement amongst the young men.* Job had made a few remarks, and he knew most of what was going on in Gundaroo.

"Me cooking's none too good but I can bake a tidy loaf."

"Perhaps if I keep you in mind. At the moment everything's alright but in a few months I may very well need some help." Mary Ann could not look at her as she said the words. She knew she would never want this girl sharing the daily round. There was something about Brigid that troubled her and although she could not put her finger on it, the sensation would not go away. Watching her walking back across the paddock only intensified that sense of unease.

"There! I told you. Stuck-up cow. 'Perhaps if I keep you in mind.' " Brigid caught Mary Ann's tone with cruel accuracy as she flung open the door of the hut. "I'll show 'er, I'll show 'er."

"And I'm sure you will, my bird, I'm sure you will. Just bide yer time," chuckled her mother.

CHAPTER 12

Mary Ann tip-toed into the darkened bedroom and gazed down at her sleeping daughter. A healthy sheen of perspiration glowed upon Cathy's brow, the clean, soapy scent of washed linen hovered over the cradle. All was well.

Why did she feel uneasy? Tucking in the sheet she went back to the parlour.

Knit one, slip one, purl one... the words echoed through her head as the wool passed between her fingers but she could not keep her mind on them.

Knit one, slip one, pass the slipped stitch over. Too complicated! Putting down the work she stared across the paddock. Why did she feel so uncomfortable with that girl? Something in her knowing glance and the set of her shoulders when she looked around the room had stirred a hint of menace.

Hastily she shrugged the sensation away. Why should she worry anyhow? George, Cathy and Bywong were all she could wish for, and of course the new little life moving inside her. Would it be the son that George wanted so much? Her sigh of contentment wafted away the last of that uncertainty and she fell once more into the reverie which had become so much a part of everyday life.

Her life had changed even more since Cathy was born. No longer did she venture out into the paddocks or help Job about the yard. George had made it quite clear that she need not concern herself with the outdoor work at all.

"You put your feet up, remember. Every afternoon, while Cathy's asleep you put your feet up."

When she protested he shook his head. "Not the place for you out there. There's more than enough for you to do about the place and I likes me dinner on the table when I get in!" A laugh accompanied this remark but it held more than a grain of truth as Mary Ann soon discovered. George expected an orderly life.

"A place for everything and everything in its place," he reiterated on more than one occasion with the single-mindedness of one who had existed all his life with so little and everything he owned having to be looked after. Every minute of the day was allotted to a task. Compared with the easy-going Guise habits he needed to work to a routine; he believed in having a plan.

Breakfast on the dot. In fact, Mary Ann laid the table before going to bed, there must be no delay. He'd be out on the property, but back sharp at midday for his dinner, ten minutes with his feet up, then off again to the far paddocks or down to the blacksmiths or searching for lost stock, any one of the myriad tasks always waiting to be done. He never returned till the light had left the sky and then, as he said, he expected his tea on the table. A few minutes nodding over the *Goulburn Herald* and then off to bed.

Long ago the house had resounded to the clamour of all those who dwelt beneath its roof. There'd been brothers and sisters busy about the place, and cousins calling in, and her own mother and Grand-mère always out in the orchard or the dairy.

Meals would be cooked, fruit preserved, beds made and piles of dirty clothes waiting for the wash, and all the time the buzz of happy chatter and laughter filled the place.

Those times would come again, Mary Ann assured herself. Once the children began to grow up there'd be other families calling in, there'd be birthday parties and picnics and Christmases and Easters and all the gatherings which punctuated life. Now she had to expect life to be quiet, almost solitary in fact, but with Elizabeth over at Woodbury, Hannah up at Barrack Street and George out on the property all day long, she could not help feeling lonely.

Occasionally someone dropped by to borrow a harrow or have a chat over when to start cutting the hay, or pose a query about some missing stock. Nowadays there were even fewer callers than in her father's day; it soon became apparent to his neighbours that George did not care to share any belongings. In fact, nobody had visited all autumn and now the frosts were beginning to whiten the paddocks.

So when she heard the clatter of hooves in the yard one early afternoon Mary Ann leapt to her feet - was George home early? What had happened for that to occur?

"Mr de Rossi!" Amazed she held out her hands in welcome.

"Mary Ann!" He'd already hitched his horse to the verandah rail. "Mary Ann, I mean, Mrs Brownlow."

"Oh nonsense, of course I'm Mary Ann still! Please come in, what an unexpected pleasure." All the negative thoughts she'd once harboured were swept aside as she welcomed him. Any thought of that fateful night was banished by the remembrance of her family's friendship with the de Rossis - that wonderful ball! Memories jostled each other as she bade him come in.

"Such a pleasant surprise, Mr de Rossi, I was only thinking visitors are not very frequent. Everyone is so busy these days."

"I'm taking the road to Melbourne, business of course, I wondered if I might take the liberty of calling on you and your husband."

"George will be so disappointed," she said, not quite truthfully for her husband regarded such as the Rossis as pampered settlers. 'Rossiville! I ask you. Perhaps I should change our name to Brownlowville,' he'd sneered on one occasion.

"And I've been carrying this around the world!" He laughed and handed her a parcel.

"For me?"

"Most certainly." He did not tell her that the white silk shawl, threaded with gold silk and hung with slivers of mother of pearl, had in fact been bought with quite another thought in mind.

He'd left the country soon after the ball and taken with him the picture of that rather solemn girl. Many another girl and woman had crossed his path but every time it was those dark eyes and the curve of her lips and the delicate arch of the brows that came to him in his dreams. Not a day passed whilst he was away when he did not think about seeing her once again. Time and again, when out in a crowd, he'd catch sight of an elegant form tossing dark curls, a cheek half turned and a finely traced brow and he'd imagined for one throbbing, glorious moment that he was looking at Mary Ann again.

Before long he learnt the truth. His father kept him well informed of all that happened in the district, but if the old man had known of the pain which would surge through his son's whole frame he would not have written as he did.

"Such a journey, all the way to Gundaroo for a wedding. I ask you. Why do they want old fogeys like me! Good present I suppose, expect something from a de Rossi. No, that's wrong, young Mary Ann would never even think of it but that

Brownlow. Can't say I'm too happy about that match.

"She's a wealthy woman, isn't she? Pity she couldn't have waited a few years. Well they say 'marry in haste, repent at leisure'. Let's hope there's not too much repentance in that match. The great shame is all those de Guises passed on so soon. Well, not the old man, but William never lived to be what you call old, and there's two sons up in St John's graveyard, and as for young Charles, a terrible accident, that drowning. Not a soul to run that property. You can't blame Brownlow, I suppose…"

Now, face to face at last, a spasm clutched his heart. Amazed, he stared at himself in the mirror which hung across from the table. He'd never realised how profoundly he would be affected.

All those other times they had met came flooding back to him. Truly he had basked in her very rare smiles and once he had tried to convince himself that her coldness might perhaps mask a little more interest than she felt it suitable to display, and all the while he carried in his heart the memory of her at the ball. The serious face, the eyes which lit up with such pleasure as she took to the floor, her soft hands and hesitant smile, every single thought of her from that first night at the inn to the terrible events that befell the family, every recollection was graven on his heart. Many a night he'd tossed and turned but then finally came to the conclusion that he must ask for her hand. She was so young, though; something told him he must wait a while. Another year and the thought of marriage might be in the air. He did not want to spoil his chances by acting too quickly. The de Guises and the de Rossis! Both dogged with memories of past grandeur and the countries they came from. He had chuckled to himself as he thought of old Richard and his father harking back to that distant, noble ancestry.

How had he been so shortsighted and delayed so fatally?

Even worse, he had been the bringer of such terrible tidings.

Perhaps he should have spoken before he left for that journey back to Corsica? But no, she'd looked so coolly at him, he had needed time. At that moment he thought he had time. Years and years stretched ahead.

Now she laughed and pulled aside the wrapping paper.

"How beautiful. I've never seen such a lovely shawl in my whole life!"

Emotion deepened her voice as she touched the silk with fingers roughened with housework. "How utterly beautiful." She picked it up and laid it against her cheek. "Thank you so much, Mr de Rossi, thank you so much."

"Frank. Do remember, my name is Frank."

"How could I forget?" For a moment she looked at him with the eyes of that young girl, entering an inn for the first time, a whole life ahead of her. That was the recollection he had taken over the seas with him, that was the Mary Ann who still ruled paramount in his heart.

"May I ask you to come over to the kitchen?"

He followed her heavy form.

Soon tea was on the table and a plate of scones before him. Spellbound, she listened to his adventures in Corsica after the dangerous sea journey around the Cape of Good Hope and the tumultuous passage to the Mediterranean. They were still talking when the door flew open and George walked in.

"Rossi! Was down by the river. Thought I saw a horse outside."

"Frank… that is, Mr de Rossi… he's back from his travels."

"So I see." George regarded him coolly, and just as coolly extended his hand and nodded. "Good of you to drop by." He smiled at the other man but his eyes remained watchful and held no hint of welcome. "What you got there?" The shawl had caught his eye.

"Something from foreign parts, such a pretty shawl." Mary Ann hastily tucked it under her arm.

"I'm taking the road to Melbourne, thought I'd call in on my way past."

"Very good of you. I see my wife's made you some tea. Hope she hasn't held you up. Light's beginning to fade."

Frank de Rossi's smile had faded too and after a few desultory exchanges he made his departure.

"Not sure I care for that fellow," George remarked as he watched him ride away. "You never know with people like that."

"People like what?"

"It's said the old man was a spy in the British service. That's how they got *their* land."

"I know there were whispers, but gossips say anything."

"Whispers? 'Tis a well known fact! All kinds of folk making a fortune hereabouts. Never had to get his hands dirty doing a day's work in the paddocks, that one."

"He's always about on his father's property… least, that's what Papa used to say. Either over in Corsica seeing to their affairs, or spending most of his days on their property here, never in one place long."

"S'pose the Rossis and your pa'd have a lot in common really, coming from the old world with all them hoity, toity ideas." George picked up a scone and ate it quickly. "Got to go. Lost two yearlings down past the dam."

Mary Ann took the shawl and tucked it at the back of one of the drawers of the chest in their bedroom. Poor George, only too true, really. He'd had to work his way up, man and boy, and certainly there'd been no helping hand there. He had every reason to feel resentful. Some were born in a privileged position, some just weren't. Hopefully Frank de Rossi didn't call in again on his way back. Nice of him to bring that shawl but seeing him stirred up memories which had been good at that moment, but now were surprisingly painful. Grand-père's stories, the Ball of the Yew Trees, her father's easy guiding arm leading her into the de Rossi ballroom. Loss! Highlighted for a moment the past was painful. A whole flood of memories washed away her composure for one moment. She had to hold on to the well-worn wood of the chest and steady herself. So much had gone for ever from her life.

Quickly, returning to her senses, she hurried out on to the verandah. Someone was calling her name. Oh no, surely Frank de Rossi hadn't come back so soon, not after that chilly farewell.

"Mary Ann, it's your sister!" George called out.

He frowned as he followed Elizabeth up the steps. "They want you over at Woodbury." Turning on his heel he left the room.

"What's the matter? What's happened? Is it Grand-père?"

"Now don't take on. Not in your condition. Don't take on!" Her sister put a comforting arm around her shoulder. "Just not himself, he isn't. He's had a couple of turns and they leave him dizzy-like, and he keeps calling your name. Well, you know how the old ones are. We just thought it'd be a good thing if you came over for a few days; it'd settle him."

"Oh, Grand-père!"

"Like I said. Don't take on. If you could get a few things together, we'll be off and away. I'll help you with Cathy."

As the gig rattled out of the yard Mary Ann waved to her husband who stood on the verandah watching them go.

"I'm so lucky, Elizabeth, so very lucky. He's always looking for new ideas too. Why, the other week he brought home a dozen of those Spanish sheep from the sales. There's nothing George can't do. You've no idea how hard he works."

"He's a good enough worker," grudgingly admitted her sister. "By the way, who's that fellow over by the well? Where's Job?"

"He's out at the wash pen."

"That's hard work for an old'un. He's usually in the yard. So who's that man, then?"

"George needs more hands, he says. He's taken on a couple of the Irishwoman's boys … Mick and Seamus."

"The Irishwoman!"

"Yes, you know. The hut down near the river. She had that one daughter and all those boys."

"And a different father for each one, some say. That girl, not that she's a girl any longer…"

"What about her, then?"

Elizabeth paused. "Least said, soonest mended. Couldn't he find better than those fellows? Rough as goat's knees, the whole family, in fact. I don't know why Papa let them stay all those years, a real blot on the landscape they've been. That place of theirs no better than a humpy. Full of brats it always was and now look at them! My Henry says 'tis a wonder none of them's had their neck stretched. No better than tinkers."

"Well, they're working for us now."

"I can't believe George would take them on. He'd know the score alright." Elizabeth frowned as she flicked the whip and set them off at a spanking trot.

That night as they sat beside the old man neither of them could make sense of his mutterings. Whilst his fingers plucked at the sheets his mind wandered along paths which only he could see. He called for his dear wife time and again. Tears so steadfastly unshed over the years spilled down his cheeks as he moaned and muttered into his pillow.

"You stay with him." Elizabeth rubbed her eyes as the first light of dawn filtered through the curtains.

"He's been calling for you all the time."

Both of them stared at the withered lips. "Makes no sense to me," Mary Ann muttered as she squeezed the old man's hand. "They say old folks get these fancies at the end … but the sea? What does he mean?"

"I'll get the girl to bring you up some breakfast, just you stay there. That's what he'd want."

Mary Ann took the old man's hand in hers and settled herself more comfortably. "Grand-père," she whispered, "you were trying to say something about the sea … that's what Elizabeth said."

A faint smile wreathed those features and a sigh escaped but no words were spoken. Instead, he squeezed his granddaughter's hand and almost at once fell asleep.

He knows I'm here. The thought comforted Mary Ann as she kept up her vigil all that day and the following night.

Rarely had she sat and done nothing for so long. Elizabeth and her maid kept Cathy occupied and increasingly she found herself dozing off, grateful for the lack of any tasks, conscious always of the new life stirring in her womb..

She allowed herself to drift into a contented reverie and, as always, George dominated her thoughts.

How had she been so fortunate? Strong, energetic, blessed with the knowledge that would keep Bywong on the path to prosperity. Already the flocks of sheep had nearly doubled, only last week he'd brought back a fine Percheron mare from the Goulburn sales.

Feeling the child move in her womb she breathed a silent prayer that it would be a boy. Like all the men, George wanted a son.

She'd be quite happy with another daughter, but years stretched ahead. Soon there would be a family around them, just as there had always been under the roof of Bywong, chattering, clattering, filling every hour of the day with their plans and arguments and discussions. George would sit at the head of the table with the firstborn son on his right-hand side.

She could feel the muscles relaxing on her face, the radiance of a smile which came from her innermost depths. Love is enough, she repeated to herself.

The hours ticked by and in the silence of the sickroom her thoughts returned again and again to her life at Bywong.

How wonderfully well everything had turned out, how happy her father would be if he could see them now, drought well behind them and flocks increasing.

Yes, he'd be so pleased, except for Job.

Wouldn't it be better if George sometimes asked her opinion? When to take the flocks up to the mountains, when to drench the cattle, when to do some of those myriad tasks she'd once shared with her father? Reluctantly, she accepted that such matters should be left with the man of the house, but, try as she might, she could not fathom George's reason for getting rid of Job.

"You're not serious?" she'd asked when George told her of his decision.

"Not for a few months, of course. There's plenty for the lads to pick up from him yet. We need him around a bit longer."

"Job's always been at Bywong!"

Before she could walk he'd dandled her on his knee. Once marooned in the uppermost branches of the big elm he'd fetched the ladder and hauled her down. He'd tucked her under his arm and carried her into Grand-mère when she'd skinned her knees in the yard. He'd taken her mushrooming and explained how you could distinguish them from the poisonous toadstools. Together they'd sat on the river bank and watched the duckbills frolic. He'd shown her where the tadpoles wriggled down by the dam and explained each change in their bodies till they were tiny frogs hopping amongst the lily pads. Job had been one of the pallbearers at every family funeral, shouldering the weight with the Guise sons and grandsons. Every Guise who lay in the tomb at St John the Baptist had been carried there by Job.

"All the more reason; we need's the new blood."

"Surely he can stop on. Won't be many more years for him and…"

"Near his dotage, Mary Ann! Mark my words. You've got used to his ways but anyone taking a fresh look can see. He ain't the full dozen any more, always blathering on. Can't keep his mouth shut."

"And why should that worry us? He's been a faithful servant all these years, it's wrong to cast him aside like that. Where can he go at his age, anyhow? We've got no secrets to worry about."

"Wait on, wait on, you never give me half a chance. He's welcome at the smithy, old Briggs'll be glad to have him."

Sitting beside her grandfather Mary Ann made up her mind. When she got back to Bywong she'd talk to George again. Explain to him that the old man was part of their family and, even if too old for work, he should be allowed to stay in his hut behind the yard.

There were times, she admitted to herself, that George did not think the same way as she did…

Impatiently her grandfather shifted in the bed, his fingers picking at the sheets. Faintly, she could hear his words.

"Grand-père, what is it about the three seas? Do you mean crossing the sea? Is it when you came here you are remembering?"

Leaning closer Mary Ann stroked the old man's hand.

"No one listens... not that kind of sea," Grand-père muttered, his eyes opened wide and he stared at his granddaughter, seeing the dark eyes and olive skin of his own long-gone family.

Impatiently, he shook her head, too late now to try and explain what he meant. Like so many long-ago events any words would be inadequate.

He muttered and his grip tightened. "You're a good girl, Mary Ann, you're a real de Guise."

Guise was the last word to pass the old man's lips. He sank into a deep sleep and when Mary Ann tried to rouse him by patting his cheeks his head rolled upon the pillow and the great sigh he gave marked his last sound on earth.

Whether the unseasonably hot weather and the funeral or the sadness of her grandfather's death brought on the first contractions, Mary Ann did not at first realise that she had gone into labour, for she had another six weeks to go.

While bending over tying up some raspberry canes she felt the first discomfort. A slight niggling at the base of the spine which went unnoticed for a couple of hours until the discomfort increased and spread and could not be ignored. Six weeks still to go!

Picking up Cathy she hurried into the kitchen. A cold drink? A quiet sit-down at the table while the little girl nibbled at a biscuit.

Reluctantly, she counted out the seconds before the next pain - nearly twenty. Once that had subsided she began counting again. Twenty. The regularity frightened her. Were they real labour pains?

Scooping Cathy up in her arms she almost ran along the path to the house and out on to the verandah. Not a soul was in sight.

Neither of the Irishmen was to be seen and Job had taken one of the horses down to the smithy. The last time she'd seen George he'd been riding off in the direction of the river.

"George!" Clutching Cathy to her she cried out into the empty air. "George!" Who was there to hear?

The little girl whimpered and struggled. "Hush, hush, it's alright, love. Mama's got a pain… a nasty tummy ache. Come along, we'll find that dolly of yours."

Insidiously the centre of pain spread, sending out its piercing tendrils further and further until the biting cramps encircled the base of her womb.

Never had she imagined her own body could give such torment. Where was George? Gasping, she clutched at the rail and cried his name time and again.

Cathy's birth had been so easy. George had ridden off for Dr Morton, Elizabeth had come over from Woodbury and then rattled off in the trap to fetch the midwife. All had been so secure and safe. People were all around, telling her what to do, reassuring her.

What should she do now, all on her own?

Up and down the verandah she walked, first of all carrying Cathy, but finally having to put her down, just keeping an eye on the little girl as she played with her dolls.

Was it best to move around, or sit down quietly? Somewhere she had heard it said that movement helped in these situations. Up and down the verandah she paced as faster and faster came the pains. As each spasm gripped she clutched at the rail for relief until it subsided. Minute upon minute went by. The minutes became quarter-hours, half-hours and hours till she no longer thought of time, only of how much longer she could stay on her feet and endure the agony.

She longed to cry out but all the while she tried to keep her voice level and calm so as not to scare Cathy.

Faster and faster the cycle of pain and relief, then relief and pain took hold of her.

"Missus...Missus..." Job's voice cut through the pall of agony enveloping her. Just at that moment her waters broke and poured onto the verandah. She had heard nothing of his approach, not the creaking of the gate nor the clatter of the trap, and as she fell back in his arms she fainted for the first time in her life.

Drifting in and out of consciousness she became aware of her husband, of Dr Morton and voices in the background. Each time after surfacing to reality she experienced the shock and the dread of knowing that more was to come.

She was in a trap. Her body had snared her in pulsing, pitiless waves of unbelievable pain. Pain that came and then went, came and went; what would be the end?

Every muscle ached with effort that she did not understand. Her body had been taken over by some giant hand which grasped and squeezed till she felt she could bear it no longer then suddenly gave a few moments complete peace. Each time the pain ebbed she gulped for air as she steeled herself for the next onslaught of agony.

As she lay and tensed against the agony beating upon her womb Mary Ann struggled to think of anything which might help her escape from the reality now gripping her. The farm, George, the orchard, the new trap smartly painted standing in the yard, even the passing of Grand-père. Rejoicing and regret chased each other around the prison that suffering had made of her body.

Faintly, she became aware of flickering candlelight and the faces above her in the dark. Dr Morton and a bulky woman with capable hands that gently pushed the strands of hair from her forehead and sponged her face.

Also she became aware that the pains, though just as fearful, were weaker in their intensity, or had she become used to them? Through a gap in the curtains she could see the first hint of dawn. Surely she did not have yet another day ahead.

"Why is she so ill?" demanded George as he followed Dr Morton into the parlour. "Last time there was none of this fuss."

"Mr Brownlow, I must remind you that your wife is six weeks early with her confinement. Her body is not really ready for the delivery yet. She is in great pain…and I might add, in danger too."

"Danger!" George's eyes narrowed, he put up his hand to his face and the other man could only imagine that it was to hide his grief.

"I grant you she's a strong woman," Dr Morton fixed him with a serious gaze and gave a no-nonsense shake of the head, "but another few hours of this and I'll not say what could happen. I should have been called sooner. This is a premature and sudden labour. It must be brought to a swift conclusion."

"What do you mean?" muttered George.

"The risk becomes greater the longer we allow this to continue. I can induce matters by intervention. You'll have to give me some understanding in the matter…"

"They comes in their own good time. Same as folks die in their own good time." George shrugged and filled his pipe.

Dr Morton narrowed his eyes and regarded the other man

with distrust. This was a time to think of life, not to put life and death in the same sentence. Did the fellow care one jot what happened to his wife? He'd seen the Guise family through fevers and broken limbs and more deaths than he cared to recall. Was this fellow prepared to leave his wife unaided, possibly on her deathbed?

"She's becoming exhausted. I need to intervene."

Had the man even heard him? He'd walked over to the window and stood staring out. "Did you hear me? Something must be done." George Brownlow continued to stare out, beyond the yard, beyond the paddocks to where a thin whorl of smoke marked the chimney of the hut down near the river.

"If she's left... well... she could lose her life."

"And the baby?"

"On the other hand there's always a risk if I intervene, but I'd save the mother."

"What's the risk?"

"The baby could be stillborn."

George did not answer. He still stared out, eyes fixed on the smoke.

"Well, answer me, man! I need to know."

Before another word could be spoken a piercing cry came from the bedroom, another swiftly followed and as the surgeon sped down the passage the nurse could be heard muttering, "Lor' bless us, Lor' bless us and keep us, now you just keep trying... We'll be alright. Push down just once more. We'll try this, my dear. I know it's no time to tell you to relax but this'll help." From a bowl of warm water the nurse took a sopping wet sponge. "Warm water, my dear, nothing like warm water."

She held the sponge on high and let the warmth trickle down between Mary Ann's legs. She did not bother that the mattress was soaked. All that mattered was that the young woman felt the comfort and for a moment could relax.

A different cry filled the room. A higher-pitched wail that wavered and paused, then peaked to an indignant howl.

Dr Morton grinned as he held up the baby. "As I always said, ma'am, 'a good midwife's worth a brace of surgeons." Handing her some cloths, he stood back with relief.

CHAPTER 13

"For Christ's sake, make it stop that noise." George shifted violently beside her. "See to the child, can't you?"

Rubbing her sleepy eyes, Mary Ann sat up. Heavy-breasted, still half-asleep, she got out of bed and went over to the cradle.

"A man needs his sleep, don't he? Can't you make up a bed down the end there... down the passage?"

Holding the baby to her breast she swallowed hard. A bad dream? A nightmare? How could life have swung from such happiness to this misery? Of course there must be reasons. George was so disappointed; she had known he wanted a son but had no idea how much he had set his heart on it. In vain did she tell him of her own father... three sons and three daughters. There was always time, always time.

Of course he had been working so hard, he'd lost patience with them. Problems abounded on the property and he'd try to keep them from her. The strain must be getting to him. Round and round the excuses went but they gave no comfort. "Of course", "of course", "of course" preluded the unspoken litany of excuses each day.

When eyes which once had smiled now scowled, or at best glazed over with lack of interest, and when words only came in barked commands, then facts had to be faced and Mary Ann had never been one to shirk reality.

At what moment had the change crept in? Time and again she puzzled. Was it when Grand-père had sickened and she'd been away at the Lintotts, or had it come since then? No, she thought again, he'd been distant before that. The first inkling of anything amiss came when he'd spoken about Job and bringing the Irishmen onto the property.

Perhaps the time had come when she must accept their presence. Certainly the baby took up more and more of her energy and there were jobs around the home always waiting to be done. She knew she was no help outside on the property. Maybe she should accept their presence gracefully.

"I'd like some help with the pruning down in the orchard," she asked. "Can Mick or Seamus spend the morning there? I'll tell them what to do." Even the names sounded foreign and vaguely sinister, but asking for help might be a way of pleasing George.

"Can't spare 'em."

"But it's only a couple of hours."

He scowled and shook his head.

"They seem to spend a lot of time out in the paddocks. I never see them round the yard except milking time."

"Stop your nagging. They've more than enough on their hands."

So no more could be said. Mary Ann decided she'd ask them herself but something in the way they looked at her held her back. She did not feel easy with them. That certain arrogance of their walk, their loud but often incomprehensible chatter and their entire demeanour made her ill at ease. Whereas she had often stopped to chat with Job, she found herself looking the other way when they passed by.

The black hair and blue eyes, and the secretive exchanges between them in a tongue she could not always follow, added to that sense of alienation. They darted about their work and then disappeared for hours on end. What were they doing half the time? The yard remained a mess. Straw littered the far corners, a pile of old boxes tottered near the well and a broken spade leaned against a rusted implement so twisted, she couldn't even see what it had once been.

"What you going on about?" George snapped each time she asked for some help. "Can't spare the lads, they've got more'n enough to get through." George's replies became more staccato as the weeks passed by but it wasn't until he went on one of his ever more frequent trips to Goulburn and she found herself alone once again that she came up against the full reality of their smouldering resentment.

She'd driven the trap back from Gundaroo. Passing their neighbours' spick-and-span driveways alerted her to the slovenly appearance of their own entrance. "That rail needs hammering back, down near the gate," she told the brothers as they slouched out of the yard.

Seamus just looked at her and Mick shook his head. "Master's never said nothin'."

"But it's hanging loose. Anything can get in."

"We're to be down the dam, Missus. Clear them reeds out, he said, that's what we're doin'."

"The reeds! Clear the reeds. Why?"

"Them's his orders."

"You'll do no such thing," she exclaimed. The dam was the home to the moorhens and the ducks, frogs croaked from the dark green banks of reeds while dragonflies skimmed over the surface and even an occasional blue heron came fishing.

"Master said by the time he gets back from Goulburn he

wants them reeds done for. Them's his orders."

Mary Ann drew herself up and faced them. "And these are my orders: that fence needs fixing, no one touches the dam!" The rail was back in place by next morning but her growing unease did not diminish as she watched them slinking about the yard.

She had to ask more times than she cared to remember for water to be brought up from the well and the yard to be swept. True, the milk awaited her in the dairy and the bucket of pig's swill was taken down to the sty, but the reek of beer caught her nostrils when she walked past the lean-to behind the cowshed and she guessed they'd been sampling the brew.

Was she a nag? She kept remembering George's words. Her life had shifted so radically, she had to admit to herself, that with the swift changes taking place she felt quite powerless. For all these years she'd been mistress of her own fate and now there were these two young demanding lives dependent on her; and at the same time countless tasks always to hand. Tending to the dairy, kitchen, vegetable garden and orchard filled every minute of her day.

Daily existence had always been arduous but there were opportunities to ride out and just occasionally people called in. Now solitude had become her lot.

No longer did she feel involved with her own property, never once was her advice sought. She could not remember the last time she and George laughed together. These days her husband was short-tempered and cold and, what was worse, she did not seem able to talk to him any more.

"George away again?" This was a red-letter day for Elizabeth had ridden over from Woodbury and brought some new clothes for the baby.

"Yes, the sales at Goulburn."

"Must be spending a mint…" her sister shook her head.

"He says it takes time to build up good breeding stock. The drought's only a while ago, after all."

"Well, you've got the little girls now, anyhow, at least not quite on your own."

"I realise how lonely it must have been for Grand-père … with Papa and me always out. Even so we'd be back in the evenings." Mary Ann confided in Elizabeth.

"And George isn't home evenings?" Her sister sniffed. "'Tis always the same when the babies come - they takes up all your time but doesn't make for that much company."

"Oh, he's very good."

"But the men, they stop by with their friends, don't they? There's things that need to be seen to…and all those sales too? Amazing all the things that have to be seen to once the little ones arrive!"

"It's not just that… it's… well, sometimes I feel like an intruder on my own property!"

"What do you mean, Mary Ann?"

"Those men, those Irish, have got a kind of resentful look about them, as if I'm in the way just being here. The other day I really had to stand my ground to get them to do as I asked. I told George, they are too full of themselves by far. He didn't like it, but he had to agree in the end."

Elizabeth opened her mouth to say something but then thought better of it. "Tell you what, my dear, why not leave me to listen for the little ones. Take yourself out for an hour or so."

"I'm tired, that's half the trouble. Just to walk down to the dam I find pretty exhausting."

"Then take my Merrylegs and go for a ride. I'll be bound you've not been in the saddle for weeks."

"More likely, months! Last time was when I found I was expecting Lizzie."

"Well, there you are. You go off now. You see, you'll feel a new woman."

"And a pretty achey one, not being used to it nowadays."

"Never mind. Be off, before young Cathy wakes up and starts making a fuss. If you're not here it won't matter but if she sees you go off without her there'll be the devil to pay."

Mary Ann had to admit her sister had been right. Ten minutes away from the house, the world looked a different place. Wind blowing through her hair and the call of the plovers in her ears she soon passed the dam and reached the bank of the river.

The cool wind blowing across the water refreshed her.

Not a soul in sight. Not a movement on the opposite bank. The Irishwoman's cottage stood still and silent. Even though smoke spiralled out of the chimney the dwelling appeared deserted.

As if to prove her very thoughts wrong the door of the hut opened and a figure appeared on the step. Mary Ann shaded her eyes. The Irishwoman herself stood there. *I don't even know her name,* Mary Ann admitted to herself. *My only neighbour, and they've been there forever, yet I don't even know her name.*

And why should you? She could hear her grandfather's derisive comment. No better than tinkers!

On impulse Mary Ann waved to the woman.

Hair awry, hands upon her wide spreading hips, feet splayed out, the woman stared back for a few moments then swung round on her heels and disappeared once more indoors.

Mary Ann winced, suddenly feeling exposed and uncomfortable. Even a nod of the head would have been something.

She turned the horse's head away from the river and set off at a swift trot and then a canter over the hill towards the furthest paddock.

Reaching a sloping eminence Mary Ann blinked in the sunlight. Beyond the rocky summit the land dropped away and the shepherd's hut nestled amongst the tumbled boulders at the bottom of the hill. Since the drought the hut had not been occupied, no flocks had grazed upon these paddocks and only a few wandering goats browsed amongst the scattered boulders and occasional clumps of bush.

Leaning back in the saddle she half closed her eyes. Many years ago she and Grand-père had ridden to just this very place. Several times they'd sat on the on those rocks and she'd listened to the old man telling his stories. Nothing had changed, all remained peaceful and tranquil. Guise lands. Just the boundless acres and the hut with the air shimmering above the bark roof.

Shimmering! She opened her eyes wide and looked closer. The air above the bark roof certainly quivered in the heat but the movement came from a spiral of smoke rising and spreading from the chimney and slowly dispersing into the atmosphere.

Smoke? That hut hadn't been occupied in several years or more. Briefly after the drought George had restocked but there had been an outbreak of scouring in the flock and George told her he had decided to move them on to higher ground. Who could be living in this remote place?

Approaching more closely she caught sight of an orderly array of implements outside the door. Two buckets, a large jar, a shepherd's crook and a rake were ranged neatly against the wall. Two dogs, lying in the shade of makeshift cover eyed her suspiciously and as she came closer one began to bark.

"Was you wantin' summat, Missus?" A rangy leather-faced man emerged, shirt hanging down and a straw broom in his hand.

At a loss for a moment she paused and then dismounted.

"Don't get many visitors hereabouts, Miss. You come from the property over the hill? Wherever you come from, would you like to sit down for a moment and I'll fetch you some water?"

"I'll not trouble you but…"

"No trouble, Missus. Plenty of water in the well," he laughed as though attempting to lighten the situation, for Mary Ann could not take her eyes from him. She stared at him. Who was this man? He appeared to be perfectly at home in their hut. What was he doing here? George must have hired this new shepherd and he'd completely forgotten to mention him to her.

"I didn't realise you had a well here nowadays. We always brought water over to this hut from the stream. Has Mr Brownlow had a well dug for you?"

The man looked puzzled. "Not Mr Brownlow, Missus, 'tis Mr Palmer I works for."

"Mr Palmer?"

"Mr Palmer brought his flock back from the mountains last month and this is where we'll stop till they drops their lambs. Mr Palmer said as how he'd had a good well dug and looks like it'll never run dry. A blessing 'tis, not a drop of rain in weeks, animals is parched half the time."

Mary Ann remained silent. How could the Palmers own these pastures? As far as the eye could see the land had belonged to her father.

Sipping the water she listened to the man as he rattled on. "You come a fair step, Missus. If you don't mind me saying, you'd best be back before them shadows start lengthening."

Every inch of the way on the journey home increased her puzzlement. How could Palmer own that land? These acres had been left to her in her father's will. Question after question flew through her mind adding to the fear that she had stumbled on something she would rather not know about.

She said nothing to Elizabeth about the matter. There must be an explanation and she'd wait till George came home.

By the time he returned the evening had set in. With Cathy tucked up and the baby asleep she sat in the kitchen watching him eat his meal. Absorbed in his food, remote at the far end of the table, Mary Ann found herself regarding him for the first time as an onlooker instead of a wife. His chin jutted aggressively, a frown creased his brow and hadn't she noticed before how close together his eyes were set? Love plays subtle tricks with memory. That first sight of him, smiling down at her, every feature graven in her mind as she felt the warmth of his embrace had never wavered. Now George could have been a different person entirely.

"I went for a gallop this afternoon," she ventured.

"How so?" Pulling his bread apart he sopped up the last drops of gravy.

"Elizabeth came over, suggested I take her Merrylegs out… fine ride."

"You've not been in the saddle for months."

"And don't I know it. Aching in every joint."

"Thought you'd given all that away. Don't have no call to go riding out these days, do you?"

"I went up past the long paddock. Have you leased that land, George?"

He pushed his plate away. "No, never lease me land."

"The shepherd there says he works for Mr Palmer."

"That'd be right."

"Well, how did it become Mr Palmer's land all of a sudden?"

George looked up and held out his hands, palms upward. "Come my love, come and sit over here. 'Tis a pity you come to hear about it like this but I'll explain."

Silently she sat beside him.

"I never want to worry you with business matters, you know that. We've had more'n enough expense lately, and wives don't need to concern themselves about such things. Think of your grandmother, she was kept busy from dawn 'til dusk. She never fretted over what was happenin' on the property, she left that to your grandfather."

"Father never sold any land. He would never agree, whoever asked."

"Not wishing to speak ill of the dead, your father had let the place go a bit, hadn't he? I've been stocking up again, and then there's the Percheron and them black saddlebacks and where'd you think the money come from for the new trap?"

Of course. How could she be so slow-witted. There'd been so many changes in the running of Bywong during the last months. The two Irishmen, those Spanish sheep and all the matters he'd mentioned. How could she be so blind? Remorse swept through her. Of course George had been trying to spare her any worry. She took his hand and held it in hers. "But couldn't you speak to me about it? Couldn't you trust me? I'd have understood."

"You've got more'n enough on your plate," he smiled at her. She realised he'd not smiled in ages. "I didn't want to worry you, had a hard time with little Lizzie and you still feeding her. It's a strain on you, I know that. Leave the running of the place to me."

"But you could have told me." She grasped his hands.

"Not easy," he muttered as he looked away.

"George!" She moved closer and took his other hand. "George, everything's going to be alright. I know the stock's been a bit run down but there's good years and bad years. Think of all those months and months of drought and we're pulling out of that now."

"Takes time." He took his hands away and rose, walked over to the window and stared out across to the dam and the distant river.

"Time, yes, but if we don't have the land, we don't have anything. Of course you did the right thing but we'd best not let any more go." She went across to the dresser and picked up her sewing, drawing the candle closer. Better not pursue the subject any more. The point had been made, leave it at that.

Silence filled the room. Silence should be emptiness, a gap, a nothing. But sometimes silence propagates more silence until it spreads and fills every corner and becomes a tangible barrier between two people. Words that cannot be said, thoughts which must not be expressed, combine to make a wall of silence.

Determined that her last words should not sound like a criticism Mary Ann took the time-honoured path of changing the subject. Shying away from the awkward to the familiar ground of everyday life she pushed silence aside.

"River's filling up. Time was not so long ago when anyone could wade across to that hut…"

"Hut?"

"You know. Where the Irishwoman lives."

"They got the punt."

"Seems pretty quiet over there."

"Lad's live down the village."

"Must be lonely for their mother nowadays. Well, I suppose she's still got her daughter at home."

Silence seeped back.

"Come to think of it, I've not seen her about lately."

"Who?"

"The Irishwoman's daughter. Used to see her in the village sometimes. I wonder what's happened to her? Remember she came looking for work last year? Maybe she's in service somewhere."

"Blessed if I know," George grunted as he picked up the *Herald* and left the room.

Two weeks later the answer came to Mary Ann's question when she called in at the general store.

The shop buzzed with the chatter of women.

" 'Ain't she a little love." Lizzie stared wide-eyed from the security of her shawl as customer after customer paused to pass the time of day with Mary Ann and give the baby a gentle pat. "And how's your big sister? You helping your ma these days, young Cathy. Always got to help yer ma."

Compounded of a whiff of this and a sniff of that, the atmosphere in the shop was heavy and yet subtly satisfying. Liquorice, ginger, soap, the sharp clean scent of paper from a pile advertising a sale and the faintly chemical odour from some cotton sheets. The sunshine slanted down upon the busy women as they touched and felt and added up the pennies and the shillings. Chatter filled the air while neighbours caught up with the news and bandied words.

Mary Ann was watching her sugar being weighed out when the door flew open. Immediately the hubbub ceased as every head turned.

Amongst the sober clothes of wives and mothers, Brigid O'Rourke's green and yellow flounced skirt and tasselled shawl glowed artfully. Not too showy, yet not to be passed over, everything about her spoke of style. Long black curls framing her delicately boned face, highlighting the sparkle in her eyes and certainly drawing attention from the faint lines around them. So fine was the arch of her eyebrows and the Cupid's bow of her lips that they might have been drawn by an artist. From the tilt of her nose to the determined set of her chin she exuded health and vigour.

"Them ribbons come in yet?" she demanded across the counter.

Gone was the uncertain woman who'd come calling at Mary Ann's door. Gone and never to return was that Brigid who had no place in the world. The new Brigid had arrived. Her eyes gleamed as she caught sight of Mary Ann and her red lips curved in a faint smile showing evenly-spaced perfect teeth which, for some unknown reason, reminded Mary Ann of a ferret. She did not speak a greeting, instead she nodded with the casual acknowledgement of equals.

There are nods… and there are nods. This nod was not a polite acknowledgement of another's presence nor a familiar greeting between neighbours. This nod was a dismissive gesture of one who scarcely has the time and certainly not the inclination to further any aquaintance.

"I said, have you got them ribbons in yet?"

The storekeeper's hand faltered, he spilled some sugar on the counter, then fumbled for a piece of paper amongst a pile of receipts and notes. "Lookin' for the invoice." Slip after slip went through his fingers, no one moved.

"Ain't got all day, you know." She glanced around the shop.

Conversation ceased. Expectancy quivered in the air, triggered by furtive glances between customers. The muttered exchanges of woman to woman took the place of the easy banter and an uneasy shifting of feet marked the distinct turning around of several women, continuing their conversations with their backs to the newcomer.

"If they ain't in, don't trouble yerself," Brigid called across. "Won't waste me time stoppin' by."

"Sorry, Miss, sorry. When's the latest… I'll send one of the boys up."

"Friday. Early, mind you. Be on me way to Bungendore Friday night."

"That'll be the races, eh?"

Not bothering to answer Brigid spun round and slammed the door shut.

Eyes that had been rivetted upon the girl now wavered, some eyebrows were raised, some lips mimed mild disgust, those that had turned their glances away now faced each other again and within seconds those same glances fell on Mary Ann.

And why are they staring at me? Every pair of eyes focused on her, Mary Ann shifted uncomfortably and turned away. Why were they so curious? Some watched covertly with their hands busy feeling or lifting or weighing up the value of a purchase, some steadfastly observed her.

She looked down at her cotton dress and pulled the crocheted shawl closer round herself and the baby. Surreptitiously she rubbed one dusty boot against the other and smoothed the wrinkles in her bodice. A wave of regret swept over her. Once her eyes had sparkled like that, once she'd had no more thought in the world than some new ribbons for her bonnet. Brigid O'Rourke didn't look a day older than herself and yet there must be at least five years between them, maybe more.

Why were they still staring? Certainly they looked their fill! How they had all stared at Brigid, a pretty woman always sets the old chooks clucking, she told herself. Well, perhaps they'd seen too that marriage and motherhood made a big difference. Perhaps they would enjoy a gossip at her expense. She turned and asked for another pound of sugar.

By the time the trap bowled into the yard she'd thrown off the regrets. They had trotted along leaving a cloud of dust, while Job chattered unceasingly. Sitting beside him, with the reins in his hands, the years rolled back. Laughing at his same old jokes, listening to his pungent comments about the carelessness of the younger generation and the selfishness of the older one, nothing had changed, had it? This was her life, a fine farm, a handsome husband, beautiful daughters. How could she feel inferior to an older woman who most likely owned nothing but the clothes she stood up in?

I've everything to be grateful for, she told herself as she helped Job unload the bags and boxes. The same happy mood lingered when George came in for his supper.

Cheerfully he had pulled up a bucket from the well and whistled to himself as he came in and sat down at the table. Lately he'd not grumbled about much at all, the baby no longer woke him. Well, she'd taken his hint and moved out on those nights when Lizzie was restless. A man needs his sleep, after all.

She watched his sunburnt hands cutting the bread with a yearning that was becoming more and more frequent. She hungered for his touch and the pleasure of his closeness, but since Lizzie had come he turned away from her on many a night.

"Can you get one of the lads to kill one of the cockerels for me? We'll have it roasted tomorrow. What do you think?"

"Hmm … hot weather comin'."

"Well, that doesn't matter."

"Won't be here for a couple of days. You won't eat up cold chicken all on your own, it'll go off, this weather."

Disappointment flitted across her face as George laid down his knife.

"You're going away again? You were in Goulburn not two weeks gone."

"Not going to Goulburn. 'Tis Bungendore, me and the lads might pick up some yearlings…"

CHAPTER 14

Smoke! The merest inkling but enough to warn Mary Ann.
"Did you put out that bonfire like I said, Job?"

"Two buckets of water I used, Missus, two buckets like what you said."

Even so Mary Ann hurried down past the homestead to the orchard. Apples and plums glowed upon the trees and in the far corner were the blackened remains of diseased crab-apple branches. She picked up the few remaining twigs. They needed to be completely destroyed so as not to spread the mould.

Certainly the fire had been put out, yet the bite of wood smoke tainted the air. She shrugged, that smoke must have drifted along on the breeze from some other property.

Back in the kitchen she moved quietly, snapping the crab-apple twigs and filling up the kindling box. She tucked it back underneath the black belly of the stove where it would remain perpetually dry – for damp kindling was a disaster if the fire ever went out. She swept up the few ashes into a heap. Soon the fire glowed and the gruel began to bubble. Lizzie was on to her first solids now; soon it would be time for her feed. Then the neck of mutton in the meatsafe must be stewed up, there'd be the pan she'd left soaking from last night's meal to scour, the hens to feed, scraps to go out for the swill and she'd have to check on the dairy - couldn't trust Job to have cleaned out the pans properly. One speck of sour milk and the cream would be ruined.

Hearing Lizzie's cries, she went in and pulled aside the curtains. She stripped off the wet binder, wiped her dry and swiftly tied on a fresh one. Then holding her tiny daughter to her breast as she walked back to the kitchen she was soon spooning out the gruel to let it cool. She'd been careful not to lose her milk; wasn't it said if you were feeding a baby you couldn't fall for another, and at the moment Mary Ann did not want a third child. In a short while of course it would be fine, but she guessed George would not be too pleased. Let him get used to the second baby, then there'd be time for others.

"Missus! Missus!"

Draping a shawl around herself she went to the door.

"See there!"

Job pointed across the paddocks to the line of hills rising from the plain.

The merest hint of smoke smudged a faint trail amongst the hollows at the base of the ridge but even as they watched, it swirled into a more distinct form and spiralled up into the sky.

" 'Tis the smoke you caught."

"A long way off."

The whites of Job's eyes showed up against his leathery face as he stared into the distance. "Don' like it, Missus. There ain't nothin' 'twixt that there fire and back o' Murrays. Nothin'."

"It looks closer than it is. That fire's miles and miles away. There's a lot of space between us. Change of wind, change of weather. Too far off to worry about."

With the confidence of youth she dismissed the possibility

of any trouble and, reassured, Mary Ann returned indoors to finish feeding Lizzie.

Two days more on her own. George and the men would be back on Wednesday. A smile spread across her features; another two days and then he'd be home. Forty-eight hours and she could be holding him in her arms again. Perhaps absence would have made the heart grow fonder?

The shadows were beginning to lengthen on the beaten earth of the yard by the time Mary Ann took an afternoon stroll down to the dam. Ducks dabbled amongst the reeds and dragonflies hovered over the water.

The column of smoke was barely visible. By the time she'd circled the dam and walked down towards the next paddock she had reassured herself once again and turned back towards the homestead.

Home. No doubt about it, home is where the heart is. From the front verandah to the covered walkway joining the kitchen to the back door, security enfolded her.

Time to get some mending done and maybe even a few moments to pluck that chicken she'd had killed for the table.

Job puffed away at his clay pipe, sitting on the bench outside his hut. As she went indoors he called out, "Wind's a-freshen', Missus, caught a sniff of that there smoke again."

"Miles away, miles away." Job certainly lived up to his name. He saw nothing but disaster all around.

But yes, the wind had freshened. What had been an almost airless morning had gusted into a windy afternoon. A baking breeze snatched at the saplings not long planted around the fence, the upper branches of the big elm by the gate twisted and its leaves shook as dust flew in all directions.

It wasn't till dusk when she put the children to bed and walked out to make sure of the henhouse door that any real danger became apparent. Shadows had gathered around the homestead, candlelight glowed from the kitchen, and the chimes of the grandfather clock heralded the fast approaching night.

Had Job made sure that the henhouse was locked as well as latched? A clever dingo or a persistent fox could nudge open any carelessly closed door. Was the barn securely padlocked?

She walked out of the yard into the home paddock. Not a sound came from Job's hut. The old man must be dog-tired, or perhaps he had some secret supply of grog, what did it matter? The smell of burning had become stronger. Where there had been a wavering hint of smoke a line of fire now glimmered. No longer was the question: 'How far away?' Suddenly she found herself asking: 'How close?'

Mary Ann leant against a fencepost and stared at the fiery line. With that common refusal to accept that the worst can happen she tried to reassure herself. Surely it wasn't coming in their direction? But the wind grazed her cheeks, full in the face she could feel its touch.

Denial after denial flitted through her mind. Night time often brought about a change of wind direction, perhaps even a brief shower might fall. Something would surely come between the farm and the fire. By the time she dragged herself indoors the myriad pinpoints of the Milky Way glimmered overhead - and the distant flames gleamed brighter.

Unwilling to get undressed and go to bed she dozed the hours away on the settle in the parlour, every few hours going to the door and peering out. Now the smell of burning came on the gusting wind.

Before first light she hurried down to the best vantage point, the knoll by the dam. The fire had leapt many miles during the hours of darkness. Now it menaced her neighbour's land. The Palmers scarcely ever came down from the city, those acres had been bought with an eye to the future. The dry waist–high grass would be devoured in a trice.

Previously the fire had seemed quite separate from them. A great conflagration way across the foothills, searing a path through distant plains. Now the vast firefront devoured paddocks, fences, trees and the clumps of bush which had always made up their world around Bywong. Flaring up into the sky, spreading ever more greedily, the monster gulped and glowed and ravaged all that stood in its path.

During that restless night fear had driven sleep from her mind. Crossing and uncrossing her legs she had fidgeted the night away. Twisting and turning, the hours had chimed by. Terrible possibilities had surfaced. In the small hours all the worries of the world had descended; she faced each one. Destroyed stock. Ruined pasture. Dairy, sheds, sties and home razed to the ground.

They must be saved. The work of three generations of her family was not to be extinguished in a couple of hours.

Mary Ann summed up all the possibilities and knew how she could save the farm.

Just as she'd watched her father poring over the old ledger, just so she summed up the credits and debits of the situation.

An unrelenting west wind. A dam half empty. A well creaking up meagre amounts by the mere bucketful. A husband many miles away, one old man, two little children, the sheep, the cows, the pig, the horses, the carts and the plough. There was the dairy, the cowshed, the stalls and the barn. All wood, wood, wood – fodder for that devouring monster. These made up a whole host of debits.

The credits? The wind could change, clouds could bring rain. There was always the last resort of flight for Job and her little family.

But in her mind's eye only too clearly she saw the blackened trunks of the trees, the leafless skeletons of a thousand branches. Henhouse, verandahs and huts crackling into flame would spit their sparks into the air until posts, rails, hay bales, barrels and boxes raged and shrivelled and sank to piles of ash. Worse, far worse, all around would lie the tortured carcasses of the animals.

Unthinkable. This must not happen.

Surely there was more to the credit side of life.

Hope. Hope burned bright in Mary Ann's mind. Hope burned more brightly than the approaching flames.

Aren't all our lives lived in hope? Mary Ann asked herself. Hope of a better understanding of others, hope of prosperity, hope of good health and happiness? And hope had always been so good for her... a fine husband, her own farm, for hadn't her father bequeathed her a life of security? All that her father had accomplished and Grand-père Guise before him, could not, must not, be relinquished to the flames.

Walk away from all that? The house, the orchard, the majestic grandfather clock, her three brothers' portraits painted by a travelling artist – so very precious now – the nodding rows of peas and beans in the vegetable garden, the roses, Grand-mère's precious roses...

And what of the Percheron mare, the shorthorns and the Dorsets? Then there were the Spanish sheep. No, nothing must be allowed to menace this inheritance, this home, this haven. Out of the ravelled turmoil of those small hours hope had come, sheer determination spawned by logic pointed the way.

Mary Ann knew she had only one chance.

One loophole remained - time. Time to prepare for the onslaught.

Standing on the knoll she knew what she had to do. Nearby half a dozen bullocks regarded her with the curiosity of their kind, their soft brown eyes wide and innocent. She could not see them terrified and burned. Gathering up her skirts she hurried into the yard.

"Missus! Missus!" Job called to her from the doorway of the cowshed. "'Tis the wind, gettin' worse by the minute. Right from the west, blowin' fit for a gale. I'll get the mare out. Cart's near the gate. We'd best be gone."

"Gone! Have you lost your senses, man?"

"Well, I ain't stayin' not to catch this lot. Give it an hour or so and it'll be 'pon us. I'll get her in the shafts, we'll take what you want. The little 'uns'll be safe. We'll be gone in no time."

"Gone! What about the house? What about the animals? What about the orchard?"

He looked at her as though she'd lost her senses.

"Missus, this ain't goin' to go away. This 'ere fire's goin' to take us with it if we stays."

"We're staying."

"'Twill be the death of us." As though to underline his words a few ashes fell upon his outstretched hands. "I'll get that there cart and…"

"And I forbid you. We stay here. We don't leave the farm." She looked back at the house. How small and defenceless it appeared against the approaching conflagration. The cowshed and barn were only a stone's throw away from the house with the well close by. For a moment it looked no more substantial than the toy farmyard that Cathy played with.

'Bywong,' she muttered to herself. 'Bywong,' she repeated as though the ancient name of the property could conjure up the strength and wisdom to ward off this threat. The old Canberri would have understood, the Ngunawal would have known how to save themselves. This had been her home as a child, she knew every inch of the ground – the flames would never reach it.

So much happiness, so much hard work, so much endeavour and so many smiles and laughs and tears had gone into this world of hers. It would not be relinquished without a fight.

She knew how she was going to save it.

"Missus!" he implored.

"Like I said, we stay." And she threw back her head and stared at the distant flames with all the arrogance of her forefathers.

A de Guise never turned his back on the enemy.

'Missus…"

"Hurry now." Not even listening to him she turned and ran back towards the house and, as if sensing her intent, the bullocks lumbered along behind the fence.

"Make sure that gate's tight shut. Make sure that trough's full. Let the dogs off their chains. Get them out in the paddock. Round up those sheep. Get the cows out of the shed into the paddock… forget about the milking. Prop the gate of the chicken run open, birds always find safety. I'll see to the girls, I'll not be long."

He started to mutter something. To protest once again about the futility of trying to fend off a fire. She spun round and briefly stared him down.

Unwillingly he checked the gate leading out onto the track. Wearily he turned the handle on the well. Bringing up bucket after bucket, carrying them over and tipping them over the fence into the trough.

Letting the dogs off their chains, he opened the gate into the paddock. No sooner had he given the long, low whistle they understood so well than they jostled the sheep together and the whole flock moved towards the trough.

That took time, sheep being giddy things at the best of times and not at their happiest when there's disaster in the air. For animals know. They know when danger threatens and when flight is their only escape. Round and round the dogs went, worrying the flock until they shifted faster, one thick mass of animals with the bullocks snorting amongst them.

A strange exhilaration gripped Mary Ann. Both children were asleep but she had left a pile of biscuits at the end of Cathy's cot - Cathy loved her biscuits. If she woke they'd keep her happy for a while.

Next door's property had not been grazed in a twelve months, a sea of thick parched grass adjoined her paddocks. Once into that swaying, desiccated mass the fire would sweep across in no time at all. Now a pall of smoke cut off any view of the hills. A persistent greedy glimmer marked the edge of the approaching fire. From left to right the firefront stretched away on all sides.

"Missus, there's still time," Job was hard put to it not to run but something in his mistress's manner, something in the certainty in her voice kept him at her side. Now the sheep were jostling each other near the trough and the bullocks barging in amongst them.

"We'll not shift."

"There's still time," he muttered again.

She stood and stared in the direction of the fire. A dense, brown pall hid the sky. The slope of the ground obscured the flames.

"Keep those beasts a-moving, keep them all moving."

He stared at her. He'd no idea what she meant.

"Get them going. Get the whole mob moving out there round the fence. Keep them moving. Don't stop for one minute."

Job had known Mary Ann, as he often said, since she was knee-high to a grasshopper. He'd served her grandfather, her father and now he was serving her husband but he'd never seen her like this. But then he'd never before seen someone fighting for their life and their future.

"For God's sake, man. Come, come on, every minute counts."

Something in her voice brooked no argument. She snatched up a switch and followed the mass of animals. Job followed behind her with the dogs at his heels. Round outside the fenceline and up past the orchard she urged on the bewildered beasts. Then down near the backyard, round the back of the barn, the dairy and the cowshed, back along the paddock and then up again to the orchard, backyard and round again.

The thundering hooves of cattle and sheep cut into the earth. Clouds of dust flew in the air. Choking, blinding dust engulfed them. In their terrified confusion the animals buffeted and lunged, hurtling on, pursued by the dogs, yelled at by Job and all the time Mary Ann laying around herself with the switch, keeping the mob on the move.

After the third circling of the farm and its yard he was quite convinced she'd lost her reason.

With sweat streaming down his face after the fourth time around, he plucked up courage to speak again. He even opened his mouth but she was shouting, yelling and pointing at the dirt scuffed up by the stampeding hooves. "This is what we have to do. This'll do it."

"Roundin' em up, Missus?" Still he did not understand. What were they being rounded up for? Where could they go?

"Fire'll never jump the dirt." Mary Ann's voice was hoarse and cracked with the heat and the effort of keeping away from the blundering beasts.

"The beasts'll perish in the heat. Missus, 'tis cruel hot."

" 't'will be hotter'n hell when the fire gets here. But it's not going to get here, is it?"

Where was she taking them? "Missus? Missus, there's still time."

"Save your breath. The flames'll never jump this."

And then he realised.

A dusty dry band of twenty feet or more surrounded the fence. The hundreds of hooves had kicked up a dust storm that had settled and spread beyond the fence.

The firebreak would save them, could save them, might save them…

"'T'won't be enough Missus. Not near enough. The flames'll jump…"

"Do as I say." And to make sure the old man understood she flicked the switch in his direction.

Circling the farm, round and round they went. Ten minutes passed, twenty minutes. She had no way of judging the time. She just knew that the sun did not shine; instead, it glowed - a red, angry disc in a grey-brown sky. A false dusk bathed the landscape. An immense pall of smoke preceded the fire, rising higher and ever higher into the heavens. All the while the animals kept moving. The stampede had slowed, some plodded, some trotted, the sheep kept together to avoid the snapping dogs and the bullocks just followed, hides blanketed with dust, the whites of their eyes flashing through the cloud of dust. Soon the animals were brown as the broken earth and many limped pitifully. Every so often she chased some aside to the trough for water for a few moments, then laid about them till they went on their way again.

Her leg muscles cramped with exhaustion, she tripped and nearly fell. "Here, keep going. I'm going to see Cathy's alright." Once inside the house she closed every window, shut every door and took a last look at the sleeping children before creeping out again and closing the door. Would the closed-up house be their salvation or their tomb?

When she returned she left him with the animals and

stumbled down to the knoll.

Though prepared for the worst, hot and sweating from her exertions, she shuddered as she stared at the fearsome enemy at her boundary.

In spite of the sweltering day a chill went through her. At least no one was there to see the shaking of her hands. Previously the fire had been a distant, though swift approaching, menace. Suddenly the peril was thundering on the doorstep.

On the outer edges of the firefront several stands of gums flared. Even as she watched, one particularly tall gum exploded, sending balls of fire in all directions. Immediately new fires shot up.

Raging across the grassy plain the flames devoured the pasture. Smoke puffed in all directions. The draught of the fire sent it whirling through the air. Fire makes its own wind. First of all a few gusts, rising to a steady blow, then a hurricane of flame beating down all that lies before it.

A small flock of corellas dived and disappeared towards open, clear country. Several kangaroos leapt across the paddock in the same direction. The flames had swallowed the distant plain, eaten up the trees. Nothing was going to stop it marching on to claim its next victim, Bywong itself.

Mary Ann ran back up the slope to the yard. Job heaved a sigh of relief, the dratted woman would agree to them leaving now, alright. She'd seen with her own eyes. She'd be begging him to hurry. He'd get that mare harnessed in two shakes.

So he could only groan when she shouted at him. "Keep on, keep on, keep those beasts moving."

Several sheep staggered helplessly. "Over here, bring them over. Over to the trough." Two sank to the ground with bleeding hooves.

Frantic minutes passed. Job's face bled from a cut when he'd blundered into the fence. Thick dust thrown up by the mob coated his entire body. His shoulders ached from the buffeting of animals. Mary Ann's hair had come loose, her bodice was soaked with sweat and one boot had lost its sole. She did not pause for a moment.

"Stop! Get them over to the trough again." This time three of the sheep sank down and nothing would get them up again. Another had lost a hoof, the flesh was bare and bloody.

"Nearly done for, they is." He stared at the exhausted animals.

Briefly she glanced at the path the mob had cut outside the yard, the belt of beaten earth outside the fence. She looked again at the sheep; they were failing fast and several of the bullocks had disappeared from the mob.

Time to get the horses out. In a trice she rushed over to the barn where the Percheron and the mare shifted restlessly in their stalls.

"Here…take her." Shoving the mare's rope into Job's hands she went back to bring out the enormous shire horse. Sixteen hands high, its huge shoulders towered over her. "Giddy-up, Giddy-up, Perchy," and soon his hooves were slicing into the soil. The iron of his huge shoes and the weight of his great body threw dirt in the air as she led him out into the press of jostling animals.

Up till then it had been sight and smell which had been bearing down upon them but now came the sound of the fire. At first a muted disturbance hit the air, then a sudden roar came up the hill as it pounced and devoured the dried-out reeds above the waterline of the dam.

She would not allow herself to look. Sometimes fear can only be faced with shut eyes - but no one can shut their ears. The terror that cannot be seen can still be heard.

Flames leapt across the dam, sizzling the reeds, burrowing

into the tussocky grass and consuming the stand of she-oaks. Soon they'd reach the belt of beaten earth.

So intent had she been upon the grass that she had not looked further. Now she could see the full fury of the inferno that would engulf them.

For the first time Mary Ann faltered. Could the cart still be harnessed, or was it too late? No, they could get through to the village still, there'd be others hoping to keep the fire at bay.

Had all her preparations been in vain? Was it time to turn tail and run?

Smoke filled the yard. The huddled sheep slumped around the trough, their last refuge. The dogs' tongues hung out but their eyes were still bright and watchful. They'd go to the very last step and beyond, faithful to the end. She looked at Job's ravaged doubting face. What if she had made the wrong decision? Had she made a dreadful, irredeemable, mortal mistake?

No. The time for pulling back had passed.

The fire attacked. It burst over the rise. Flared up. Red and orange tongues challenged everything that stood in its path.

Gusts of hot air scorched their faces.

"Look Missus! Look."

Burning leaves and twigs flew through the air. Mary Ann could have wept. So intent had she been upon the advancing firefront that she'd thought nothing of any danger from the sky above.

Like burning lances cast by a savage tribe, balls of blazing twigs and glowing cinders showered down upon them.

With a flicker of yellow the roof of the cowshed sent up a plume of smoke. Immediately red tongues of fire shot from the shingles.

Panic-stricken bellows from a sick cow still inside told its own story.

"Get that animal out!"

The enemy was in their midst.

"There's still time, Missus. We could still..."

"No." Mary Ann squared her shoulders and stood stock still for one moment. She'd meet the foe head on.

CHAPTER 15

Tears of relief scalded her cheeks as she stood upon the verandah and watched the fire streaking by, to left and to right.

Flames leapt from the cowshed, the pigsty smouldered and the dairy roof still blazed but within that oasis of safety surrounded by the churned-up paddock no more buildings burned. Barn, lean-to, henhouse, verandah and the precious home remained unscathed. Now the firefront moved away as swiftly as it had approached. Grasping the smutty rail for support she leant against it, too tired to move, too exhausted even to go in to her daughters.

"Never would have credited it," Job muttered as he gathered up the burnt remains of a couple of chicken. "Like they say, truth's stranger than fiction and no one would credit it, no one. Nothin' like. I'll see to the yard. Got to get them cows back and that hay's all alight down near the sty. You goes indoors now. You've done more'n any other mortal woman could."

Her legs no longer supported herself as she clung to the rail. The deep breaths she took sent smoke deep down into her lungs and she coughed and choked till her body shook with the effort.

Eyes watering and chest aching, she stood for a full five minutes taking in the destruction all around. So much had gone, but so very much remained. Grass would grow, rails and fences could be repaired, the gum trees would sprout once more.

Finally she kicked off her boots and opened the front door.

Oven-like the sweltering atmosphere engulfed her. Hurrying from room to room she threw open the doors and windows. Not a sound came from the bedroom. She paused, stood stock still and listened as smoke swirled around her. Common sense told her that nothing could be wrong but such disaster had surrounded them she could not even turn the handle of the door for dread. She gripped its smooth surface and waited. Unable to marshall the effort to turn the doorknob, she just stood and listened.

Cathy was sitting up chewing a biscuit. She did not even seem frightened by her mother's wild appearance.

Mary Ann could hear the edge of hysteria as she stood and laughed - what else could she do? To think this dainty bedroom could have been a fiery tomb! The baby stirred and almost at once began to cry. Mary Ann scooped her up and went onto the verandah.

"You poor little mites. Oh Lizzie, you must be starving. Just think, four hours ago you had your last feed. Look what's happened in that time? Never mind, here we go…" She unbuttoned her bodice and held the baby close.

But her milk had gone. Those hours facing the fire and watching the terror creep closer and closer had drained her body. What was it she remembered hearing? Many a baby died for want of its mother's milk. Mary Ann fumed as Lizzie nuzzled at her breast and complained relentlessly. Milk, the milk must come back!

Such conflicting emotions gripped Mary Ann that she could

not think straight. Triumph at having saved the home, despair at the ravaged farmland all around; but underlying those two extremes lurked sheer exhaustion and solitude. I know how a climber feels, she told herself, struggling up to a peak, achieving a great feat but being all alone upon the mountain.

Times like this, you needed people round you. Some helpful older woman who'd come up with tried and true homely advice, anything to help bring that milk back.

The farm was saved, most of the animals had survived and within a few weeks there'd be shoots of new grass. Inside a month or so tiny leaves would sprout along the bare arms of the gum trees. As the shoots multiplied they'd fill out into balls of greenery, becoming larger and more luxuriant until fresh growth cloaked the entire tree. Fed and succoured, the skeletons would green up again. Then, when the tree had recovered, the balls of greenery would give way to its usual twigs and leaves. That was the way with gum trees. They mended themselves.

But what of the baby? Trees could take their time to recover. Babies did not have a second chance.

She'd tried once before to give the little one a feed of cow's milk. She'd not been well and her breasts had become so swollen and lumpy that she shuddered and winced with pain when the baby sucked. In desperation she'd diluted milk with boiled water and, filling a bottle, fashioned a teat from a plug of clean rag.

Suck! Suck! She'd almost shaken the poor little mite. Suck, damn you! All the while trying not to think of those tales about babies starving to death for want of their mother's milk. But the baby had turned her head away and screamed her rejection louder than ever and Mary Ann had gritted her teeth and let the baby suck again.

Wearily Mary Ann sat on the doorstep clasping the screaming

infant to her breast. What had Grand-mère said? In her young days there had been wet nurses. Oh, to have that comfort for my little one.

Through a fog of exhaustion and despair Mary Ann forced herself to remember Grand-mère's words.

"Many genteel women never fed their infants at all…but a working woman could make a living as a wet nurse."

"Ugh!" Mary Ann had shuddered. "That is just so disgusting. A wet nurse! They'd be more like a cow."

"For years on end a poor woman can support her family just being a wet nurse."

"How can they keep up the milk all that time?"

"They bathe their breasts. Milk will go on for ever if you don't bind the breast. That, of course, is how you get rid of the milk. To dry milk up you swab your breasts with vinegar, bind yourself very tightly and don't drink. To keep it coming you drink and drink as much water as you can, you loosen your garments and you bathe your bosom, first in hot water, then in cold. Several times over you do this and before long the milk will flow once more."

She laid the child aside in its cradle, forcing herself to ignore the screams and the hopeless whimpering that followed. Too tired herself, she instructed Job to stoke the fire and boil the water and then fetch more from the well.

Painstakingly she bathed her breasts, first with hot water, then with cold, and when the baby slipped into an uneasy, complaining slumber she let herself relax and dozed off, sitting at the table with her head in her hands and the bowls of water before her. Three times she repeated the bathing, first in hot water, then in cold, until exhaustion overcame her and she fell asleep.

A tingling in her nipples woke her.

Wake up! Her breasts swelled when she lifted the baby up in

her arms. Mary Ann clutched the downy head against her body with enormous relief.

Clever Grand-mère. Grand-mère, like Grand-père, knowing so much and understanding everything. What Mary Ann would have given to have that old grey head nodding off over her crochet hook as she sat in the corner of the kitchen.

By the time George and the men returned next day the baby had settled and Mary Ann was busy out in the yard helping Job replace some of the burnt palings round the pig sty. As the gate creaked open she flew across the yard.

"My bloody oath!" George shook his head as he stared at the burnt roof of the barn, the blanket of dust and the bare branches of the gums. "My bloody oath!"

"George! Oh George!" She threw her arms around him.

"Give over, girl, give over." He patted her shoulder and placed a kiss on her forehead, "Where's the mare? Where's them Spanish sheep?"

Every detail tumbled out. The long wait, the anxious hours as the flames approached, the animals, Job's endless toil and the fear, above all, the fear.

"Never seen nothin' like it," he kept repeating, while the Irishmen shook their heads and muttered between themselves.

"The Missus saved the day, she did," Job stated, eyeing the two men warily. He did not look at his master. Mary Ann sensed the old man's distrust. Did he suspect George's intention of getting rid of him?

"You did well, you certainly did, but there's a mighty bit of work needs doing now. Look at that stable roof, and the fencing over by the trough." He freed himself from her arms and moved away, calling to the men to follow him.

What did all those myriad details matter? Mary Ann stood back and watched the men following their master. The important thing was that they were safe – and Bywong remained as it had always been. The house, the orchard, the dairy, nearly all the sheds – a bit damaged and sooty – but they were there. Grand-père and Grand-mère's beloved home had been saved.

Although she would not put it into words, all Mary Ann asked for was that George turn to her, put his arms around her and make her feel like a woman again, instead of one who washed and cleaned and mopped and cooked while he fell into bed each night in silence and snored the night through..

Now, as day followed day and George, the Irishmen and Job laboriously set about righting so much which had been destroyed, Mary Ann felt her husband slipping further and further away.

Angrily, he stamped indoors for his meals and ate them in silence. He fetched in the buckets from the well resentfully if he could not find Job to do it for her. Not once did he pick up either of his daughters, instead he frowned if they made any noise and many a night Mary Ann paced up and down with young Lizzie to stop her from crying.

On those occasions when she turned to him at night and pressed her face against his shoulder he'd yawn and roll over. Words that cannot be spoken in the harsh light of day can be whispered in the dark when encircling arms give the comfort that ushers in sleep, or love. But scarcely a syllable escaped his lips, no longer did she hear those comforting words.

"Dear George, you work so hard. It's all so worthwhile and you are so good."

A stifled yawn came as a reply and he burrowed deeper in the pillow.

Night followed night with the occasional punctuation of sheer animal release on George's part, but tenderness and care had flown away and that travesty of contentment which can cloak a marriage now ruled the day.

Casual exchanges, the weather, the state of the paddocks, the whereabouts of some lost stock, all the patina of life which masks the real questions that need to be asked, were their sole communication.

Was this the way of marriage? Who could she ask? She'd not want to discuss such a subject with either sister and there were no other women of her acquaintance close by. Isolated and very sad, Mary Ann turned the subject over time and again as she sat with the baby in her arms watching Cathy playing with her dolls.

It was all there. Even a tiny human being like Cathy was already tending to another, brushing her doll's hair, changing its clothes. Is this all that we are here on earth to do? The words remained unspoken; who would listen?

Yet she remembered Grand-père had always spoken to Grand-mère with love, and when she recalled the past there had been many times when he had put his arm around his wife's shoulders and laughed with her. And, for all their occasional tiffs, they were happy enough, certainly still husband and wife, not just master and servant. And Hannah and Edward, and Elizabeth and Henry certainly shared many a confidence and there'd always been a loving embrace each night when husband returned to wife.

A sham! Why am I living a sham, Mary Ann asked herself. And yet, perhaps she was wrong, perhaps she had jumped to conclusions. Times were difficult, the fire had brought about so many extra tasks. George worked so hard, always out from dawn to dusk; she certainly could not point a finger.

Rain started to fall again and continued over the next weeks. Good, solid, steady rain raising the level of the dam and bringing the ducks quacking back from wherever they'd flown.

A green sheen spread across the paddock by the end of the week, and at the finish of a second week a hint of fresh verdure touched the stricken gums. Some trees were gone for good, the elms Grand-père had planted along the drive remained blackened and stark, the she-oaks would never recover and several apple trees had been reduced to mere stumps. But Mary Ann marvelled at the land's recovery.

"Never seen anything like it, Job." They were chatting in the dairy as he moved some heavy buckets for her.

"Well, you've not seen a fire before, have you? Drought's come through but not fire in many a year and you'd be too young to remember."

"Little fires perhaps, nothing like we had."

"Your grandpa reckoned we'd bin completely wiped out back when they started to build the new house," Job maintained. "That time the barn went down to the stumps and them fence posts all went too, not a gate left neither. You wasn't even born then but I remember, alright. Never seen nothin' like it but we wasn't wiped out, and we ain't now."

"I just can't believe the paddock's nearly green again."

"Good sweet grass. Still, don't do to let 'em fill their bellies too soon, they'd be scouring in no time. We'll move them wethers out the far paddock a-whiles."

"You leave all that to me," George said when she repeated the old man's words that night. "You've had more'n you can handle lately. Course we'll shift the wethers, don't need no advice from that old wiseacre. Never knows when to hold his tongue, that old 'un."

"Hold his tongue?"

"Always ready for a gossip, he is."

"Well I suppose as he's getting on he's more inclined to have a chat."

"I'm glad you come round to seeing it my way, Mary Ann. Time for him to move on, I'd say. Like I said before."

Mary Ann stared at him. Hadn't the subject been relegated to the past?

"When folk get too old there's always work can be found, a bit of woodchopping, or something down the village."

"We can't get rid of Job. He's been with our family since he was little more than a lad, as I said last time. He's lived with our family all his life."

"Too long, some might say."

"Have you forgotten the fire? If I'd not had Job here we'd have been finished."

George smiled at her. "What happened during the fire was all your doing, Mary Ann. A miracle, I grant you that. He, after all, just did your bidding, didn't he, but if you ask me it was about his limit. Time to put him out to pasture like the old grey mare."

"You can't put people out to pasture just as if they're animals. He needs some work. He's always had that hut at the back of the sheds. He can go on living there and just helping out. I always need a hand with the orchard, the digging with the vegetables and the chickens anyhow."

George fixed her with a disapproving stare. She never used to stand in his way like this. She'd given way over the selling of the land, she'd said no more when Mick and Seamus came, she usually stepped back from any argument and held her tongue.

George's hostile gaze didn't falter. Job had to go.

Job was the ears and eyes of Bywong. The old man knew everyone who came and went, some might say he knew every blade of grass on the property. George did not want someone looking over his shoulder all the time. Job had to go.

"Briggs down at the smithy's looking for someone. Easy work, just fetching and carrying and seeing to the horses. Little room out the back, all he could need."

"He belongs here," she muttered stubbornly.

"Think, Mary Ann. 'T'would be a good place for him in his old age; work he can manage, place to live in the village."

"I think not." To preclude any further argument she left the room, shutting the door exceptionally gently - a far more subtle rebuke than a slam.

Nothing more was said though she wondered if any hint of the situation had filtered through to the old man, since he remained unusually silent in the following days.

He didn't call by the kitchen to ask her what he could bring up from the vegetable patch, he turned away and appeared quite deaf when she took out the bucket of pigswill. So she was surprised when a couple of weeks later he called out and hurried over to her as she came back from the well. "You never ought'a be carrying that weight, not you in your condition."

Amazed she put the buckets down at once. No one knew she was expecting again, not a word had been spoken. She regretted she'd listened to those who said that when you are suckling an infant you cannot conceive again. She was nearly two months gone but had not even told George. The right moment will come, she kept telling herself, but he always hurried over his meals, sped off to the pastures or fell into bed and snored almost immediately. "I've not said anything, Job, no one knows, no one."

"Ain't seen you day in day out since you was in swaddling clothes without knowing a thing or two. I know, and you leave them buckets for me."

That night she'd tell George. The new life which she had

hugged to herself would be a secret no longer. But somehow that right moment never came.

A strange remoteness crept into Mary Ann's life. A subtle detachment from daily life as she began to think about the new arrival. She was tired. So tired that the very thought of another birth, another life to care for, filled her with dread. If only she could have laid her head on George's shoulder and shared those fears, then all would have been bearable.

The birds did not sing as sweetly as she recalled, the scent of roses scarcely touched her nostrils, the sky was not as blue, the grass not so green. *I'm imagining all this*, she told herself as she sat listlessly shelling pea pods at the kitchen table. A veil of uninterest had fallen over so many of her days. Whereas before she'd eagerly asked George about the doings out in the paddocks, now she felt no curiosity at all. He'd taken on that life. He always answered her in monosyllables, almost putting her in her place and that place was the kitchen.

Left with the house and its surrounds she'd filled her days with the usual domestic chores, trying to convince herself all the while that she was experiencing contentment, whereas a sneaking feeling told her that resignation would have been a truer description.

Perhaps the coming birth produced this strange lethargy? Her second birth had been so frightening, this must be the reason. The pangs had not been forgotten, nor the dread, even though she told herself over and over again that next time she would not be so exhausted, next time it would be different... and all the while she hoped beyond hope that she would have a son. George may have shown little interest in Cathy and Lizzie but the mere mention of a son brought a rare smile to his face. Surely this time she would be lucky and that might change his whole attitude. So she tried hard not to fear the birth, and stepping back from all the worries, becoming more of an onlooker, regarding her daily life from a distance.

While the grass grew thicker in the paddocks and the trees shaded the ground once more there were very few changes to those other casualties of the fire. Admittedly, the dairy had a roof again - it had been a first priority - but the cowshed still gaped wide open to the elements and the cows were brought into the barn for milking nowadays. The trap remained in the open, prey to all the vagaries of the weather, and tools with their wooden handles burnt off lay scattered just as they were when the fire had pounced on them.

"Are they going to start on the sheds soon, George?" She asked, for she hadn't seen either of the men for several days. Job milked the cows and she helped him out when Lizzie slept and she could take Cathy to the barn with her.

"They can't be everywhere at once, Mary Ann. Those rails down near Palmers are taking every moment. We'll be down there today till nightfall. Give us time."

Something about the 'us' snagged at her consciousness, as she watched him leave the yard with the two men. Laughing and chatting the three men disappeared past the dam, leaving her with a sense of exclusion. They would be away all day, George would come home exhausted and silent and once again he'd fall into bed and snore beside her.

Men had the best of it, she told herself as she put the breakfast before him next morning. He would be off round the property but she would see nothing but the same as she had seen for days and days. Pots to be cleaned, floors swept, children's demands.

'Anyhow, they'll have their work cut out for a while. I'll need to go to Yass - yearling sale."

"Yass? A yearling sale? I thought you'd seen those beasts over at Bungendore. Didn't you say you'd make an offer and…?" Mary Ann ladled out the porridge.

"You got it wrong. You misremembered again. What I said was…"

"Couldn't we come with you?"

George looked suitably shocked. "What are you thinking of Mary Ann?"

"We could take the tarpaulin, we could camp out under the stars like Grand-père used to do. Cathy would just love that. It's only for a few days. Such a difference, just to do something different for once in a while."

"You know what I think," he regarded her carefully. "I think 'tis time for a visit to your sister up in the city."

"Oh, George!" So he'd listened to her after all. A journey to Hannah, a while in the city. Now he had those men he must feel he could leave the property. "Oh, George." she hurried over and threw her arms round his shoulders.

"I was thinking for you and the little 'uns. Can't expect me to leave the property, can you?"

CHAPTER 16

Several times during her journey Mary Ann regretted she had agreed with George. Never more so than when they passed through Bargo Brush. The coach hit a rock and came to a crunching halt, straddling the narrow road with a ravine on one side and a solid wall of rock on the other. Everyone had to get out, the horses were released from their traces and by the time the pushing, shoving and shouting had finished she made up her mind this would be her last journey away from Bywong.

"Dunno what you're complaining about, Missus," one of the other passengers wryly observed when finally they were back on board. "Last week's mail was bailed up good and proper. Now, that would be something to carry on about, wouldn't it? They took the mail, took the horses, tied the driver to one wheel and his passenger to the other! We've not had nothin' like that, have we?"

"There's potholes in this road you could lose a haystack in," muttered Mary Ann as she cuddled her daughters to her. Lizzie began to drop off to sleep but Cathy never stopped scratching. For the inn where they'd spent the previous night crawled with lice and bugs. Foetid air and grey sheets had been their lot. Grand-père's words over the years came back clearly to her.

'Nothing but a bloodhouse!'

Well, that bloodhouse certainly lived up to its name.

Wistfully she recalled her last journey to the city. Their nightly camps under the stars with Job tending the fire and their blankets rough and welcoming, then that one night in the homely inn. That was how journeys should be. The old Guise coach had gone now. George had sold it months ago.

"Best shift the old thing before its wheels fall off." A smart little trap had taken its place, though now its paint was blackened and blistered. All those happy memories of family excursions had rumbled off into the past with the ancient coach.

"Four days since you left home. You poor angels, oh, how you must have suffered. You look exhausted, my dear." Hannah gathered them in her arms when they arrived. "A good night's sleep, that's what you all need. You'll be as right as rain in the morning. Here, let me have Lizzie. The little love."

Taking the baby from Mary Ann she led the way to their room.

Mary Ann tiptoed down the passage behind her, grasping Cathy's hand. Once again that feeling assailed her. For a second time she felt like a wild thing from the bush that had strayed into a paddock full of prime stock. She became acutely aware of her dusty boots and crumpled clothes. Catching sight of herself in the mirror which still hung outside the parlour did nothing to dispel that illusion. Admittedly the dark curls still framed her face, just as they had on that last visit, but now dark smudges of exhaustion spoke of disturbed nights, tiring days and endless toil. Brushing aside her hair she stared for a moment at that reflection. The slight indentation from cheek to chin would soon become deeper just as the faint lines near her eyes marked the beginnings of a wrinkle. Perhaps Hannah was right and a good night's sleep would wash away those signs of fatigue but she'd seen the changes for enough months now to doubt they'd ever be reversed.

Mary Ann followed her sister with the uneasy sense of intruding upon hallowed ground. Once again the scent of pot pourri and beeswax greeted her and the bedroom smelt of freshly washed linen and lavender.

"What a shame George could not accompany you," her sister commented as she patted the counterpane and held the baby close. "Now there's water in the jug and all you need over there on the washstand. I'll help you with the little 'uns. Make yourself comfy and then we'll go down to the kitchen. Young Cathy must be as hungry as a hunter."

Later when the baby was curled up in her cradle with Cathy fast asleep in the big bed and the two women sitting in the comfortable morning room, Hannah repeated her remark.

"What a shame George could not accompany you." Hannah looked curiously at her sister over the rim of her cup of tea.

"Oh yes, such a shame, but he insisted that we have a little holiday. That terrible fire set him back so much, and then of course I've been so occupied with Lizzie I haven't been any help at all. It's been so demanding with repairs and shifting stock and so on. Poor George is out there from dawn to dusk and it is easier if he doesn't have to worry about us for a little while. Poor George, he never stops."

Sagely Hannah observed to herself that her sister spoke too fast and repeated herself too often.

Mary Ann could not tell Hannah her real reason for agreeing to this visit. The last thing she had wanted to do was leave Bywong, leave George and travel up to the city. Night after night as she had tossed to and fro, every thought had been punctuated by George's snores as she searched this way and that for a way ahead.

A change must come about. Anything to break the routine of tasks and silence. If she went away for a few weeks surely the joy of her return would overturn that weight of indifference which had taken hold of her husband. As she thought of Cathy's eager face and felt the baby's fingers curl about her own she longed to share those moments with him. Surely he would look at them afresh and realise the loneliness of life at Bywong too and see the beauty in their daughters and long once more for the warmth of her embrace.

And she would tell him about the baby then. Of course it was a gamble, there might be another daughter on the way, but families were large, she was strong, there certainly would be sons one day.

"We hear a little news from Gundaroo," her sister's gaze did not falter. "Mrs Palmer visits her mother in Hyde Park Crescent from time to time. Mrs McAllister, you remember her, don't you? Well, she's a great friend of Mrs Palmer's mother. We hear that the Palmers are increasing their acreage."

So everyone knew about the sale! The network of chatter which linked those from the remote properties to their city cousins had functioned as efficiently as usual. Birth, death, disgrace, prosperity and failure travelled from country to city and back to the country, fodder for all those who sat at the banquet of life. Mary Ann swallowed hard and then smiled brightly.

Obviously Hannah was fishing for more information. "Yes, we sold some land to the Palmers a while back. George wanted to be rid of it. There'd been scab down there… best forget it, he said.

"What he doesn't know about sheep isn't worth knowing. All those years on other's properties… that's what experience does for you."

Her sister sniffed but said no more. At least no more to

Mary Ann but she certainly had plenty to say to her husband as they settled down for the night in their four-poster with the mosquito net pulled tight.

"Not a decent rag to her back!"

"Oh come, my love, you know how everyone lives down there. What would they do with frills and furbelows."

"There's always Sunday best, isn't there? Admittedly, Mary Ann was a bit of a hobble-de-hoy, but she's a married woman now – with property too."

"Girls can't be hobble-de-hoys."

"Well, she was always out and about on the farm, down in the paddocks and…"

"Can't blame her if she's not very stylish then, can you? She's happy enough. Don't unsettle her, leave her be."

"Living in a fool's paradise. I'd like to ask her about that land they've sold. Papa would be turning in his grave if he knew. Are they in trouble?"

"Well, ask her. You've a tongue in your head." Edward sighed to himself.

"I did. She just said George had decided it was best got rid of, not good land or some such, but I can tell you, Honoria Palmer hinted there's a lot more baggage attached to that George and she says things are happening as would make your hair stand on end."

"Don't read too much in to what you're told, my love."

"Sometimes it's what you're not told, isn't it? Mrs McAllister said things were changing at Bywong, or so some say, but then she wouldn't utter another word. I'll just have to come face to face with our Mary Ann, I can see that."

"Now then, Hannah, not right to meddle."

"There's a mite of difference between meddling and giving some sound advice and I'm beginning to wonder if that isn't what our girl needs right now. I'll find an opportunity."

Each day Hannah's housemaid and the girl who helped in the kitchen spirited the children away.

"You need a real rest, my dear. That's what holidays are all about, aren't they? In a few days we'll pay some visits. Everyone's agog for news. So much has happened since your last spell in the city."

So much! When, three days later, Mary Ann glanced around the tasteful parlour of Mrs McAllister she found it difficult to enter into the conversation. The latest journal, a successful new addition to a family, the shocking lack of good nursemaids or even kitchen staff as so many women joined their men at the diggings – the currency of everyday life dominated every conversation but the values and demands of her own life at Bywong would be so completely foreign to them that she could only sit in silence.

No one would even be able to visualise all that made up her daily round: the sole care of her children, the orchard, over forty chickens, the mixing of the pigswill and the orphan lambs to rear. And like a shocking backdrop was the memory of the fire, the desperate hours that saved their home. No, she could not even begin to tell them of her life.

Every room at Mrs McAllister's basked in the sheen of the current trend in sophisticated furnishing. Displayed on the lacquered table in the parlour the latest journals spoke of all that was *à la mode* in London and Paris. Casually tossed over one of the chairs the colours of a Spanish shawl glowed in the sunlight and the ivory keys of an upright piano gleamed shiny and white.

Obviously Mrs McAllister cherished every single item, every nook and cranny was scrupulously cared for, every piece of wood, brass and silver burnished to perfection.

"What a lovely piano." Mary Ann felt that some comment was expected.

"Ah, yes, so many of our friends like to sing, you know. The pianoforte is a great delight. I am sure you'd find that in the country too. I make sure the keys are cleaned with milk each week."

"Cleaned with milk!" Mary Ann exclaimed.

"The vapours of the city, Mrs Brownlow. You have no idea the dirt we have to put up with. The only way to keep ivory nice and white is to rub it with milk. Our windows need cleaning every fortnight, I may say. You'd have no such problems in the country, would you? I daresay your windows would not need attention more than once a month?"

Mary Ann bit her lip. Once a month! Lucky to get to them once a year. Wryly she observed to herself that, anyhow, glazing was still something of a luxury. Perhaps she might mention to her hostess that she had to make do mostly with open windows and shutters. "My days are very full," she managed to reply.

"Full! Well, we all know how that is, once we have a family. Ah, it seems only yesterday when you were here with your dear grandfather. So much has happened, hasn't it? Mr McAllister's not enjoyed the best of health, you know but still, he has perfectly amiable business partners to share in his duties. Yes, that has been a constant concern for us. Then of course we had some extensive work done on our home, not nearly large enough for such a suitable position as Mr McAllister's. But handy for Government House, so convenient. And then there has been the most unfortunate plague - one could almost call it a plague - of the shingles. That made certain that many of us have had to curtail the visits we usually make. Oh yes, plenty has been happening here, we have all had to make such sacrifices. The whole Colony suffered with the drought - the price of

lamb! But then the city is like that, isn't it? I really envy you
your life down at Gundaroo. So peaceful after all the hustle and
bustle up here. So restful by comparison, don't you agree?"

Before Mary Ann had time to open her mouth the ladies
were nodding and agreeing and moving on to the next subject.

"Now you have the little ones, you really will have to come
up to the city more often. You owe it to yourself, you know."

"More often?"

"Well, no one spends their life buried in the country, do
they?"

"My grandmother was always very happy, and our mother
too."

Mrs McAllister cast a pitying look at Hannah then smiled
at Mary Ann. "But times change, my dear. We must all move
with the times. It is said that following that terrible drought the
farmers are entering a most prosperous time. You must speak
to your husband. Now is just the moment to think of buying a
house in town. After all, think of the years to come when your
daughters will need a good school and then you'll be glad…"

Houses, husbands, new carriages and the latest news from
the old country dominated the conversation. Occasionally a
novel recipe was mentioned or the name of the best dressmaker
bandied about. Certainly after several days of calling upon
Hannah's friends Mary Ann's head was bursting with all the
advice so freely given.

"You'll have to have a new dress for the Governor's Cup.
Only ten days, Mary Ann! I've got some delightful sprigged
muslin. It won't take more than a few days to have it made up,
then we can find a bonnet."

Mary Ann recoiled from the thought. A sudden change in
the weather had ushered in one of the chilly southerly winds to
the city. The day had been hot but suddenly the temperature

dropped and the coolness brought remembrance of sitting on the verandah at Bywong before winter chased them indoors. A determination had been growing inside her. A deep conviction that she needed to be back at Bywong. George would be facing each day with the same tedium that she had felt herself. She wanted to see his face light up as she walked onto the verandah. She longed for his arms around her and his breath upon her cheeks. This was no place for her, she did not belong, she could not share in her sister's life. Her own awaited her. How foolish she had been to turn her back.

"I was thinking," she paused as she dreaded the reception her remarks would have, "I was wondering if I shouldn't return to Bywong... I think..."

"Return!" Hannah exploded, tight curls bobbing up and down on her forehead, indignant eyes flashing. "You've only been here just over a week. What are you thinking of?"

"Dear Hannah. I should be at George's side. I know he'll be working all hours of the day and night. The fire's weeks ago, I know, but he's still replacing fenceposts and the cowshed's waiting to be rebuilt. He's working from morn to night. I'm so selfish enjoying myself up here when he has so much to do. We came to see you, we came to enjoy life in the city. Well, I've enjoyed every minute but I fear I have been too self-indulgent, I really must return to Gundaroo."

"Are you sending off a letter by the mail?"

"There's hardly time, is there. I'll stay till the end of this week, no matter. It will be a lovely surprise for George. We'll just be there, he won't be on his own."

Her sister shrugged. Made very little difference to her own life, of course, but she wanted to shake the girl, take her by the shoulders and rattle her from side to side like a wayward child. Speak firmly to her just as Grand-père would have done but she was a married woman now, a woman with two children and a husband whom she unfortunately idolised. Why couldn't her sister just enjoy herself for once, be like other young women and make the most of the drapers and the milliners and the haberdashers, take advantage of all that the city had to offer?

"She's always been like this," Hannah grumbled to her husband that night as she pulled up the sheets and tied the ribbons of her night cap a little tighter. "Not like the other girls. Always wondering about what's happening out on the wretched property. I thought this visit'd show her a more genteel way of life. Why, I bought a whole length of chenille for her – lovely delicate material that would have been perfect for a gown – and what do you think she said?"

"I don't know, dear, I really don't."

"She said, 'If I back it with something more serviceable it'll make a beautiful runner for the table!'"

"Uum," he muttered as he turned over.

"Have you seen her shoes? She was going to wear her boots to the races, I ask you. Mrs McAllister would have swooned if she'd known and now she's finding every excuse to make that awful journey back to Bywong. What do you think?"

With a sigh Edward rolled over. "Can't say, dear. Second time she's ever been away from the place. Homesick, that's the trouble I'll be bound and fretting for that husband of hers."

"But she's a mother now, she needs the company of other ladies. Surely she can think of something beside that wretched property and fussing over that George? Gets an idea into her head and goes at it headlong. Never thinks. Like Henry said at the wedding, our French blood's the trouble, either up and floating around with her head in the clouds or down in the dumps. Passionate, that's the word."

Argue as much as she liked, Hannah could not shift Mary

Ann's resolve. Disappointed, she waved farewell to the coach and agreed amongst her friends that Mary Ann had become an out-and-out country wife.

No music could sound sweeter than the rattle of the wheels and the creak of the woodwork, no fragrance more enticing than the fresh scent of the gum. As every milestone passed by so Mary Ann's heart beat faster, the eternal jolting, the tedious delays and Cathy's complaints mere annoyances compared with the growing elation gripping her.

Soon she had put all memories of the city behind her and passed the tedious hours totting up in her mind all the tasks awaiting her shortly. What should she do first? Should she turn the apples, take out the damaged ones, make them into rings and string them up to dry or should she make the new dress for Cathy? There'd sure to be a pile of mending and by now some of the hens would have gone broody and would have to be set upon their eggs. Should she start making the new cushions with the peach brocade she had bought? Or would the plums be ripe and ready for jam making?

The very thought of George sent her senses spinning. The sight of him, the roughness of his jacket, the touch of his hands, such pleasure would be hers again. Before long she'd have the kitchen filled with the smell of fresh baked bread, the soup bubbling and plopping in its pan as she sat recounting all the novelties of the city in the soft glow of the candlelight. Best of all, she would be able to tell her husband they were nothing compared with the joy of being home once more and sitting opposite him. Camden, Picton, Berrima, Paddy's River passed by; three days later when they rumbled down the hill into Goulburn her heart thudded in time with the horses' hooves. *Home, home, home, George, George, George.* Home is where the heart is and the joy of returning made those two weeks away almost worthwhile.

And then would come the moment when she would tell him her wonderful news.

Enquiries at the inn quickly found a couple of men taking a dray out to Gundaroo the next day so early in the morning they left Goulburn, on the last leg of their journey home.

Wings on your heart, wasn't that what the old folks said? When you are journeying to meet your loved one, you have wings on your heart.

Even before the cart turned the corner she heard the sound of hammering. One of the Irishmen stood, tool poised, about to drive home a nail into the gatepost. The other lounged nearby, pipe in mouth. Both stared at her, neither said a word.

"Can you open the gate …?" They stood transfixed, "The gate?" Glancing at each other, one shrugged his shoulders and the other raised the latch. Mick or Seamus, Seamus or Mick? She nodded as the cart passed between the posts, identical cold blue eyes in identical long bony faces framed with identical shocks of black hair just watching and saying nothing.

"Where's Mr Brownlow?"

"Master's down the long paddock," one of them muttered. No word of greeting, not even a welcoming smile.

"And where's Job?" She'd brought a new waistcoat for the old man. A present chosen with much pleasure.

The man with the hammer shifted from one foot to the other, the other one looked away.

"Well, where is he?"

"Down the village. Fetchin' and carryin' for the blacksmith."

Something faintly like amusement flitted across the men's features. An emotion akin to the superiority felt by the young and strong for the elderly.

Rage spurted through her. Rage which she quickly

dampened down to disappointment. Had George been having problems? Could he not keep the old man on? She must not judge, she told herself. Even so she felt a bucket of cold water might just as well have been thrown over her.

She bit back the words which were on the tip of her tongue. She could not allow herself to spoil the next few hours. Nothing must spoil the meeting with George that she'd dreamt about and longed for.

But she had also looked forward to seeing the pleasure on old Job's face as he undid the parcel she had brought for him.

Firmly stopping her thoughts from going further she allowed the patina of civil words to conceal that sudden fury.

"One of you find Mr Brownlow for me," she called over her shoulder.

Those damned Irishmen! George would explain, she knew exactly what he would say. Yes, of course they'd agreed about Job's failing strength, but she'd imagined after she'd expressed her feelings that the old man would remain on the property. His hut and vegetable patch would have been enough for him. Perhaps George had approached the subject awkwardly, maybe the old man had taken umbrage and walked off the farm.

I mustn't come home with a complaint on my lips, she told herself, *jumping to conclusions never helps.* Irishmen or not, the farm had run smoothly and George would have made the right decision.

Her heart ruled her head. Even though reasoning and common sense told her she'd been disregarded, the whirlwind of emotion experienced now, as she was almost in his arms, once more swept aside any doubts.

She'd have his meal on the table. The little girls would be in bed by then. She'd have him all to herself and as she hurried her daughters indoors Mary Ann rejoiced to be back where she belonged.

"We'll get a bite to eat and then it's bed for you two," she hurried them along to the kitchen.

The same homely smell greeted her, wood smoke with a faint memory of roasting meat on its breath. The cups and saucers gleamed from the shelves and pans were piled on top of each other in the washing-up bowl. All so familiar, this was home again and she felt herself smiling from ear to ear as she looked around. Home again.

Then something caught her eye. A straw sun hat, tossed casually beside a pile of apples on the table, its pink ribbons lay crumpled and twisted as though whoever had worn it had snatched at the brim and hastily thrown it down.

Visitors? We've had some visitors. Well, he won't have been entirely on his own then, that's good, Mary Ann thought.

How thrilled George would be to see them back again, a whole week earlier than expected. Her body glowed with anticipation as she rattled out the ashes, set out the kindling and wood in the stove then watched the flames take hold.

First of all, feed the little ones and get them to bed. Cathy grizzled with tiredness and the baby kept nuzzling for her breast as she hurried round the kitchen, not wanting to put her down in case she started crying. Some said a good cry got the appetite going, but Mary Ann just thought it filled them up with wind and made for more trouble.

"You wait here, lovey, you just watch over our Lizzie while I go and fetch us some milk from the dairy. Just you be a good girl and wait."

Cool and cavernous the faintly animal scent of milk, butter and cheese enveloped her as she reached the threshold. How neat and tidy it looked. But how different. A stack of cloths and butter pats took up the space where usually she kept clean bowls, a pipkin of cream stood on the cold marble surface and whey slowly dripped through the cheesecloth suspended from one of the beams.

George must have been busy, but he did not usually bother himself with the dairy. She'd expected to find a trail of disorder left by Job but of course, she pulled herself up. No Job now, must be the work of one of the men.

Perhaps I should go away more often, she smiled to herself. *They certainly have managed very well - for the time being.*

Cathy and Lizzie were tucked up and fast asleep well before she heard the crunch of George's boots upon the path. Her heart leapt as she turned to the door.

"What's up?" He stood staring at her. Rigid, hands at his sides, his gaze flitted around the kitchen.

"I'm back. Oh George, I'm never going away again. Isn't it wonderful, I'm back."

She threw her arms around him.

Wooden as a post he stood there. Then he patted her on her back and gave her a slight squeeze. She raised her face to his but somehow his lips were not there and if she had seen the expression she'd have seen his startled reaction when he glimpsed the straw hat. But the flood of relief at being once again in her husband's arms had transported Mary Ann beyond ordinary everyday matters. The very feel and smell of him!

Pulling back she held him at arm's length, her eyes bright with excitement. So broad-shouldered, so bronzed and so completely the man of her dreams, and also so different from those milksops up in the city. Never ever again would she leave him. Next time they'd make the trip together.

"Oh George! Look what I've brought you." She took out several little packets from her bag. "Look." Impatiently she waited for him to undo the string: his favourite tobacco, a new necktie, some exotic lures for his rod. The thrill of seeing him unwrap the gifts matched her pleasure of choosing them.

"And I've brought Job a new waistcoat, he'll look such a swell."

Then she paused. Job! Hastily she rattled on, this was no moment to bring in a discordant note.

So much to talk about, so much time to make up. As she hurried around the kitchen laying the food out, she barely noticed his silence.

"…and most of all, it's wonderful to be back. I'll never, never go away again."

Of course George had never been one to chatter, had he? And if she did feel he was a little quiet… well, the poor fellow had been forced to make do with his own company these two weeks anyhow with only those fellows to talk to.

Even by the time they laid beside each other that night the subject of Job had not been brought up.

When she called by at the smithy two days later old Job did not come out at first.

Eventually George had got round to the subject and she'd listened to his reasons for putting off the old man. Reluctantly she'd nodded but could not bring herself to agree. Now she watched the back door of the smith anxiously. Would the old man come out and talk to her, or was he mortally offended with her family?

"Job! Job! Out 'ere mate!" the blacksmith shouted again, but he had to call three more times before the old man came out.

"Job! Look what I've got for you…" She held out the package, smiling broadly. "You know how sorry I am, but certainly there'd be less heavy work here. You'll find that a blessing. I'll never forget the fire, never forget how you saved the day. We'd have been lost without all you did. Bywong's not the same without you, though. Here, cut that string…"

The old man stared at the waistcoat.

"Brass buttons, those brass buttons caught my eye. The moment I saw that waistcoat, I said to myself, 'That's for Job'."

He mumbled his thanks but his eyes did not meet hers.

"Perhaps you could come and spend a few hours helping in the orchard? One of those days when work's quiet?"

He still said nothing, just fidgeted with the string, finally winding it into a neat ball.

"There's always the pruning. I know there's Mick and Seamus but they're often busy. There's a lot of work going on up at Bywong after the fire of course, Mr Brownlow has his plans."

"Oh aye, he has his plans alright… and he ain't the only one."

CHAPTER 17

"There was a lonely drummer boy and he loved a one-eyed cook!

"With a hey! And a ho! And a hey nonny no!"

Mary O'Rourke sang loudly and triumphantly as she swept out the hard dirt floor, beaten down and resilient from the earth of ancient anthills pounded down over the years. "And when that rascal came to call the very timbers shook!" She stopped and chuckled to herself.

"Ma, I'll thank you to stop singin' yer filthy ditties. Me only just back from town and lookin' for a few hours peace and quiet."

"And I'll say you may be thinkin' you're on yer way to being a fine lady but the time's comin' when the kid gloves is coming off over at Bywong, my bird. Time's comin', dirt's got to fly!"

The Irishwoman looked at her daughter with satisfaction. "Didn't I tell you to bide yer time, wasn't I right? This time next year we'll be singing a different song over them pastures. You listen to yer old ma. Things's working out very nicely, thank you. Now come and help yer ma. There's a load of pegging out to be done. Rain's on its way, can feel it in me knees."

Brigid stared across the paddock with a smug gleam in her

eye. "The lads'll be back soon. They ain't sayin' much."

"Don't need to. They know which side their bread's buttered and, like you say, they never says much, but things ain't the rosiest over there. Still, that old fool isn't hanging around no more, carryin' tales and the like. Best place for him down with that Briggs. What the eye don't see, the heart don't grieve after."

Job's departure had certainly made Mary Ann's life even more arduous. She did not feel comfortable with the Irishmen, she could not come to terms with George's decision. Job had certainly been slow and often forgetful. If he could end his working life fetching and carrying for the blacksmith in the village, then perhaps that was his lot and, after all, everyone reaches a stage when heavy labouring is beyond them. Yet a stubborn sense of loss pervaded her daily life and a conviction of something amiss constantly nagged at her.

The old man had always been there. They'd shared many times together; now when she went out to the yard she missed his cheery greeting. From the days when she had help him with the milking and he had grinned up at her from his stool and squirted her with a stream of milk from an overflowing udder, to the times when he had grumbled and complained, he had been part of their family.

"I'd like a hand with that wire down in the chicken run. Look at those clouds. Don't want to be out looking for those hens in the wet," she said. "Can Seamus spend a while there, I'll tell him what to do."

"Can't spare him."

"But it's only a couple of hours. Two hens have already got out. They're broody and if they make their nests out in the paddock the dingoes will get them."

"No, he's got more than enough to do."

"When he comes up for the milking perhaps he could spare a minute. It's the only time I catch sight of him."

"Those lads have more than enough," he repeated and shut his mouth tight.

Mary Ann decided she'd ask them herself but something in the way they looked at her held her back. Their walk had a certain arrogance, when they spoke she found them difficult to understand. That black hair and blue eyes accentuated their sharp features. They darted about their work, then disappeared for hours on end. Nor was the yard even tidy any more.

"Why are those lads so unwilling?" Mary Ann grumbled on yet another day to her husband. He'd returned from a journey to Goulburn and they were sitting over their meal in the kitchen.

"Different folks has different ways."

"I suppose it's like Grand-mère used to…" but she did not finish the sentence. The door opened and Seamus stepped into the room followed by Mick.

"An' where's me winnins?" He held out his hand to George while his brother waited a few steps behind.

Mary Ann stared in amazement as the three men put their heads together and when Seamus, with no bidding, drew up a stool and joined them at the table she stood up and retreated across to the dresser. In confusion, she busied herself tidying one of the drawers while the three men immersed themselves in the details of horses, finishing posts, wagers and handicaps.

When Mick took out his pipe and began filling it she left the room.

"What were you thinking?" she demanded later. The men had gone and she'd returned to the kitchen, now smelling of tobacco and beer fumes.

"What's the matter?"

"How could those fellows just walk in? And smoking, no

one smokes indoors here."

"No one did, you mean. Times change, my girl. Move with the times, same as the rest of us, eh?" He fixed her with a challenging stare.

"And the money… that money… where did it come from?"

"If you want to know, Mrs High and Mighty, it come from the old gee-gees and there's plenty more where that come from."

"The horses. Was that what you went to Goulburn for? Was it the races? You told me…"

"Never knew I was marrying a nag. Here am I, working all the hours God gives a man. Taking a few hours for me pleasure and here's you putting the boot in, as usual."

As their voices rose Cathy ran over to her mother, then the baby started to cry.

"My bloody oath. Can't a man have some peace in his own home?"

Own home? That was the crux of the matter.

All the excuses in the world came flooding in. Overworked, worried about owings to the bank, hoping to make some easy money and put things right.

Feeble, hopeless excuses that shied away from the one inescapable fact - he was not the man she had always imagined him to be. And she had become a stranger in her old home. A foreigner in the family kitchen with its streaky walls and scrubbed table.

A fierce tide of disgust flooded through her. Abhorrence at her own feelings, her own weakness and her sudden helplessness. Trampled upon and insignificant and strangely unclean as though she had betrayed all those who'd gone before. The ancient name of de Guise had been dishonoured.

Tipping water into the basin she scrubbed her hands. Round the nails, round the knuckles, then time and again she rinsed them in the soapy water as the discord of her thoughts clamoured in her ears.

What had Grand-père often said, something about water finding its own level? Were those Irish louts the level where George Brownlow really belonged?

Something of her confusion must have communicated itself to her husband. He glanced at her curiously. For a moment he just looked at her, then he walked across and knocked out his pipe on the window sill.

"Look, my dear, you know how 'tis. Time's been difficult… we'll pull through. I never meant no harm and that's a fact. Believe me, I'm always tryin' to do the best for you and the little 'uns, and maybe it don't seem so clever but that's the way of things."

He put a tentative arm around her waist and pulled her closer.

Oh, you weak fool, something inside her said, but even so she pushed the doubts from her mind. She wanted to believe him, wanted to go about their daily life as they had always done, needed the world of cooking, mending and afternoon strolls.

"I've been a bit sharp," she muttered burying her face in his shoulder.

"Well, 'tis always said there's a touch of curry in the Guises," and he laughed as he ruffled her hair.

"But those lads, they're taking liberties that's what I don't understand."

"Look at it this way, my love, them Irish is all the same. Butter wouldn't melt in their mouth one moment and the next they'd have the shirt off yer back. But we need hands about the place, time's so difficult. Where've the shepherds all gone? There's no one to tend the beasts hereabouts. We're lucky to have the smith still, one over Bungendore's up and gone. There's only old men like Job left. Everyone's shot off to the goldfields. We should be countin' our lucky stars for what we've got. At least we've got them lads and that's a fact."

Reluctantly Mary Ann agreed. Gold fever had not subsided a single bit. Some had said at the time it was a passing madness but men still left everything and made for the diggings. Anyone who could get to the goldfields made their way there. Everywhere employers were bitterly complaining.

"If we lose these lads, Mary Ann, then we're in a bad way."

"They're sly. They always seem to be up to something. I don't…"

"High spirits, my love. That's all 'tis, high spirits. You've been used to that old codger these many years past well, look at him, one foot in the grave! These lads may be a bit rough but that's all 'tis, high spirits."

Of course George must be right. Times certainly were changing. Up till now daily toil for the working man had been the necessity. Routine, regular work and skills learnt from the very earliest days of life. Now this delectable option had appeared. The luck of digging up a golden nugget could transform a working man into a millionaire overnight. Everyone had heard the tales. Those fortunates who could light their cigars with banknotes, the lucky ones who tossed away their tents and pots and pans and headed for home. Well, you'd be mad not to have a go! You've got to be in it to win it.

Yes, they were lucky to have two able-bodied men on the farm. Instead of bemoaning her lot she should be grateful. *You fool*, she told herself, *you've a fine husband and two lovely daughters, you have your acres around you and your beasts out in the paddocks. Why be so discontented?*

Discontent was not the right word. A deep uneasy malaise of the spirit had taken hold of her. Like a swimmer who's waded into the sea and finally takes their foot off the bottom, and finds themselves at the mercy of strange currents and rips pulling them this way and that. Never once did she manage to get her head up and see where the best direction lay. Instead, from day to day and week to week she vascillated between agreeing with George and a conviction that strong undercurrents at Bywong were distorting their lives. Helplessly she sensed that tide in the life of all humans that can sweep them inexorably towards the maelstrom.

Was she imagining their insolence and sideways looks? Why did George have to travel to Goulburn or Yass or Bungendore so often, and should the farm be left in their hands so much? Some days none of this mattered; George might be at hand, the men could be working out on the property and all seemed normal. But in his absence the pair of them took over. Any request she might have made would be met with a shrug, they'd scarcely appear, except at milking time.

How could life have changed so radically at Bywong? How could the servants suddenly come to rule the master? The Irishmen appeared to make the choices and George complied without a murmur. Matters came to a head with the rebuilding of the barn.

The roof of the dairy had been patched up, the sides of the cowshed had been cobbled together, but the barn remained a cavernous travesty of itself.

For a couple of months since the fire the blackened walls had gaped, roofless, at the sky. During all that time everything was left open to the elements, even the new trap remained outside. No room, no shelter anywhere else. Several times Mary Ann mentioned rebuilding but the reply remained the same.

"Bide yer time, Mary Ann, bide yer time. The lads have

enough to do, they'll come round when things is slack."

But that time never arrived. As the new harrow lost its shine and the paint on the trap blistered she held her tongue - until the day when she went to fetch the sickle and found it yellow with rust and the handle split.

"We'll just have to get that roof mended. Look at this, George. We can get the wood for those rafters any time. You must tell them to get on with the job."

"They ain't much hand as carpenters."

"Neither was Job, nor were our boys in their time, but they could always fix a roof."

"I'll have a word with 'em."

"Not 'have a word', George.' Tell them! Half the day they're nowhere to be found, they're sheer lazy."

"You'd better watch your tongue, Mary Ann. If you speaks ill…"

"Speak ill! What are you talking about? You give the orders, you don't take them, for heaven's sake."

"We're that lucky to have those lads. Half the labour in the place has gone to the goldfields."

"Yes, yes, so you've said before but the truth of the matter is they've not gone only because they're bone idle. That's a fact."

"I'll speak to them."

"Sometimes I think you're scared of them."

The moment she made the remark she'd wished it had never been said. George's face suffused with a dark tide of resentment and he threw himself out the door, slamming it violently behind him.

He did not come back midday, by mid-afternoon he still had not returned.

He did not come home all day. He did not come home that night.

Next day silence enveloped the house, even Cathy whispered as she played with her dolls. The house had never been so quiet and all she could think of was getting out of it, taking herself and the girls off for a spell, at least talking to another human being.

"Now you brush your own hair Cathy. I'll see to our Lizzie" Laying the baby down, she left the little girl sitting beside the cradle while she went out and put the mare between the shafts of the trap. Soon they were trotting down the main street. She breathed a sigh of relief at being out and away from the chores, if only for a short while.

"Good day Mrs Brownlow," the storekeeper nodded, "and what can I be doing for you this fine afternoon?"

She nodded and took out her list but immediately became aware of his sideways glance at the only other customer in the shop. A look exchanged, a slight pursing of the lips and the hint of words that hung in the air – she sensed that she had interrupted some titbit of gossip. Had they been talking about her as she'd hitched the mare to the post outside?

The few minutes she spent at the counter were no longer a pleasure. She hurried through her purchases and made her way to the smithy.

"Those brackets, Job, remember those brackets in the kitchen? Well, I've brought the broken one and if you can get Mr Briggs to copy it, that's just what I need. But while I'm here, can you open up this hook for me? It's closed up tight and I can't hang anything on it."

Job had settled into his new occupation with the usual resignation of his kind. He'd been given a room at the back and had the use of the yard whenever he wanted. The blacksmith knew a good worker when he saw one.

"Settled in, Job?"

He did not reply. Instead he picked up some pliers and took the hook from her.

He did not say another word till he handed it back to her, then the ghost of a smile flitted across his features.

"Little'un can stretch her legs, eh? Let me give her a lift?" Children were always welcome in Job's world. Cathy scampered across the yard and, with Lizzie in her arms, Mary Ann leant against one of the rails watching the old man stack some firewood.

"Them Irish givin' satisfaction?"

Mary Ann shrugged. Many times she'd wondered if Job thought she had known about his dismissal before going up to the city, left George to do the dirty work in her absence. "Job," she began, "Job, I hope you realise I never wanted you to leave Bywong."

He put down the broom and lowered himself down on to a nearby log. "Never thought 'twas your wish Miss Mary Ann. Never for one moment."

How lovely to be Miss Mary Ann once more. She bent down and touched his shoulder for a moment as though to reassure herself that her past was still intact.

"I'm sorry."

"Yes, I'm sorry too but most of all I'm sorry for your pa… and thinking back, his pa before him, and all the rest of 'em. Proud they were, proud as peacocks and what…" He stopped. He'd said too much.

"What do you mean?"

"'Nough said."

"No, it's not enough. What do you mean?"

"There's folks who's always on the lookout to better themselves, Miss Mary Ann. Your pa and old Mr Guise and all them family worked hard and earned every penny. But there's those who just sits about and waits for an opportunity and then jumps in and makes a killing."

"Who are you talking about?" The needless question had to be asked.

"Them… them Irish."

"That family have always been down by the river. That's been their life, they never changed."

He nodded. "But they're looking to change it now." The glance he gave Mary Ann spoke volumes. "Just have a care, Miss Mary Ann… have a care."

The shadows were lengthening when she drove the trap into the yard. The milking had been finished – two full pails stood on the table in the dairy. Otherwise the house and yard were just as she had left them - empty.

Task after task swallowed up the next hours. The mare unharnessed, fed and watered, the lamps lit, the girls fed and put to bed, George's dinner to prepare. Finally by the light of the stable lantern, she went about her work in the dairy - butter made, milk skimmed, buckets washed and all left ready for the morning's milking. She finally made her weary way back across the yard.

Would George come home tonight?

The day had been long and every bone ached but she did not want to go into that empty bedroom and lie in the bed, alone. A sense of unreality pervaded her thinking, a sense of being completely out of her depth and at the mercy of tides that she did not understand.

Perhaps it was the coming baby? She'd delayed too long, she must tell George tonight. Whether he was pleased or not there was no more time to lose as she knew it was beginning to show.

She laid the table for George's meal in the kitchen and sat

with her sewing on the settle. She waited till well past the usual hour of his return, working away steadily tacking and hemming by the light of two candles. A growing sense of purpose slowly, inexorably, took hold of her, steadying her will. Questions must be asked. Answers must be given.

When she heard the grating of George's boots upon the step her resolve almost dissolved, but she bit her lips and waited. Wives and husband always had problems, there were no perfect marriages. When she told him her news he'd have to take notice.

"Still up?"

"You're late." She did not ask him where he'd been, it might bring forth another torrent of complaint. Instead she fetched out the bread and took the chicken and vegetables from the oven.

"Just busy."

She put off the moment and tried to gather her thoughts together.

"Had the trap out, I see."

"Went into town today. Called at the blacksmiths. Saw old Job."

George uttered a laugh. "That old scoundrel. He's lucky to be there…"

"He always did an honest day's work."

"Meanin' what?" His eyes narrowed as he watched her.

"Something's up, George. He was strange, different. I feel people are talking about us. There's something up, isn't there, and I don't know what it is."

Her husband gave a sigh.

"I must know. Is there trouble? You don't need to sell any more land, do you? What's the matter."

He gave another sigh and then leant on the table and smiled to himself.

"S'pose the trouble could be the way you go about things."

"Me? The way I go about things! What do you mean?"

"There's got to be some changes made, Mary Ann. You need that much help about the place, you need someone as can work with you, help with the little'uns and such."

She listened in silence.

Now was the moment to tell him about the coming baby. But strangely she could not find the words.

"Have you looked in the mirror lately, my girl?" Picking up the candle he laid a hand on her shoulder and pushed her across to the small looking glass on the wall. "Look at yerself, worn to a frazzle, you are."

The light cruelly highlighted her gaunt cheekbones and hair all awry.

"You've more than enough on your plate." She could hear the conciliatory tone in his voice, a false concern. "The dairy, the hens, the orchard, the house, the little 'uns – you're hard at it from morn to night you are, just like me. You need some help you do. Fact is, we need's another woman about the place."

Another woman? Two words. Two simple words that shattered the fragile façade she had fashioned around her fears and doubts.

How could mere words cause such pain?

Gathering up her skirts she wrenched herself from his hand and flew down the path to the privy. She flung herself to her knees, retching violently into the pan.

Even in her distress Mary Ann's reasoning still held. She found herself amazed and utterly confounded by the pain. That emotional pain could translate into sheer bodily agony added to her distress.

Rejection, rejection, rejection! She muttered the word again and again. Her stomach shrank into a ball and she vomited once more. Immediately the agony spread from the stomach to the heart. Heartache, hinted at and spoken of almost lightly in songs and stories was no fictional state. All the buried fears that had banked up and remained unspoken were released in a gigantic wave of emotion. The desperate, gripping physical pain amazed her. A cramping that bit into her left side and clamped a cruel band around her heart.

Uncontrollably she threw up time and again, then her bowels loosened and she had to sit there, tears streaming down her face. "My God, my God, what's happened to me?"

She clutched her hands together as though seeking reassurance, reassurance within herself. There is a place beyond suffering. There is a place where despair writhes in the mind to such an extent that it takes its tortures out on the body. You'd like to be done with that body. Love and passion can turn into sheer hellish pain.

Hard on the heels of pain came fear. Too far from the safe shores of everyday life, never again would the solid world of reality be there beneath her feet. Instead, the maelstrom had snatched her and all around deep peril surged.

Yet all the while, that logical Guise mind ticked off the facts just as though, all along, some secret tally had been kept, an inner account compiled. The arrival of the Irishmen, the blowsy mother's defiance, the sunhat and the memory of that other woman's greedy eyes. The constant trips to Goulburn and the sale of the land. All along George had wanted the property, he wanted Bywong and he had achieved that desire. She, herself, was part of the deal. The deal once made left her expendable. Now this other woman waited in the wings.

In the wash house she splashed water on her face and ran her fingers though the dark, wild hair. Stumbling across she threw open the door of the kitchen. George sat at the table, a chicken bone in his fingers. He looked up questioningly.

"Did you mean that?"

He put the bone down and half rose. "You need help Mary Ann. Too much you've got on your plate. The lads'll back me up, you need help and they reckon their sister…"

"Give her her name!"

"What?"

"Her name!"

"'Tis Brigid."

"Brigid! All along I've wondered what she was called. All these years they've lived down there and I've never known. Just fancy that…" she added with a hollow laugh, "just fancy that… I never knew that one day she was going to have my home."

"Now wait on, Mary Ann, don't take on like this…"

"And that old harridan will come too. I suppose we'll give her Grand-père's room, eh? And I'll have the girls in with me, is that so? And time will come when everyone takes their orders from your Brigid and even my daughters will turn to her because she'll be the mistress of this house!"

"Wait on, Mary Ann, I never said nothin' like that."

"You don't have to. They'll take over, that family, Brigid and her brothers, and that will be the end of it."

"I told you, you need help about the place, that's all 'tis."

"No, thank you very much, George. I don't need help and I don't want her in my home. You can tell her she's not needed." Mary Ann's hands shook as she brushed some crumbs off the cloth and then sat down opposite him.

George sat back. He narrowed his eyes and rocked to and fro as he tried to make up his mind. There'd been trouble on the horizon for a long while. There'd been hell to pay on occasions with Brigid and it would only get worse if he didn't fall in with her plans. Why did women have to make such a fuss about everything. He'd been quite happy with matters as they stood. Those secret meetings, the trips which had been such a delight, then there were always those eager arms awaiting him when he went across the paddock and over to the hut. At the same time home had always been there, welcoming, a good meal and a warm bed. Why did women constantly have to make these demands? Only last week Brigid had delivered an ultimatum. "And would you be thinkin' I'll be content to spend the rest of me days with our Mam livin' in this humpy, eh?" Before, there had only been hints, now they'd reached the crux of the matter. "I'll be off and away to Goulburn meself soon, find a good situation and a good master no doubt. Our Mam always says there's bigger fish in the sea than ever come out of it."

Marriage had become a habit, George accepted that. A vaguely tiresome exchange of thoughts, but a decent enough habit. And hadn't it brought him all he'd desired? But every time he caught sight of Brigid his heart lurched. Maybe that was a habit too but it showed no signs of easing. From that first moment when their eyes met across the street in Gundaroo he'd wanted her. First of all a casual greeting, then a lingering down near the river and a wave and a smile. An offer of help to move some fallen timber, a visit to inquire how the family had fared when a sudden flood surged over the river bank. All such simple steps towards the much more complicated dance of love.

No hurry, no impatience, small favours, chance and not-so-chance encounters and then the first touch, a hand on a shoulder then an arm around the waist. George was no stranger to the moves and knew too well that time was needed in all affairs of the human heart, and daily business, if full satisfaction was to be gained. Hadn't he proved that? All that time dancing attendance on old man Guise had certainly paid off dividends.

But, cunning as he was, George did not fully realise that

two could play at that game and the other participant was even more skilled than himself. By the time he called by the hut one day and found Brigid on her own, matters had already reached a point where each understood the other's motives but no one had in fact taken the first step.

"Keep 'im waitin', me bird, keep 'im waitin'," chuckled the old woman, "but you needs to pick the right moment. Can't expect him to be around for ever, there's plenty younger than you round these parts!"

The right moment came on that day when he'd ridden out past the dam and across the paddock. Lazily the smoke spiralled out of the chimney and the hut was bathed in that strange light that rivers can give off, the miasma of slow relentless progress. Whether these thoughts were the touchpaper which lit George's deepest desires it would be difficult to know, but something in the laziness, the power, the mystery of the hut and all it could mean to him urged him on.

Brigid came to the door. No word was spoken. She held out her arms and he stepped across that threshold.

Neither were strangers to the art of seduction, but then seduction had already been completed: the words, the smiles, the random meetings. No need to tarry any longer and lifting her into his arms he carried her past the hessian curtain and threw her down on the bed.

He tore at her bodice as she reached down and grasped at him. Within seconds he was inside her and she cried out in ecstasy, which in all truth she did not particularly feel at that moment, but Brigid knew what a man needed to hear and she was giving it to him.

Coming back from Gundaroo Mary O'Rourke saw the horse tethered to the rail and sensibly went back along the path to sit down and wait in the shade of a she-oak for a little doze.

But each time she ventured along the riverbank again the horse was still there, so she just went back and dozed a little more. *No worry, give 'em time. A bit of hanging about now would pay off in the end. A sprat to catch a mackerel!*

Time and again George fell upon Brigid. She cried, she moaned, she hugged and held him close – Brigid held nothing back. While certainly she enjoyed herself, it was nothing compared to the absolute abandon of her lover and his ecstasy.

Finally exhausted, the shadows lengthening, George lay back and stared up at the drooping bark of the roof.

Nothing. Nothing in the whole world could be allowed to come between himself and this wonderful experience, this frenzy and perfection. Nothing.

It was a few weeks later that the little favours began to be requested: some repairs to the roof, a new washtub. And favours have to be repaid. Brigid delighted in their repayment as much as he yearned for every secret rendezvous.

A wife! Brigid did not waste much time pondering over the question. She'd known quite a few men with wives, they didn't amount to much and rarely knew what their husbands were up to. A flirtation here, an assignation there, she'd often smiled to herself. She could tell the wives and mothers of Gundaroo a thing or two! Old Mam had trodden that path, but Brigid winced when she looked at the body bloated with childbearing and the hands gnarled from years at the tub. No, if she was going to do better then that she'd steer clear of poverty. She'd find herself a real man, with a real living to offer and she'd deal with the wife later.

Off and away, there's bigger fish in the sea than ever came out of it – those had been her words and they echoed around George's head. He could not let that happen.

Now he found his wife staring at him. Mary Ann was for the

first time really looking at George Brownlow. It wasn't dismay or distress that he saw in her eyes - it was sheer disgust. The truth was out, he knew she would never trust him again.

No more rambles at night, when he'd absented himself from the fireside with excuses of lost cattle or marauding dingoes, no more tumbled sheets in some wayside inn. Well, why couldn't he have both... Brigid and Bywong?

"I say you need help around the place. I say she's coming."

"No, George. She is not." Mary Ann clenched her fists.

He paused and looked at her white, strained face. He reached for the knife and sliced off a piece of chicken breast. "A man's master in his own home, Mary Ann."

"This is my home, George."

He half rose and glared at her.

"She's comin' and you'd best make the best of it!"

"She's not coming."

"And I say she is." He pushed the chair back and went into the yard.

At that moment from the house came the chimes of the grandfather clock striking nine o'clock.

To Mary Ann each stroke sounded like the voice of her ancestors. The deep, notes rumbled out strong and firm and utterly rebuked her for the low level to which the family had come.

In that instant she vividly recalled her grandparents. Even more vividly she remembered Grand-père's words as he spoke of the doomed queen. A Guise never turns his back on the enemy.

Now she faced her enemy. Hastily she put that word aside. She must not think like that. He was the father of her children. He must understand, he must understand.

Mary Ann stood stock still for a whole minute. She picked

up the knife and started to wipe the blade upon her apron. It was sticky from the chicken. Then another thought struck her: she must tell George her news. That might put the whole of their life into perspective again. Wiping the knife on her apron she followed him into the yard.

"Wait, George… wait!"

He grunted some unintelligible words, his back firmly turned as he started to walk away.

"I've got something to tell you."

"Go tell it to the birds, tell it to them jackasses. Leave me be! Brigid's coming here to live, make no mistake."

"Where are you going, George?"

"Where do you think?"

Gripping the knife she leapt towards him.

CHAPTER 18

Lord Justice Alfred Stephen glanced at the prisoner in the dock. He rearranged his papers and shuffled some of them to one side, making a neat pile of the rest.

Squirming, he shifted uneasily. The night had been most uncomfortable. Admittedly his bed had been clean and the covers adequate but, above in the roof, the rats scampered and squeaked. Now a queasy stomach was beginning to make itself evident. Could it be the water or the food?

The inn, albeit the best in town, proved a far cry from the comforts of his home in Hyde Park Crescent. Dinner had been an even further cry from the repast of a few evenings ago at Government House. Then there'd been every variety of fish, flesh and fowl, hock and claret flowed like water, sweet wines had been served with the syllabubs. Last night's roast fowl of indeterminate age and cold bread pudding rumbled ominously in his guts. Sighing to himself he admitted his life to be one of extremes and wondered briefly what this woman's life had been like.

But only briefly, for Sir Alfred Stephen was a true man of the law. He had a reputation for extreme fairness. His mind functioned on two levels, as a tireless legal administrator and a devoted family man, but he lacked that element of imagination to glue the two together and make for compassion.

The clerk, a fussy little man with a perpetual dewdrop on the end of his nose and eyes that gimleted each prisoner in turn, prided himself on his local knowledge.

"One of the Guise family, sir, very early in the district."

Sir Alfred nodded. "Heard of the family. French, of course."

"Oh, we have every nation in the world come to the Limestone Plains and roundabout, sir."

He glanced at her again, a dark-haired young woman, not much meat on her bones. Skinny, in fact. She'd sat there throughout the morning without looking once in his direction, her eyes cast down or just occasionally scanning the courtroom where friends and relatives anxiously gathered.

Lot of interest in the woman he noted, even if she did not appear particularly concerned. Strange remote quality about her. Not one supplicating look in his direction, not a single tear. Unwomanly. Definitely unwomanly.

But then to kill your husband wasn't exactly in the normal course of events. Not the way to proceed with married life. And Alfred Stephen considered himself an expert on married life. Wasn't he about to be presented with his eighteenth child?

In the midst of the respectful hum of the court his thoughts flew for a moment to that event possibly taking place at this very moment far away in Sydney. Dear Eleanor, would she prove stronger than Ginny had been? In bringing her ninth into the world poor Virginia had lost her life – and the child. But Eleanor had so far proved to be made of tougher material.

He smilingly reflected on that bustling home. God, justice and family, what a fortunate man he was to have such a rewarding life. Eighteen children! Would it be a boy or another girl? How wonderful were the rewards of duty and fidelity. All those sparkling eyes and rosy cheeks.

Of course some looked askance at such a large family, at least in the home of a Supreme Court judge. Some would say an educated man might have managed a smaller family?

Well, let them titter behind their hands. Oh yes, there were ways, ways that were known to many, ways to limit the Will of God. There were herbs and shocking stratagems to regulate the size of a family. There were restrictions for the man – certainly not condoned in the Bible – and there were devices for the woman – he'd hesitate to use the word 'lady'. Yes, shocking devices that interfered with God's work.

The French were adept at such matters. Why, it was said they even used pig's bladders to… well, to contain the problem. Ah, nicely put. And weren't there said to be sponges for their consorts? Wasn't it maintained that for a French nobleman to have his mistress with child was regarded as the most shocking and ignorant behaviour? The French! Well, we all know about the habits of the French!

So, a descendant of the de Guise family? Well, that might account for her distant demeanour. A cornstalk perhaps, but not a sturdy one. Not a typical currency lass. Everyone knew the French were given to romantic notions of the extravagant kind. They even spoke of passion, passion for men and passion for women.

He shuddered. Passion for women! Sir Alfred blinked as he thought of either his first or second wife even reaching up and… and… oh no! He closed his eyes momentarily.

What were they saying? Firmly he pushed away his wandering thoughts and listened to the evidence.

A cause for jealousy, the hint of an errant husband? Well who could say what the truth of that might be but certainly if every wife who caught her husband playing away from home immediately knifed him, then the population of the Colony would soon be seriously depleted.

The place was going to the dogs. All these Continentals—Germans, Italians, French and heaven knows what else. The place was filling up with them. Always disputes when you had people like that to deal with.

"Mr Fawcett is her lawyer," the clerk told him.

Why, the woman did not even appear to be listening to her own lawyer! Her family had procured one of the best legal men in Colony; why didn't she at least acknowledge him? Sir Alfred could not understand such behaviour. He expected a variety of emotions, to see the face of the accused display some sort of reactions: fear, supplication, resignation? Craven glances were called for, not this aloof bearing.

She just sat there, silent, without the slightest trace of humility, staring into the distance with her gaze miles and miles away. Tall, dark-haired, sombre-featured, submitting but remaining detached from the proceedings.

"Constable Nugent!" The first witness was called. The policeman had been told to make a few notes but his ability with the pen did not match his ability with saddle, handcuffs, lock-up or carbine.

"Prisoner stated…" He fumbled with the paper.

"The very words, Constable," Sir Alfred demanded.

"She said, 'I wish I had done it better. If he gets over this I'll do for him yet'."

A gasp went round the court. The Lintotts and the Cantors looked at each other and shook their heads, Frank de Rossi muttered to one of his neighbours, someone at the back of the court cried out, "Shame."

"Silence!" shouted the clerk.

They heard how George Brownlow had staggered along the

road and been able to reach some houses where his cries drew attention to his plight. One, Edward Hines, had taken him into his home and sent for the doctor. Andrew Morton, surgeon, testified that he'd suffered a wound on the left side between his ribs, closer to the spine than the front of his body. George Brownlow had lingered on at the house of Edward Hines, who had persuaded the dying man to make a statement two days later.

"Dr Morton said that he'd best make his peace with God and leave a statement explaining what happened. He told us Mr Brownlow did not have long to live."

"And what was stated?"

"Mr Brownlow said his wife, Mary Ann that is, attacked him as he was crossing the yard in the night time."

"And why did she do this?"

"The victim said he'd told her he was bringing a lady to live in the house."

"A lady?"

"Well," the good sergeant hesitated, "she wasn't quite described as that."

"Go on, man, go on… the exact words!"

"There was Mr Hines there and Dr Morton and he was failing, failing fast. I just writ down what was said, Sir. He said he was bringing his fancy woman to live at Bywong."

Fancy woman! A crime of passion! Jealousy and passion were foreign emotions in Sir Alfred's own world. Passion distorted the judgement. Reprehensible in a man, quite shocking in a woman. The embrace of a woman was every man's right but women were expected to control their emotions. It was not their place to dictate to a husband, however wayward, what his actions should be.

Sharply he brought himself back to the proceedings in hand.

Dismissing the sergeant he sat back as Dr Morton was called to the stand.

Andrew Morton's words came loud and clear.

He agreed with all the sergeant's words. That night after attending to George Brownlow he'd gone over to Bywong.

"I examined the woman and found that she was with child."

With child! Had he heard rightly? Why that was, let's see, he checked on the months that had passed since the date of the crime. The child would be no more than a month at the most now. She already had two children; how could a mother commit such a crime?

Sir Alfred peered at Mary Ann. Not a vestige of feeling showed on her face. He turned a page and penned a few more lines. Painstaking and meticulous, he wrote down her actions in his own careful shorthand, each outline etching yet one more fact in the depiction of her character. Black was black, white was white, but the unfortunates who ended up facing him were usually those who had stumbled into a zone where only grey prevailed.

Mary Ann looked up at the mention of her child. Her lips tightened and she frowned. Even to hear the word mentioned in this cold, shabby place sickened her. Babies were soft and warm and smelt of fresh linen, woollen bootees and bonnets. They had no place in this grim gathering where the air was filled with a mixture of mothballs and musty drapery overlaid with a patina of stale sweat. She made an involuntary gesture to push away the thought of little George, and return him to his milky sweet world.

The long awaited son!

Somehow if she clung to the thought of her son she found the strength to look back once more upon that night. The night when a lifetime of daily chores, early morning canters with her grandfather, working in the orchard, searching for straying beast, listening for her husband's step upon the verandah, a whole lifetime made up of the daily round and cherished in the depths of her being came to an abrupt halt.

George had flung himself out of the door and started across the yard. With one hand she'd picked up her skirts, the knife was still in her other and her apron still wrapped round its blade.

"Stop," she'd called but only the flickering candlelight from the window and the faint lifting of the branches bore witness to her desperation.

He could not leave! She had to tell him her secret, she had to let him know another life stirred within her, she had to urge him to stay away from those who were waiting to swoop down upon the lands of the Guise family and gorge themselves upon the feast, like the crows who circled overhead and then came to rest in the branches where they can watch and wait. Just as the Irishwoman had watched and waited ten, twenty years? How many years had she awaited her chance.

"George! George, listen!" She ran after him.

He'd spun round and stood still. "Listen? You ain't got nothin' I want to hear. Brigid's coming here to live, that's my last word."

She put out her hand and grasped his shoulder but he pulled away and raised his arm as though about to strike. "Get away from me."

Stepping back for one second Mary Ann raised her hands and the apron dropped away. "I've got something to tell you."

"Go tell it to the birds, tell it to them jackasses. Leave me be! Brigid's coming here to live, make no mistake."

"Where are you going, George?"

"Where do you think?"

Gripping the knife she leapt towards him.

Mary Ann sighed and shifted uncomfortably. Her bodice was tight, the milk was beginning to flow and young George would soon be crying out for his feed. How could the questioning drag on like this? Everyone knew what had happened. Why this endless charade of question and answer? Couldn't they take Sergeant Nugent's word, couldn't they accept Dr Morton's statement? Why all this to-ing and fro-ing of argument and counter-argument.

Dr Morton had known all of the Guises, hadn't he seen both Cathy and Lizzie into the world? How she'd wished he had been there to bring her son into the light of day. There had been nothing to relieve those hours on that rock-hard bed, for the most part on her own, as the pains came closer and closer together. To stop herself crying out she had bitten her lips and only when they held up that tiny boy did her emotions overwhelm her. The longed-for boy… too late, too late by far.

Familiar faces crowded the court. Her sisters and their husbands, many of the neighbours and Frank de Rossi. Even Job had managed to get himself brought all the way to Goulburn, wearing his new waistcoat, bobbing his head to all but resolutely not meeting her eyes. Everybody knew everybody else. Doctor, policeman, landowner, and then there were those who had just come for the spectacle.

She lifted her head up high and stared at them. Muffled against the cold seeping into the courtroom, all squeezed together from lack of space, for all the world no better than the caged monkeys in Ashton's Circus. Some had eager eyes which peered at her as though they could see into her very soul, others were vacant in their glances.

"Yes," said Dr Morton. "I saw George Brownlow on the night in question I was called to the house of Edward Hines. The victim was a healthy man about thirty. He had staggered towards the village and been taken in by Mr Hines who had immediately sent a servant to my house. In spite of the depth of the wound, on the left side between his ribs towards the spine, there wasn't much blood, but there would have been copious bleeding internally."

"Did the victim explain his condition?"

"My lord, he was in extreme pain, nothing could be said. Two days later, still at the house of Edward Hines, I urged him to make a statement. I said to him, 'You are in a very dangerous state. Do you want to make any statement with reference to your injury? You'd better make it now as there is the prospect of death. Your life is fast drawing to a close.'"

Sir Alfred dipped his pen in the inkwell and wrote at a furious pace to keep up with the doctor's words.

"George Brownlow said, 'I was aware all along from the time of getting the stab' and then he made a statement which I took down correctly, hurriedly too, because I feared he'd become insensible. I read it over to the victim afterwards in the constable's presence and he agreed with it."

"Read it, sir." For a moment only the scratching of the judge's pen could be heard in the courtroom.

"George Brownlow said his wife followed him after an altercation with her about a fancy woman came up. She had a knife concealed and stabbed him."

Elizabeth Lintott drew in her breath. "Fancy woman! Fancy woman! Why don't they speak the trollop's name, that Brigid? Makes our Mary Ann just seem like many another jealous wife. But why don't they speak about him selling off the land…? And think of having her living there, under your own roof…eh?"

"Hush, my love." Glancing round nervously Henry Lintott nodded to Frank de Rossi. They'd gathered for a while in the parlour of the inn, waiting together during an adjournment.

"My poor Elizabeth's beside herself, beside herself with worry."

"Never fear, Mrs Lintott." Frank de Rossi sounded confident. "They've not hanged a woman in thirty years."

"It's that old devil I'm afeared of, that Sir Alfred. He's got a nasty reputation, very strict, they say. If she'd have come up for trial earlier it'd been easier. If she'd have been tried before the baby was born, it would have been different. Everyone knows you can't hang a woman as is expecting. But what do they do? Let her have the poor wee thing and then they tries her. I tell you, our Mary Ann's being made an example of."

"We don't know, my love," her husband shook his head. "'Tis hearsay, we don't know. Take a bit of this." He pushed a piece of pie towards her, but she shook her head.

"Stomach's turned to iron, it has. Don't want a thing."

"Come, Mrs Lintott, now is the time to keep your strength up. All day with not a bite passing your lips, now, that's not doing your sister a service, is it?" Frank de Rossi held out the plate once more. Elizabeth grudgingly picked at a crumb.

"Don't know how we'd have managed without you, sir," Henry Lintott shook his head. "Our Hannah'll be down with her husband, as you know, but at the moment they can do more to help up there in the city. Her husband Edward knows everyone who's in the know, so to speak, as we've said before. But we've a lot to thank you for, getting that Mr Fawcett for one thing. "

"Fawcett's one of the best. Reputation second to none. Not that there's any doubt about it. No one in their right mind would... would... would take the wrong path, so to speak. We all know the facts of the matter - your poor sister-in-law was being swindled out of her inheritance. But it's best to make certain sure and I'm very pleased the way he's handled the whole matter. Top of his profession. A couple more days at the most and Mary Ann'll be on the road back to Bywong and we'll all be remembering this as a bad dream." He nodded at their two anxious faces. "Now come on, Mrs Lintott, that pie, remember."

Reluctantly she slipped the slice onto her plate. "I'll try, but to tell you the truth, my insides feel rock solid."

Sir Alfred had quite the opposite problem. Cursed place, he muttered out in the privy as he buttoned himself up. Sooner I'm back in civilisation, the better. Bad food, bad beds, bad people!

When he took up his pen once more he was in no better frame of mind. When he addressed the court he had, in his own opinion, a complete grasp of the case.

A crime of passion, of jealousy, did not provide sufficient excuse for such a violent act. The murder was premeditated, evidence showed the knife had been concealed in her apron and she followed the victim before striking the blow. Out of her own mouth her words condemned her. Had not Constable Nugent heard her state she would do it again if necessary?

Beside the evidence in his notes he wrote his judgement.

"I sentence her to death."

CHAPTER 19

"Hush, hush," Mary Ann sighed as she cradled her son in her arms. Gradually his screams lessened and his tiny body relaxed as he gulped down the milk. The relief at being back in the solitude of her cell almost cancelled out the misery of the last hours – almost, not quite.

Stiff with dread since early morning, she'd sat and listened throughout the long day while witness after witness testified. By mid afternoon every detail of her marriage had been exposed and the closely-knit raiment of love, birth and death unravelled.

Friends and curious onlookers crowded the court. Keeping her head held high she did not allow her gaze to meet that of any other. Any glimpse of pity would have been unbearable.

Even when Sir Alfred delivered his verdict she did not flinch. Her only concern had been getting back to the baby, giving him his feed, making sure he was dry and comfortable. That other Mary Ann who'd followed George Brownlow into the yard, who'd raised the knife and plunged it into him, that other Mary Ann was another person from another world... that other world of months ago.

Overwhelmed she had not even noticed as George had stumbled away into the darkness. Cathy and Lizzie were all she thought about as she hurried indoors and went to their room. She was still kneeling beside the sleeping children when the house began to fill with people. Some voices hushed, some harsh. All around, disjointed words and phrases added to the confusion in her mind. "Murder," "wicked shame," "seen it comin'," "who'd have thought," "respectable folk"…on and on they went.

The kaleidoscope of sounds battered her ears till finally a pattern of coherent thought emerged from the chaos. She faced them, white-faced and unrepentant.

"I wish I had done it better," she cried out. "If he get's over this I'll do it again."

As that fierce tide of rage subsided all the snags of their marriage became exposed and visible on what had once been the enchanted shores of love. Like rocks that had lain concealed until the tide receded, now they were laid bare for all the world to see. Every devious action was revealed. The sale of Guise land, the sacking of Job, the visits to Goulburn and the other towns, and small lies giving way to larger ones. But, just as the hazards of a rocky shore are exposed on the ebb, so they will be covered up again by the next flood. And following her furious outburst Mary Ann felt the tide turn in her emotions.

She must remain calm, she needed to be strong for her daughters' sakes.

Hadn't it been said that even the doomed queen's accusers were chastened by her dignity? Mary Ann found herself strangely calm when she finally made the journey to Goulburn Gaol.

Even so the agony at the parting from her daughters nearly broke down her firmest resolve.

"Keep up your spirits, my love," Elizabeth had hugged her and searched for anything she could think of to lessen the blow. "Right'll be done, right'll be done. They've just got to hear your side and believe me, we all know what that is."

The letter of the law had to be followed. A death had occurred and she must make the journey to Goulburn Gaol until the future was decided.

How often she had ridden along that dusty road with Grand-père, with Papa, with brothers and sisters; now she rode with the unsmiling troopers. Familiarity surrounded her every inch of the way. The thick stands of boxwood, the towering monolithic rocks, some as steep and sheer as the tower at St John's, the expanses of thin poor grass barely covering sandstone outcrops and barren stretches where only goats browsed.

"Whoa there!" The sergeant reined in his mount as they reached a bluff overlooking the lake. "Time out, lads." Then he nodded to one of the men. "Get her down," for her wrists were manacled.

Refreshed with a draught of water she leant against the hard surface of one of the many boulders. Weereewaa stretched into the distance. Ancient and eternal it belonged in her mind to those who had lived along its shores since the dawn of time, the Canberri and the Ngunawal. King George, troopers, fences, huts and great hooved creatures mere insignificant newcomers to its great cycle of death and rebirth.

The vastness of the lake comforted her. Her sin – for over the past few days she'd been made continually aware that she had indeed sinned – her sin was dwarfed by the magnificence laid before her. How many had lived and died, loved and sinned and existed as the lake swelled and shrank with the rhythm of the elements which no one understood and yet everyone must accept.

She smiled as she caught the flash of white from a heron fishing amongst the reeds. A tiny white dot in a universe of shimmering water. As she wrapped her arms around herself and hugged her unborn baby to her, Mary Ann felt the first soothing touch of healing enter her soul.

The cycle had been completed and the magnitude of the scene brought its own peace. She wrapped her arms around herself, still hugging that secret which she had tried to share - a son. The certainty had grown within her as day succeeded day: George would have his son. That was her only repayment, he would be called George.

As she now sat with the sleeping baby so many worlds revolved around Mary Ann. Was she a mother, the owner of Bywong, a widow, a wronged wife, or a criminal? Would the bare walls of a cell become her home, would she lose her life? Everyone assured her that the sentence would never be carried out; she'd not lose her life like that poor queen.

At least Mary Ann could hold her son in her arms; Marie Antoinette never saw her own son during the final imprisonment, never once held him in her embrace when she endured those last months in the Conciergerie. She had not even been able to say goodbye to her husband when he went to the guillotine, neither had she been allowed to take leave of her son.

At thirty-five her hair had turned white. Dressed in common cloth, even her name had been changed. Reaching back to a previous dynasty her accusers had given her the name of the Capets. No longer Queen of France, she'd been called Marie Antoinette, the Widow Capet.

For two days the Widow Capet had faced the Tribunal. A pointless charade of words, the outcome already decided. Soon she would follow her husband's path up the steps of the guillotine. Reduced, by two years of captivity, from the vivacious, dancing queen to this frail, snowy-haired woman, body infirm, womb bleeding each day as though willing itself already dead, she listened impassively to the accusations.

The young woman who had chattered and pirouetted beneath the chandeliers in the Galerie de Glace had become a wiser and sadder human being facing her gloating accusers without fear. During the long hours of questioning she had learnt to curb her naturally quick tongue, and did not rise to their taunts. She thought very carefully before replying to every single question.

Try as they might she could not be tripped up. The charges of treachery, plotting with her Austrian relatives, and misuse of money from the nation's coffers were parried and thrown back.

But when the ultimate charge came she did not reply.

Unnatural practices with her own son. She remained silent as the shocked onlookers waited – and wondered. No hint of this had ever been dropped before. Marie Antoinette's faults had been bruited abroad in pamphlet and broadsheet: extravagance, treachery, nepotism, adultery and every sin a queen could commit – but incest?

"Your son has spoken of his nights spent in your bed between yourself and his aunt Elizabeth when unnatural practices occurred."

She said nothing.

"Did you hear the words?" the judge asked. She nodded, but still said nothing.

"You must reply. You must reply to the charge."

She stepped forward. Palms upwards she raised her hands in a gesture of disbelief. The disdain on her countenance silenced the assembled company as her gaze travelled from face to face.

"Reply!"

"A child can be frightened and persuaded to say many things."

"You have not answered the question."

"If I have not answered, it is because my very nature refuses to answer such an accusation. How can a mother answer such an accusation?"

A mother appealing to all other mothers. A groundswell of acknowledgement rose and filled the air as every woman in that court felt, for a moment, their kinship with the wasted figure before them.

Marie Antoinette had entered the court as the Widow Capet but, head held high, she left it as the Queen of France.

CHAPTER 20

"There, there," Henry Lintott patted his wife's shoulder and shook his head, "nothing'll be helped with you taking on so."

"Our Mary Ann! How could they do that?"

"Like Mr de Rossi says, it'll never happen."

"He's an old devil, that Sir Alfred. You could tell, the way he spoke. He wanted to make our Mary Ann an example. Make sure all married women knew what they'd be in for if they stood up for their rights."

"That's a judge's job, Elizabeth. But mark my words, they'll reduce that sentence! He has to go by the letter of the law, you know."

"What about those two men? Convicted of murder they were, but they aren't condemned to hang!"

No one could answer her.

"And why'd he give that other woman no more'n a slap on the wrist by comparison? That Catherine Reid got just six years for manslaughter! She wasn't even married to that butcher she'd been living with when she went for him with the knife. He was dead within the hour! What's the difference?"

"Mrs Lintott, the difference is that the man had been violent for many years and also she just picked the knife up and stabbed him, she didn't follow him."

"But she killed him all the same, didn't she, Mr de Rossi? She wasn't even married to him, and our Mary Ann's a respectable married woman."

"The fact that she followed him out of the house and she'd had the knife under her pinafore. those were the points he took on the side of the law."

"Wicked. He's a wicked old man sitting in judgement on us ordinary folk and he's not taken into account all that speaks for poor Mary Ann. 'Tis still my belief he came down harder, her being a married woman. Let that trollop behave like any other trollop and it's excused, but if a married woman stands up for herself… well. They're making an example of her. Saying what she did was foul and brutal, those were his very words, weren't they? Nothing about how she'd been deceived."

"He did take it into account when he spoke of jealousy and passion."

"That just makes it sound like any quarrel between a husband and wife. How about a serious cause beyond the fancy woman, how about deception over our lands, our Guise lands? He married our Mary Ann and then he deceived her. Mark my words! When there's trouble the woman always pays the price!"

"And it's up to us to see that doesn't happen, Mrs Lintott. You've heard the uproar outside! We're not the only ones. Every street corner in Goulburn's buzzing with it. You haven't been out in the town but, believe me, they're talking about it in the shops, at the market, just everywhere."

"What good'll that do?"

"Just shows how people feel. A petition, that's what's needed. I'll see to that myself. We'll take it to the Governor up in

Sydney. I'll ride over to the Murrays. Mr Murray'd be better than anyone. He knows us all and of course he'd know all the high-ups. Being our member, he'll be able to do more than anyone. You can't go much higher than the Legislative Council. Tomorrow I'll speak to the sheriff. Don't worry, we'll start the ball rolling."

"But the time…we've not got long and…"

"Mrs Lintott, your place is with your sister. Leave this to us. Mr Lintott knows everyone of note in the area; together we'll plan a course of action."

"We need more than the local bigwigs!"

"True, true. As I said, there's talk of a petition. There was talk of it before Sir Alfred came to town. A petition to the Governor-General himself. Never had that round these parts before, no one got that worked up. But everyone's on poor Mary Ann's side."

"…and so everything'll be right in no time at all," Elizabeth later reassured her sister. She said it on her first visit, she said it on her second and then repeated it each time she walked into the narrow cell and perched beside Mary Ann on the low bed. "Mr Murray's spoken to that Mr Plunkett, the Attorney-General. Well, you can't go much higher'n that, can you? Then they'll be sending our petition to the Governor himself. You'll not be seeing our Hannah, she's gone back up to Sydney with Edward for there's another petition being got up in the city, think of that! It's on everyone's lips, had a letter from her by Friday's mail. Having her and Edward up there's a godsend at the moment.

"She was that upset at having to go back with Edward but, 'Hannah', I said 'you can do much more for our Mary Ann up there where all the bigwigs are than down in our part of the world'."

"How are… they?" Mary Ann asked. Suddenly her lips couldn't say her daughters' names. To hear their names in these grim surroundings was too much. "How are my girls?"

"That happy they are. The old tabby had her kittens last month; they're that took with the little kitties, nothing else counts. And growing, I can't tell you. Cathy's got some legs on her, that one, have to keep our eyes on her, alright and young Lizzie, she'll be the same."

"And little George, what of my Georgy?" Mary Ann's eyes were dark with worry as they searched her sister's face.

"Never fret, never fret, lovey. Our little Georgy's alright. Happy as a sandboy, gurgling away every time he sees his sisters. Have to keep little Cathy away or he'd not get a mite of sleep. They'll be alright, all of them."

"But his feed?"

"Winny, our dairymaid, she's just had her fourth. Plenty of milk there, plenty and to spare."

"A wet nurse! I remember Grand-mère speaking about wet nurses."

"Sometimes I think our Gran spoke about too much. Lived in the past she did, like Grand-père and took you along with her."

"Do you remember how she said history repeats itself? The poor queen."

Elizabeth sniffed. "'Twas on account of Marie Antoinette they called you Mary Ann but that don't mean a thing."

"But they took her son away from her, didn't they? They've taken my son away from me!"

"Coincidence, just coincidence, and you'll be out of here and away before too long when those in the right quarters have had their say. Mark my words, it'll be different for you, my girl." Elizabeth shut her mind, anything else was unimagineable.

"Well, he'll be cared for, never you upset yourself. You've got to keep strong, to keep up that strength for when you're back with us."

Another visitor came to Goulburn Gaol. Hesitantly he waited as the gaoler unlocked the gate. He was not sure, yet he had to speak to her.

"This way, this way, sir," the gaoler spoke almost as one would speak to a child for he sensed the other man's reluctance. Gentry did not often come calling here!

As the door of the cell clanged shut behind him and the man's retreating footsteps echoed down the passage Frank stood staring at her and found himself completely speechless. Although he'd thought this over many times, he'd even rehearsed some words of comfort, now that he stood here, he remained tongue-tied.

What words of comfort could you give to one in the condemned cell?

Mary Ann had been sitting on her bed, the prayer book in her lap and the Bible close by. Compared with the last time he had seen her she was even thinner and the shadows round her eyes highlighted the pallor of her features. But those eyes still held the same faintly inquiring light they'd held when she first walked into that inn, when she'd started off on her journey into adulthood so eagerly, not so many years ago.

"Mrs Brownlow." he held out his hands.

Immediately she rose and held out hers. "Not Mrs Brownlow please. Do you remember, it's Mary Ann."

"How could I forget?" he laughed and the sound echoed round the barren walls and brought a smile to her face. "You know I'd never forget that Mary Ann... but I did not want to appear presumptuous."

"Oh, look, the time for niceties and fine words is long gone. I have to thank you for so much. Sit down, at least there's a chair. Sit down and let me speak."

Amazed, he did as she said. This is how she would have welcomed him to Bywong. She was speaking to him in language of the hostess, not in the tongue of a prisoner awaiting... his mind refused to go there.

"You've nothing to thank me for," he mumbled. The tables had been turned. He was expecting to talk and console and it was she who took the matter into her own hands.

"Oh yes, I have. Elizabeth's told me it was you who found Mr Fawcett for us. We are quite unversed in legal matters."

"He's not been much help," he muttered bitterly.

"You can't blame him. Sir Alfred's a powerful speaker. The point he made was very convincing. Anything that appears to have any forethought is criminal... or so it seems."

"How can you be so matter of fact, Mary Ann? How can you just take it like this?" he blurted out.

"I'm not matter of fact. Don't think I don't pick over every word that's been spoken every minute of the day and most of the night but don't let's dwell there. I was thanking you, wasn't I? For finding Mr Fawcett, for standing by my family. I believe you suggested so much... the petition, the letters..."

"This should never have happened."

"Never have happened! Why did I pick up that knife? Why did I follow him? Of course it should never have happened."

"No, I mean our lives should have been so different."

Silence hung heavily between them. She clutched the prayer book and held it to her breast like a talisman. "I think you'd better leave," she whispered.

"May I come again tomorrow?"

For a moment he thought she would refuse for she frowned slightly, she did not look at him; instead, she pushed the hair back from her forehead and smiled to herself. "Please come."

Just two words but he knew he'd found the key to her heart.

Each day that the mail coach sped into town a crowd awaited it anxiously. "Of course nothing could be expected so soon" was the comforting phrase on everyone's lips as the days passed by. After the second week still no word had come.

"A reprieve, that's what she'll get. Takes time though, takes time for those high-ups to come together and make up their minds."

Mary Ann never asked. Her world had disappeared, she existed in an alien place. Four bare walls, a bed, a table, a chair and the glimpse of a patch of blue sky high up in the window. Memories flooded back, days of haymaking, months of riding down to the river or up to the mountains and years of watching the seasons roll by. The crows would be winging their way across the Bywong paddocks, the frogs croaking down in the dam and the cows shifting impatiently in their stalls waiting to be milked.

Each memory spanned so much time. By comparison she had been in this wretched place for only a moment. What did that count against those years of freedom?

What of that other cell where the Widow Capet had waited? Were the walls as bare, the sky as far away, and did she listen just as anxiously to every footstep in the passage outside? Did her thoughts fly away from the straw, the rough boards and the dusty bricks of her cell? Instead, did she once again take a proffered arm and make her way to the dining table? Did she gather her skirts together and join the dancers, did she walk the paths in Versailles and once again look upon the fountains and the statues?

A strange tranquillity took hold of Mary Ann; others mistook her silence for despair. They eagerly told her of the letters that had been written, the hopeful remarks of those in power, the certainty that decisions could be overturned, mercy would be shown. Her ears rang with their protestations, she smiled and listened but all she wanted was for them to be gone - to leave her with her thoughts.

Day followed day and she looked forward to Frank's visits ever more keenly. He'd ridden to the city, he'd petitioned every person of note he could approach. He'd knocked on every door where help could be sought and he'd finally returned to spend time at her side.

Mary Ann would have liked to lose count of the days but instead each one came and went with a finality she could not ignore but there was always hope. Just as she'd hoped that night of the fire, and hadn't she been proved right?

Each time he came she could not help herself searching his face for an answer. If anyone could turn the world around it would be Frank. The Lintotts, Dr Morton and Mr Sowerby came and went from her cell and she could only wish them all to be gone. With Frank she felt peace and hope return when the door clanged shut behind him.

"What is that noise?"

"Noise?" Frank did not want to answer.

"Oh, thank you, thank you so much." She took the mug of coffee he held out for her and put it on the table. He hoped she would not ask again.

"That hammering. They started this morning and they just keep on and on."

The words did not come but when she looked more closely the answer was in his eyes.

"Oh yes, I understand. How foolish of me."

He took her hands in his and felt the tremor which passed through her body. "Mary Ann…I…"

"Oh, please don't say anything Frank. I haven't lived twenty-three years without learning something of the ways of the world. I should have realised, I should not have had to ask."

He sat down beside her, still holding her hands.

"There is still time, Mary Ann. No one has given up hope. There is…"

"Don't let us keep going down that road. Only this morning Mr Sowerby came and spoke of so much. Let us talk, Frank, don't let's worry about the morrow."

"Talk!" he exclaimed bitterly, "I should have spoken at the right time, I should have spoken years ago. I was a fool, I should have talked!"

"Ah, but would I have listened?" A faint smile passed over her features.

"What can I say?"

"You can tell me if the Canberri and the Ngunawal men have gone off up to the mountains yet I fancy it's a little too early for the bogongs but who knows? You can tell me if the spring leaves are shooting on the apple trees and whether it's been a good year for the lambing, there is so much you can tell me." She smiled at him, gently let go of his hands and rose. Slowly she paced up and down.

To and fro she walked as Frank talked on. Each time he paused she urged him on – his voice shut out the hammering. Up and down she paced as though in time to the distant beat of a drum which only she could hear. Her feet were treading a path which had been trod before. With each step a certainty grew inside her, a feeling of slotting into place with time and becoming part of the cycle of life.

She did not feel frightened, she did not even feel alone.

Warmth spread through her, soft fingers entwined in hers.

Another led the way, looking over her shoulder and smiling at Mary Ann… "Fear not, I have trodden this path before you."

CHAPTER 21

Elizabeth put little George on her shoulder and took her first steps along the hallway. Up and down she walked each day, just as she'd walked with her own babies. Soon he'd be sleepy, soon he'd be ready to drop off.

So occupied was she that she did not notice Henry slipping into his study, but when she passed the open door the crackling of the newspaper betrayed his presence.

The execution of this unfortunate young woman for the murder of her husband took place at 4 o'clock on Thursday afternoon on the scaffold erected for the purpose within the precincts of the prison.

Momentarily he put *The Herald* down. There were several columns to come. He'd have to make sure Elizabeth did not see it… set her off again, more than likely!

"The time appointed for her sentence to be carried out was 9 o'clock in the morning and on the previous evening the anxiety for the arrival of the mail from Sydney and to obtain intelligence of the arrival of the reprieve became intense. But Alas! No such reprieve arrived.

"One of her sisters a respectable married female named Lintott had

been frequently to visit her and her distress of mind can more easily be conceived than described. Another sister also married and in respectable circumstances arrived in Goulburn by the Sydney Mail on Tuesday but so exceedingly overwhelming was her grief and distraction on entering her condemned sister's cell that she fell into violent hysterical fits which succeeded each other.

"*On the night preceding her execution the deceased seemed to continue in a sort of half slumber and in the morning sparingly partook of some coffee brought to her by Mr Rossi. The Rev Mr Sowerby was constant in his attendance upon her and although weak in body she expressed herself resigned to meet her fate with becoming submission.*

"*She was too feeble to mount the ladder without assistance and when she had reached the platform she turned round and with a graceful inclination of the head said Goodbye.*

"*At the moment when the dreadful rope was being adjusted round her neck a trial which might have unnerved the stoutest frame unless perfectly submissive awaited her, some of the females confined in the prison (probably beholding the proceeding through the windows) commenced loudly shrieking and wailing but her fortitude never forsook her; the cap was drawn over her features, the bolt withdraw; she fell through the aperture and died instantly…without a single struggle.*"

"What have you got there?"

His wife peered round the door, little Georgy's head resting on her shoulder.

"Nothing dear, nothing!"

"Since when was *The Herald* just nothing? No good keeping things from me. It'll be about our … our girl, won't it?

Henry Lintott laid the paper aside. "Perhaps one day, dear, perhaps one day you'll want to know what they said."

"Makes no difference now, does it? Nothing can ever bring her back, I'm not a simpleton, Henry, I know that. You're right, though. Too many people poked their noses in, just made it worse, like that last day. Should have been first thing in the morning, and what did they do? Delay it till four in the afternoon well, admittedly they were hoping the mail would bring a last minute reprieve. But, think how she must have felt, waiting all day, poor love. Go on, tell me what they're saying."

Reluctantly Henry picked up the paper again.

"Go on...what do they say?"

"*The Herald* says ... *a body of police were under arms and stationed around the foot of the scaffold, ten householders had been summoned to witness and certify to carrying out of the sentence and a number of other respectable persons were allowed admittance by the deputy sheriff.*"

"Respectable persons! Our Mary Ann so brave, so very brave."

"That's true, brave to the end. I heard Mr Sowerby say as how her dress caught on something, when... when you know she was going up... and she stumbled. And how she spoke up and said she wasn't frightened, her dress had just caught on a nail."

Elizabeth Lintott gasped. "What happened? Tell me again!"

When her husband had finished she remained silent for a moment. "You know what Grand-père told us once...that when the Queen went up to the steps to that, that, you know... well, her foot caught and she stumbled. She begged the executioner's pardon for standing on his foot. She turned and faced them to show she wasn't flinching. 'My slipper caught on a nail,' she said."

ACKNOWLEDGEMENTS

The description of the fire is based on
Dame Mary Gilmour's short story FIRE.

Excerpts covering the execution are from
The Goulburn Herald.

Photography by Daphne Salt

REVIEWS OF ANGELA'S FIRST NOVEL, CHARLOTTE BADGER - BUCCANEER

Dislocation, cultural fear, alienation amid landscape, and the abuse of authority come together in (this) novel…The vivid imagining of Charlotte's adventures makes this a lively narrative.

– Sydney Morning Herald

We know a happy ending is impossible and Badger does an excellent job of portraying the horror of the convicts' lot, the desperation of life in the 19th century, and the cruelty of the social and political system in which they were enmeshed.

– The New Zealand Herald

Euan Rose wrote a play about Charlotte Badger. Angela collaborated on both the musical, and the film script by Euan Rose commisioned by Screen West Midlands.

MORE TITLES BY ANGELA BADGER

The River's Revenge (junior fiction)
Poles Apart (junior fiction)
The Boy from Buninyong
Charlotte Badger – Buccaneer
The Water People

THE HANGING OF
Mary Ann

Angela Badger

ISBN 9781922175526   Qty

RRP   AU$24.99   .....

Postage within Australia   AU$5.00   .....

TOTAL★ $_____

★ All prices include GST

Name:..

Address: ....

....

Phone:..

Email: ....

Payment: ❑ Money Order ❑ Cheque ❑ MasterCard ❑Visa

Cardholders Name:...

Credit Card Number: ....

Signature:...

Expiry Date: ....

Allow 7 days for delivery.

Payment to: Marzocco Consultancy (ABN 14 067 257 390)
                        PO Box 12544
                        A'Beckett Street, Melbourne, 8006
                        Victoria, Australia
                        admin@brolgapublishing.com.au

BE PUBLISHED

Publish through a successful publisher.
Brolga Publishing is represented through:
• **National** book trade distribution, including sales,
marketing & distribution through **Macmillan Australia.**
• **International** book trade distribution to
    • The United Kingdom
    • North America
    • Sales representation in South East Asia
• **Worldwide e-Book distribution**

For details and inquiries, contact:
Brolga Publishing Pty Ltd
PO Box 12544
A'Beckett St VIC 8006

Phone: 0414 608 494
markzocchi@brolgapublishing.com.au
ABN: 46 063 962 443
(Email for a catalogue request)